HUNGARY

Marxist Regimes Series

Series editor: Bogdan Szajkowski,
Department of Sociology, University College,
Cardiff

Further Titles

HUNGARY

Politics, Economics and Society

Hans-Georg Heinrich

Lynne Rienner Publishers, Inc.
Boulder, Colorado

© Hans-Georg Heinrich 1986

First published in the United States of America in 1986 by
Lynne Rienner Publishers, Inc.
948 North Street
Boulder, Colorado 80302

Library of Congress Cataloging-in-Publication Data

Heinrich, Hans-Georg, Univ.-Doz. Dr.
   Hungary: politics, economics, and society.
   Bibliography: p.
   Includes index.
   1. Hungary—Economic conditions—1945–
2. Hungary—Economic conditions—1945–
3. Hungary—Social conditions—1945–   .   I. Title.
DB959.H45   1986   943 ´.05   85-24178
ISBN 0-931477-66-2
ISBN 0-931477-67-0 (pbk.)

Printed in Greàt Britain

Editor's Preface

Most observers and analysts agree that Hungary is on a point of change. This, the first comprehensive book on Hungarian politics, economics and society, provides the reader with an in-depth analysis of the background, current state and prospects of success for the various experiments taking place in the country's economic, social and political life.

The publication of this book coincides with the thirtieth anniversary of the Hungarian Revolution of 1956, which was a milestone not only in the country's history, but also in the development of the communist movement as a whole and Eastern Europe in particular. This book sets the Revolution and its aftermath, including the much heralded recent economic reforms, into ideological and political perspective.

It is also a timely and important contribution to overall analysis of Marxist regimes. The study of Marxist regimes has for many years been equated with the study of communist political systems. There were several historical and methodological reasons for this.

For many years it was not difficult to distinguish the eight regimes in Eastern Europe and four in Asia which resoundingly claimed adherence to the tenets of Marxism and more particularly to their Soviet interpretation—Marxism–Leninism. These regimes, variously called 'People's Republic', 'People's Democratic Republic', or 'Democratic Republic', claimed to have derived their inspiration from the Soviet Union to which, indeed, in the over-whelming number of cases they owed their establishment.

To many scholars and analysts these regimes represented a multiplication of and geographical extension of the 'Soviet model' and consequently of the Soviet sphere of influence. Although there were clearly substantial simi-larities between the Soviet Union and the people's democracies, especially in the initial phases of their development, these were often overstressed at the expense of noticing the differences between these political systems.

It took a few years for scholars to realize that generalizing the particular, i.e. applying the Soviet experience to other states ruled by elites which claimed to be guided by 'scientific socialism', was not good enough. The rela-tive simplicity of the assumption of a cohesive communist bloc was ques-tioned after the expulsion of Yugoslavia from the Communist Information Bureau in 1948 and in particular after the workers' riots in Poznań in 1956 and the Hungarian revolution of the same year. By the mid-1960s, the totalitarian model of communist politics, which until then had been very much in force, began to crumble. As some of these regimes articulated demands for a distinctive path of socialist development, many specialists studying these systems began to notice that the cohesiveness of the communist bloc was less apparent than had been claimed before.

Also by the mid-1960s, in the newly independent African states 'democratic' multi-party states were turning into one-party states or military dictatorships, thus questioning the inherent superiority of liberal democracy, capitalism and the values that went with it. Scholars now began to ponder on the simple contrast between multi-party democracy and a one-party totalitarian rule that had satisfied an earlier generation.

More importantly, however, by the beginning of that decade Cuba had a revolution without Soviet help, a revolution which subsequently became to many political elites in the Third World not only an inspiration but a clear military, political and ideological example to follow. Apart from its romantic appeal, to many nationalist movements the Cuban revolution also demonstrated a novel way of conducting and winning a nationalist, anti-imperialist war and accepting Marxism as the state ideology without a vanguard communist party. The Cuban precedent was subsequently followed in one respect or another by scores of regimes in the Third World who used the adoption of 'scientific socialism' tied to the tradition of Marxist thought as a form of mobilization, legitimation or association with the prestigious symbols and powerful high-status regimes such as the Soviet Union, China, Cuba and Vietnam.

Despite all these changes the study of Marxist regimes remains in its infancy and continues to be hampered by constant and not always pertinent comparison with the Soviet Union, thus somewhat blurring the important underlying common theme—the 'scientific theory' of the laws of development of human society and human history. This doctrine is claimed by the leadership of these regimes to consist of the discovery of objective causal relationships; it is used to analyse the contradictions which arise between goals and actuality in the pursuit of a common destiny. Thus the political elites of these countries have been and continue to be influenced in both their ideology and their political practice by Marxism more than any other current of social thought and political practice.

The growth in the number and global significance, as well as the ideological political and economic impact, of Marxist regimes has presented scholars and students with an increasing challenge. In meeting this challenge, social scientists on both sides of the political divide have put forward a dazzling profusion of terms, models, programmes and varieties of interpretation. It is against the background of this profusion that the present comprehensive series on Marxist regimes is offered.

This collection of monographs is envisaged as a series of multi-disciplinary textbooks on the governments, politics, economics and society of these countries. Each of the monographs was prepared by a specialist on the country concerned. Thus, over fifty scholars from all over the world have contributed monographs which were based on first-hand knowledge. The geographical diversity of the authors, combined with the fact that as a group they represent many disciplines of social science, gives their individual analyses and the series as a whole an additional dimension.

Each of the scholars who contributed to this series was asked to analyse such topics as the political culture, the governmental structure, the ruling party, other mass organizations, party-state relations, the policy process, the economy, domestic and foreign relations together with any features peculiar to the country under discussion.

This series does not aim at assigning authenticity or authority to any single one of the political systems included in it. It shows that depending on a variety of historical, cultural, ethnic and political factors, the pursuit of goals derived from the tenets of Marxism has produced different political forms at different times and in different places. It also illustrates the rich diversity among these societies, where attempts to achieve a synthesis between goals derived from Marxism on the one hand, and national realities on the other, have often meant distinctive approaches and solutions to the problems of social, political and economic development.

University College   *Bogdan Szajkowski*
Cardiff

Contents

List of Illustrations and Tables

Preface

The time-honoured controversy about objectivity in the social sciences has preserved its topicality until today. The problem is particularly acute in communist area studies, where the observer's social experience, his political convictions and his actual relationship with the communist world tend to predetermine the outcome of his analysis. At the same time, an author writing in this field is expected to swear a political oath of disclosure, to openly declare whether he is 'for' or 'against' communism. Yet, the choice is not between objective but lifeless description on the one hand and biased but meaningful evaluation on the other. I have tried to solve the dilemma by offering alternative points of view whenever possible. Only the entire spectrum of perspectives—those of the rulers and the ruled, of the partisans of the regime and the dissenters, of 'normal' citizens and marginal groups—can be a reliable basis for both description and evaluation. For the critical evaluation of regime policies, I have primarily referred to official Hungarian sources. In contrast to other communist one-party states, public intra-regime criticism is strong and excludes only a few areas. Still, the goal of this book is neither to condemn nor to praise the policies of the HSWP leadership but to present a picture of contemporary Hungary which is as complete as possible. It is an instant picture of Hungary in 1985, but one that arises out of the historical dynamics of the Hungarian society, one that offers explanations and exposes trends that will shape the country's future.

I am indebted to all my friends inside and outside of Hungary who have contributed to this volume by helping me to collect data, offering advice and inspiration, and eliminating Germanisms and Hungarianisms from the manuscript. Needless to say the responsibility for faults and omissions is entirely my own.

July 1985   *Hans-Georg Heinrich*
Vienna

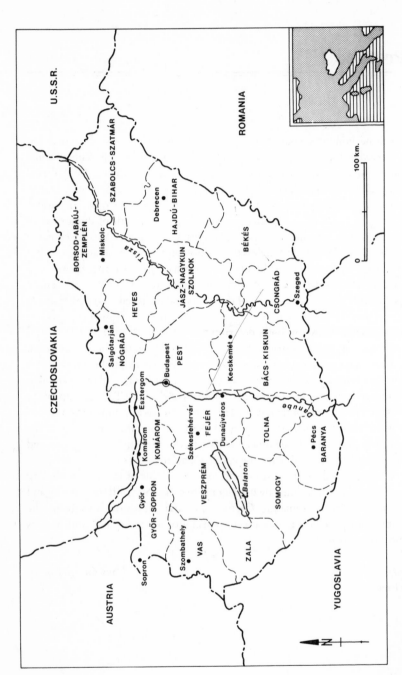

Hungary: county boundaries

Basic Data

Official name	Hungarian People's Republic
Population	10.65 million (1985)
Population density	114.6 per sq. km.
Population growth (% p.a.)	−2.0 (1984)
Urban population (%)	56.4 (1985)
Total labour force:	4.9 million (1984)
Life expectancy	
Men	65.6 (1983)
Women	73.5 (1983)
Infant death rate (per 1,000)	20.2 (1984)
Child death rate (per 1,000)	0.5 (1984)
Ethnic groups:	Germans 170,000; Slovaks 117,000; Serbs, Croats 50,000; Romanians 21,000, Gypsies 400,000
Capital	Budapest 2 million (1985)
Land area	93,034 sq. km of which 17.6% woodland and forest, 50.4% arable land, 13.6% pastures (1984)
Official language	Hungarian
Administrative division	19 counties, Budapest, 109 towns, 2,955 villages (1985)
Membership of international organizations	UN since 1955, GATT since 1973, IMF since 1982, CMEA since 1949, member of more than 800 int. organisations
Foreign relations	Diplomatic and consular relations with 129 states
Political Structure	
Constitution	As of August 1949
Highest legislative body	National Assembly of 386 members
Highest executive body	Council of Ministers
Prime Minister	György Lázár
President	Pál Losonczi
Ruling party	Hungarian Socialist Workers' Party
Secretary General of the Party	János Kádár (since 1956)
Party membership	870,992 (1985): 10.7% of the adult population

Growth indicators (% p.a.)	(1983)	(1984)
National income	0.7	2.6
Industry	1.4	3.0
Heavy	1.2	3.0
Consumer	1.4	3.2
Agriculture	−7.5	4.3
Food production per capita	0.6	3.3

Trade and Balance of Payments

Exports	US$8.6 billion (1984)
Imports	US$8.1 billion (1984)
Exports as % of GNP	42.3
Main exports (%)	Raw materials, semi-finished products, spare parts 30, machines and transport equipment 25, agricultural products 22
Main imports (%)	Raw materials, semi-finished products 46, energy 21, machines 26
Destination of exports (%)	Socialist countries 53.9, non-socialist countries 46.1
Main trading partners	Soviet Union, FRG, Austria, Czechoslovakia
Foreign debt	US$8.8 billion (1985), official US$4.1 billion
Foreign aid	0.06 per cent of GDP (US$10,125,000 in 1984)
Foreign investment	US$83,300,000 (1984)

Food self-sufficiency	Self-sufficiency in major food items (grain, meat, dairy products, vegetables, eggs)
Armed forces	Regular army 105,000 (1985), 1.6% of working-age population; border guards 15,000; workers' militia 60,000

Education and health

School system	Compulsory education 6–16
Primary school enrolment	99% of school-age children enrolled (1980)
Secondary school enrolment	90% of 16 year-olds have finished 8 grades (1985)
Higher education	56 universities and colleges; 6.6% of adult population have university education (1985)
Adult literacy (%)	99 (1985)
Population per hospital bed	106 (1984)
Population per physician	903 (1983)

Economy

GNP	US$23.050 billion (1983)*
GNP per capita	US$2,150 (1983)*
GDP by %	Agriculture 19.1; industry 46.6; services 34.2
State budget (expenditure)	566.7 billion ft (1985)
Defense expenditure % of state budget	6.1
Monetary unit	Forint (ft)
Main crops	Grain (62.1% of cropped land in 1984), industrial crops 12.3: sugar beet, potatoes
Land tenure	0.5 ha for private plots, 100 ha for private holdings, in practice up to 20 ha
Main religions	Catholic (85%), Reformed and Lutheran Churches
Transport	372 million t, 4.045 billion persons (1984)

Sources:

UN Department of International *Statistical Yearbook*, New York.
UNESCO *Statistical Yearbook*, Paris.
Central Statistical Office *Magyar Statisztikai Évkönyv* (*Hungarian Statistical Yearbook*), Budapest.
Central Statistical Office *Statistical Pocket Book*, Budapest.
A Magyar Szocialista Munkáspárt XIII Kongresszusa (The 13th Congress of the Hungarian Socialist Workers' Party), Budapest 1985.
The International Institute for Strategic Studies, *The Military Balance*, London.

Population Forecasting

The following data are projections produced by Poptran, University College Cardiff Population Centre, from United Nations Assessment Data published in 1982, and are reproduced here to provide some basis of comparison with other countries covered by the Marxist Regimes Series.

---

* Calculated on the basis of the official exchange rate. In order to minimize contributions to international organizations, official figures tend to underestimate GNP (GDP) size.

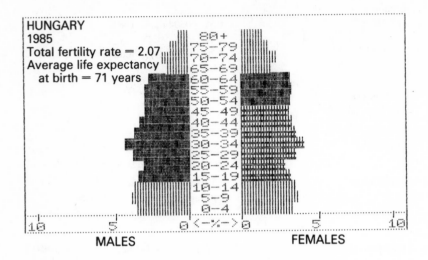

MALES   **FEMALES**

Projected Data for Hungary 1985

Total population ('000)	10,877
Males ('000)	5,297
Females ('000)	5,580
Total fertility rate	2.07
Life expectancy (male)	67.6 years
Life expectancy (female)	74.3 years
Crude birth rate	14.3
Crude death rate	12.0
Annual growth rate	0.23%
Under 15s	21.58%
Over 65s	12.54%
Woman aged 15–49	23.65%
Doubling time	308 years
Population density	117 per sq. km.
Urban population	58.5%

List of Abbreviations

AFP	Agence France Press
ÁVH	Államvédelmi Hivatal (State Protection Authority)
ÁVO	Államvédelmi Osztály (State Protection Department)
CC	Central Committee
CMEA	Council of Mutual Economic Co-operation
C.o.M.	Council of Ministers
COMECON	see CMEA
CPH	Communist Party of Hungary
CPSU	Communist Party of the Soviet Union
CSA	Central Statistical Authority
DOSAAF	dobrovol'noe obshchestvo sotrudnichestva s armiei, aviaciei i flotom (Voluntary Association for Co-operation with the Army, the Airforce and the Navy, USSR)
EEC	European Economic Community
EWC	Economic Work Community
ft	forint
GATT	General Agreement on Tariffs and Trade
GDP	Gross Domestic Product
GNP	Gross National Product
HPR	Hungarian People's Republic
HSWP	Hungarian Socialist Workers' Party
HWP	Hungarian Workers' Party
IMF	International Monetary Fund
KB	Központi Bizottság (Central Committee, CC)
KISZ	Kommunista Ifjúság Szövetsége (Union of Communist Youth)
MOM	Magyar Optikai Müvek (Hungarian Optical Works)
MTI	Magyar Távirati Iroda (Hungarian Telegraphic Agency)
MSzDP	Magyar Szocial-Demokrata Párt (Hungarian Social-Democratic Party)
MSzMP	(Magyar Szocialista Munkáspart (HSWP)
NATO	North Atlantic Treaty Organization
NEM	New Economic Mechanism
Nsz Népszabadság	('People's Freedom'—the Party Gazette)
OEW	Osteuropa-Wirtschaft
OKISZ	Országos Kisiparosok Szövetsége (National Union of Small Artisans)
PB	Political Buro

PC	Presidential Council
PCG	Professional Co-operative Group
p.p	percentage point
PPF	Patriotic People's Front
RAD/BR	Radio Free Europe Background Report
RFER/SR	Radio Free Surope Situation Report
RSFSR	Russian Socialist Federal Soviet Republic
StZsK	*Statisztikai Zsebkönyv* (*Statistical Pocket Book*)
SU	Soviet Union
TSz	Termelőszövetkezet (Producers' Co-operative)
UN	United Nations
US DoSt	United States Department of State
WTO	Warsaw Treaty Organization

1   History and Political Traditions

Geographical and Historical Setting

To a certain extent, a country's socio-economic and political development is determined by geographical, climatic and other environmental factors which are not amenable to social choice. In the case of Hungary, favourable soil and climatic conditions have generated a variety of rural societies, from one of shepherds and horsebreeders to an 'industrial' society whose population for the most part still live in village-type settlements and one-half of which is involved in agricultural activities. The main problem of social organization has always been the quest for a viable system of agricultural production and, sooner or later, agriculture became a major concern of all the regimes and political systems that Hungarian society has produced or that were imposed on it. Even today, under a modernizing industrialist regime, agricultural problems loom large on the agenda of political decision makers. They are responsible for many of the unique patterns of social and political development that Hungary's socialist society has experienced since the Second World War.

Hungary is situated in the Carpathian Basin which is formed by the Alps, the Carpathian and the Dinarian mountains, almost exactly in the centre of the European continent. Since 1919, when it lost the Croatian coast, Hungary has been a landlocked country. Its climate, however, is influenced by the Mediterranean sea, the Atlantic ocean and by the cold East European and Asiatic air currents. As a result, Hungary's weather is characterized by abrupt changes and extremes: the difference between the coldest temperature in January and the average temperature in July exceeds 20 degrees centigrade. However, Hungary's skies are blue most of the time: annually, an average 1,950 hours of sunshine are recorded; in the south the average figure is as high as 2,000 hours. Precipitation varies between 500 and 900 mm/year. As the mountain ridges surrounding Hungary keep out cold storms and rain clouds, precipitation tends to be lowest in the centre of the Carpathian Basin. The water supply problems resulting from this geographical situation have been solved through a well-developed irrigation system. In other places the water supply approaches the optimum for agricultural activities. Two major rivers (the Danube and the Theiss) and their tributaries together with Europe's largest lake (Lake Balaton) provide favourable irrigation conditions. Moreover, the country is rich in hot water springs. There are over 500 thermal springs that yield water with a temperature above 35 degrees centigrade which is used for medical and heating purposes, above all for greenhouses.

Hungary's greatest natural resource is its fertile soil: of a total area of 9,303,200 hectares, 6,783,000 are used for agriculture and forestry (50.9 per cent arable land, 4.6 per cent horticulture and 17 per cent forests). Thus, the percentage of land under cultivation is twice as high as the mean value for all European countries. About 60 per cent of Hungary's territory consists of plains that were originally covered by grass, swamps and watershed areas mixed with large stretches of sandy ground. The plain's topology has changed as a result of centuries of efforts to bring new land under cultivation. The great steppes and plains were ideally suited to the lifestyle of the semi-nomadic Magyar tribes who needed pastures for their sheep and horses. (Even today, sheep and horse breeding is still a standard feature of Hungary's image.) But with the shift to new forms of agricultural production a far-reaching transformation of the original environment ('the first nature') was inevitable. Under the impact of industrialism, Hungary's landscape was subjected to even more radical change. During the second half of the nineteenth century, travellers still described the Great Plain as a piece of Asia in the middle of Europe: malaria-infested air, impassable roads and giant villages. The transformation of this exotic landscape was a precondition for the introduction of intensive farming. The present patterns of industrial location and urbanization are a result of adaptation to given environmental conditions, as well as of a particular configuration of socio-economic and political conditions and decisions. Thus, agriculture is mainly concentrated in the central plain region (Hungary's south-east) whereas the main industrial belt stretches through the central highlands (north-west), reflecting priorities such as proximity to natural resources and to markets, or the availability of labour.

Unique historical constellations are also responsible for Hungary's peculiar pattern of urbanization, where one large administrative, industrial and social centre (Budapest with approximately 2 million inhabitants) faces a number of much smaller regional centres (Miskolc, Szeged, Pécs, Debrecen, Székesfehérvár and Győr with 102,000 to 180,000 inhabitants) and about ninety towns with a predominantly rural character (between 4,000 and 82,000 inhabitants). Much of the country's area is also used for tourism with centres in the Lake Balaton region and in the northern mountain belt where Hungary's highest peak is situated (Kékes, 1015 m). Thus, very little has been preserved of the original landscapes and even natural parks such as the Hortobágy Puszta (on the left bank of the Theiss River) are more of an open air ethnographic museum than a 'first nature' conservation area. However, the farther the transformation of natural into cultural landscapes progresses the more obvious it becomes that society's dependence on its natural environment can be changed only in form and not in substance.

The Magyars

When the Magyar tribes, numbering around 250,000 people, took possession of the Carpathian Basin at the end of the ninth century—according to a twelfth century chronicler, the Land Seizure (*honfoglalás*) began in 896 under the leadership of Árpád—they already had a clear-cut tribal organization and a distinct linguistic and cultural identity. As the first reliable evidence, namely reports by Arab, Persian and Byzantine travellers is from the same period, much about the Magyars' origin and their prehistory must be left to speculation. Comparative linguistics indicate that the Magyar tribes had originally lived in the region between the Volga, Kama and Belaia rivers and the Urals. The Hungarian language belongs to the ural-altaic group and is most closely related to the Finnish and Turkish languages. The Magyar tribes started their westward migration in the fifth century, when they came into contact with Turkish and Slavic peoples. Their eventual homestead, the Carpathian Basin, had been inhabited by the Celts, the Romans, and after the disintegration of the Roman Empire, by various Avar, Hun, German and Slav tribes. The Magyars, a people of horsemen, who depended on pastures and the spoils of war for survival, quickly broke the weak resistance of the Slav plowmen, who were enslaved and later diluted into the seven Magyar tribes. This historical process is still reflected in the vocabulary of modern Hungarian, whose agricultural terms are mostly of a Slav origin. For more than half a century the Magyars continued their old lifestyle, undertaking swift raids deep into the neighbouring territories of Byzantium, Italy and Germany, destroying and plundering cities and villages as far as the Pyrenees Mountains. Several centuries before, the Huns had devastated Europe in a similar way and thus the Magyars were believed to be their offspring. This is why most European languages allude to this imaginary relationship in the names given to the Magyar nation ('Hungarians', '*Hongrois*', 'Venger', etc.).

Eventually, a series of military defeats (Augsburg, 955) forced the Magyars to abandon their semi-nomadic warrior lifestyle. European fighting techniques had eventually proved to be superior. Thus, Prince Géza (972–997) and King Stephen (997–1084) opted for a wholesale imitation of the Western military, socio-economic and cultural traditions. This decision had far-reaching implications. A society of warriors with little social differentiation was to become one of settlers who tilled the soil. In order to underline his determination to follow Western patterns, Stephen took the Christian faith (AD1000). It took another century for Hungarian feudalism to become firmly established. New institutions such as land ownership, the Church and taxes met with the desperate resistance of the partisans of the original Magyar way of life, which erupted in a series of 'pagan revolts' (*pogánylázadások*). The transition to agricultural-feudal production resulted in a deep economic and social crisis, characterized by the breakdown of the traditional community structures and by rapidly increasing social differentiation. During the raids, the Magyar tribes had been exposed to Western luxury, but it only became a permanent feature of Hungarian feudalism in the thirteenth century, when German influence dominated King András II's court. In the nineteenth century, J. Katona used this episode to foster Magyar national consciousness, juxtaposing the evil German influence with the true values of traditional Magyardom in his drama *Bánk Bán*.

At any rate, the appearance of marked class distinctions was also a consequence of the all-out competition for survival and status exacerbated by rising expectations. Those who took to agriculture first or had a stock of slaves or large families proved to have an advantage over single warriors. The latter became tenants in return for services rendered to the landlords. Although they did not lose their personal freedom immediately, a gradual process of enslavement began that culminated in the emergence of a nation composed of two classes. This fundamental social cleavage began to disappear only towards the middle of the nineteenth century. The lower classes—the serfs, shepherds and servants—virtually disappeared from the scene to re-emerge only sporadically, during outbursts of violence such as the peasant revolts directed against the ruling class. The 'groups without history' seem to have preserved features of traditional Magyardom until the twentieth century. As Gy. Illyés, in his classical piece of literary sociology on the life of manorial servants and shepherds (*The People of the Puszta*) describes, these people lived in a world that was entirely separated from upper and middle class luxury and orderliness. Their religious convictions were still mixed with pagan elements, and violence ending in homicide was a regular feature in their lives. Private property and state authority did not enjoy the same degree of respect as with the middle classes: on one occasion, a gendarme was crucified on the tavern door of the village of Ozora because he had dared to intervene in a brawl. Generally speaking, our image of Hungarian history and Hungarian society is due to the traditional focus on the life of the upper classes who were a numerically small albeit very significant part of the tragic tangle in Hungary's social development.

Militancy, however was still held in high esteem in medieval Hungary. The empire, which also included territories that now belong to Romania (Transylvania) and Czechoslovakia (Slovakia), was under constant military pressure, culminating in a devastating Mongol conquest in 1241–42 that almost extinguished Hungary as a nation. Béla IV (1235–70) had to resort to a policy of large-scale immigration in order to bring fresh manpower to the depopulated and deserted areas. Hungary emerged from the Mongol invasion as a multinational and multilinguistic state with the German-Jewish element predominating in the towns, and large areas with Slavic, Romanian and Turkish-speaking groups.

Due to the strong centrifugal forces and the sheer overweight of her neighbours and military opponents, Hungary did not succeed in maintaining its independence. In contrast to Russian or Asian feudalism, the King's attempts to centralize his power failed in the final analysis. Already in 1222 András II had tried to limit the privileges of the aristocracy, whose territories threatened to become independent of the supreme sovereign. In the 'Golden Bull'—Hungary's Magna Charta—he tried to win over the gentry by laying down their rights, including the right to resist in case the solemn royal promise was broken. However, Hungary's feudalism was also different from the West European model. This was primarily due to the weakness of the towns as a political force.

A great number of towns had been founded for strategic purposes following the Tartar raid of 1242. However, the influx of peasants into the towns was impeded by the rule that only free peasants who had satisifed their obligations *vis-à-vis* their landlords were allowed to settle in the cities. The West European principle '*Stadtluft macht frei*' ('town air makes free') did not prevail in Eastern Europe. The growth of Hungarian towns is due to the settlement of non-Magyar townsmen, above all Germans. The city of Buda had remained an ethnically mixed community practically up to 1945, although the non-Magyar elements were assimilated much more swiftly in towns than in the countryside, where separate settlements encouraged ethnic separation. Of course, ethnical homogeneity would have greatly boosted the potential for political action of the Hungarian town. Moreover, the King did not try to make the towns his allies because of their insignificance and because they were constantly threatened by the landed aristocracy. The towns were unable to conclude lasting alliances among themselves because their interests were too diverse. Thus, they failed to agree on a common representation in the Diet (Országgyűlés) which would have increased their political leverage and considerably reduced representation costs. In contrast to the towns, the aristocracy had already formulated their common interests by the thirteenth century. The abortive peasant revolt of 1514 dealt the

Hungarian towns a deadly blow: only the citizens of towns that had not supported the revolt were exempted from the large-scale enslavement of the population. The landed aristocracy had thus succeeded in cutting off the towns from their hinterland, as henceforth any peasant migration to the towns was prohibited. In the course of the Turkish wars, many noblemen fled abroad or settled in the towns. In the seventeenth century the Diet passed a law that forced the towns to grant free settlement and to respect the aristocracy's privileges, thus eroding the status of the towns even more. In the territories under Turkish occupation, gigantic villages had come into being. As a result of these developments, most Hungarian towns had a definitely rural character and Hungary's bourgeoisie was too weak politically and socially to meet the challenges of the twentieth century.

Hungary and the Superpowers

Since her integration into the European balance of powers, Hungary had been exposed to the pressure of other big European powers that wanted to gain control of her strategically important territory. Her central position made her a permanent battleground of the superpowers from West and East. Throughout most of her history, Hungary had been a big power, but the plans to achieve a position of dominance within the Habsburg countries materialized only partially under Mátyás Hunyadi (1458–90). Under the Jagellonians, a union between Poland and Hungary was forged. However, this peak of royal power (both internal and external) was at the same time a period of crisis. The Turks, who had reached the Hungarian frontiers by the middle of the fourteenth century, threatened to involve Hungary in another war of annihilation. When, in 1514, the peasants were armed for a crusade against the Turkish onslaught, they turned against their masters. They were eventually conquered, their leader György Dózsa was burnt on a red-hot iron throne and the complete enslavement of the peasantry laid down in István Werböczi's *Liber Tripartitum*, a law book and a sort of Constitution, in which it was spelled out unambiguously that the peasants had forsaken all their previous rights 'for all eternity'. In 1526, the Turks destroyed the Hungarian army at Mohács and for the next 200 years Hungary was divided between Austria and Turkey. The Erdély (Transylvania) became a Turkish vassal state with considerable autonomy. The Magyars had a choice between two oppressors or allies, but actually they had to wage a two-front war in a series of revolts (some of these were triggered by peasant uprisings).

When the Austrians finally drove the Turks from Hungarian territory, their rule was by no means more benevolent than the Turks'. The Hungarian nobility lost their traditional rights and privileges and the peasants were exploited just as mercilessly as before. The eighteenth century gave rise to an extremely uneven distribution of land ownership—most of the land was in the hands of big landowners—and to an unprecedented immigration of non-Magyar groups (above all Germans, Serbs and Romanians). This forced the Magyars into a minority position within their own country, a fact that greatly contributed to the chauvinistic attitudes during the centuries to follow. Hungary emerged from the Turkish Wars and the Habsburg reconquest as a depopulated and depressed area with a semicolonial status within the Habsburg empire (to which they had belonged since 1547 when the Diet had accepted Ferdinand I as their ruler—protector). However—and this fact is increasingly acknowledged by modern Hungarian historiography—Habsburg rule eventually led to economic growth and steady social progress in the wake of similar developments in the German parts of the monarchy. During the 'Reform Period' (the first half of the nineteenth century) the Hungarian nobility produced a number of reform-orientated personalities, who were the trailblazers of economic and social progress. The most outstanding personality among them was Count István Széchenyi who stood for the abolition of feudal obstacles standing in the way of a modern economy. He built the Chain Bridge (Széchenyi lánchíd) and the Academy of Sciences in Budapest, carried through the regulation of the Danube and Theiss rivers and introduced the steam mill into Hungarian industry, thus symbolizing a fresh departure from the torpor that had befallen Hungarian society.

National and social tensions erupted on 15 March 1848 in a revolution that was put down by Emperor Francis Joseph with the help of Russian troops on 13 August 1849. A period of renewed Habsburg repression followed; the leaders of the revolt were either executed (as in the case of the thirteen 'blood witnesses' of Arad) or fled abroad (like the leader of the uprising, Lajos Kossuth). The revolution's spiritual leader, Hungary's national poet Lajos Petöfi, had died on the battlefield. The breakdown of the revolution was primarily due to the Magyars' isolation in their own country—Slovaks, Romanians and Croats did not join them because they were afraid of Magyar chauvinism—and their radical demands were unacceptable for the Court in Vienna (e.g. the dethronement of the Habsburgs). The unfortunate example of the uprising reinforced a main feature of the Hungarian nation's image: that of a brave rebel with extremist leanings.

The following years, however, were to prove that Hungary's leaders were also capable of moderation and circumspection. A reformist faction under the leadership of Ferenc Deák discarded the constitutional demands advanced in 1848 and expressed its willingness to compromise with Vienna.

Under the impact of military defeats, Emperor Francis Joseph I had to resort to negotiation after a last attempt to rule Hungary with a heavy hand. In spite of its relative backwardness, Hungary had in the meantime undergone a slow but steady economic and social modernization. After the Habsburg reconquest, Austria had imposed a discriminatory tariff policy on Hungarian produce in order to provide Austria's industries and factories with cheap raw materials. However, treasury investment into the Hungarian mining industries had laid the basis for industrial development in the Magyar lands. The peasants' lot had gradually improved as their corvée duties were brought under legal control following the end of the eighteenth century. This large group (85 per cent of the population) was granted personal freedom in 1848. Thus, the modern bureaucratic state had taken the lead in creating a modern bourgeois society through a step by step revolution from above. Yet, as a result social forces were unleashed, throwing all their political weight behind a new deal in the Magyar-Austrian poker game. The new settlement achieved was the *'Compromise' of 1867* which actually created a market of fifty million people for the already existing or incipient capitalist economy in both halves of the Monarchy. On the level of political organization, each part of the Dual Monarchy was autonomous with the exception of the common ('k.u.k.'—*kaiserlich und königlich*) Departments of War, Finance and Foreign Affairs. As the Hungarian economy rapidly gained strength in the years following the Compromise, it clearly emerged as the winner; some authors even maintain that 'it can safely be said that Hungary exploited Austria' (János, 1982, p. 231).

Hungary in the Modern age

The economic setup under the Compromise provided Hungary with a guaranteed market for its agricultural exports and with administrative measures protecting the emerging Hungarian industries. This resulted in an hitherto unprecedented boom in economic development. At the time of the Compromise national per capita income was 86 Crowns and by the eve of World War I, it had quadrupled. The average annual increase amounted to 3.5 per cent, which matched the European standard but fell short of the German rates of increase (Berend-Ránki, 1979, p. 79). In 1867, agriculture had produced 79 per cent of the national income. In 1913, this proportion had shrunk to 61.9 per cent. During the same period, the proportion of uncultivated land decreased from 22 per cent to 5 per cent. Wheat yields per hectare had increased nearly 60 per cent in 1890, indicating large-scale agricultural modernization had taken place. The total length of railroad track grew from 1,350 miles in 1866 to 13,625 miles in 1913. Banking institutions had multiplied rapidly: from forty-one (1867) to over 600 by the early 1890s. Industrial development was lopsided, however, and confined to a number of successful branches. Mining and machine production experienced a swift upsurge and saw rapid technological progress. Many of the industrial giants of today are a product of this first industrialization drive, such as the Ganz-MAVAG (Hungarian State Iron, Steel and Machine Factory) or the Diósgyör State Iron Works. On the other hand, the level of development of the chemical and light industries was generally very low because they faced stiff competition by Austrian and Czech manufacturers and found little official encouragement. The lack of a protective tariff system soon led to demands for Hungarian customs' autonomy and led to considerable social and national tensions. Due to the overall backwardness of the Hungarian economy, the initial investment had to be financed with foreign capital. The first substantial Austrian investments were made immediately after 1849 and went mainly into railway construction, shipping and mining. Austrian capital also launched coal mining and the sugar industries. Only gradually did the economy build up sufficient strength to finance its own expansion. During the entire period of Dualism (1867–1918), 40 per cent of all investments came from abroad.

Economic development and organized public health led to swift population increase. The towns began to swell, although the traditional agrarian character of Hungary was still ubiquitous. In 1870, only 7 per cent of Hungary's fifteen million inhabitants lived in cities with a population over 20,000. In 1910, the figure had risen to 17 (out of a population numbering 18,264,000 of which 54 per cent were Magyars). Nonetheless, the general pattern of strong regional differentiation and discriminatory investment is reflected in the spatial distribution of urban centres. After the 1872 merger of Pest, Buda and Óbuda, Budapest became the political-administrative, economic and cultural centre of the country: the only metropolis, a focal point and the urban counterweight to rural Hungary. Great buildings and bridges were constructed, partly in an effort to match similar undertakings in Vienna. Only Budapest had a distinctly urban character, and a large proportion of Hungarian citydwellers was engaged in agricultural activity.

Hungarian society, which had experienced centuries of near-immobility, began to develop and differentiate itself under the impact of industrialization and a stronger market orientation in agricultural production. Social development lagged considerably after economic development because such conventional channels of mobility as the military and civil service were closed to the lower classes. On the top of Hungary's social pyramid stood the 2,000 large estate holders, who possessed approximately one-fourth of the country's territory. Eight hundred of these landed proprietors were aristocrats, and as most of the nobility was held together through marital and other kinship ties, one can speak of about fifty to one hundred noble families that were most influential socially and politically (such as the Károlyi, Esterházy, Pálffy, Zichy, Pallavichini and the Festetich families). The aristocracy produced political leaders, but also shareholders, bankers and members of the Academy of Sciences. They controlled legislation because the Upper House of the Diet was recruited from the aristocracy. In addition, about 10 per cent of the House of Representatives came from their ranks. They were the main conservative force in the political spectrum, as they were interested in conserving and consolidating their holdings, which were protected by special legal guarantees of indivisibility and non-negotiability. Their natural allies were the 1,000 families of the lower nobility (*köznemesek*) who together with the Church and a few urban proprietors made up the bulk of Hungary's landowning class. On the next rung of the social and political ladder were the members of the *haute bourgeoisie*, concentrated in fifty to one hundred entrepreneurial Budapest families. Some of them were of a humble petty bourgeois origin, many were immigrants from Western Europe and others were descendents of Jewish grain dealers. Their residences, styled after the palaces of the aristocracy, still form the core of Budapest's traditional architecture. However, their wealth opened no doors leading to the aristocratic strata; they were denied the coveted social acceptance and respectability and were despised as *nouveaux riches* by the aristocrats. The middle class (smaller entrepreneurs, higher-level civil servants and the professionals) was, in contrast to other societies, a closed stratum. They drew a sharp dividing line between themselves, the gentlemen (*úriember*) and the lower classes. Mobility into this class from below became possible only with the availability of more jobs (between 1870 and 1918 the number of civil servants increased from 25,000 to 230,000) and with the emergence of a broad critical intelligentsia around the turn of the century. A politically important part of the old Hungarian society's higher classes was the gentry which comprised both impoverished noble families as well as noblemen without sufficient landed property such as the so-called 'seven plumtree nobles'. For the most part, they were the economic victims of the peasants' liberation, as they had been left without the necessary means and organizational skills to engage in agricultural production under market conditions. They were under constant pressure to survive as a class and lived under the permanent threat of status reduction. Consequently, they clung tenaciously to their way of life as country gentlemen, trying to associate with the high aristocracy. As the latter used them as a go-between in relations with the public, the gentry enjoyed a high degree of attention and visibility in public opinion; the 'gentry problem' was considered to be the most urgent social issue of the time. The state reacted to this selective social perception by expanding the bureaucratic apparatus and thereby creating employment opportunities for the gentry. It was the attitudes and the lifestyle of this group that the outside world generalized into the image of the 'Hungarian': the moustached cavalry officer who smashes glasses in the restaurant while listening to gipsy music. In fact, the gentry became the backbone of Hungary's middle class, which was deeply permeated by aristocratic values.

In contrast to these small groups the majority of the Hungarians lived a different life, far from the glittering facades of Budapest, the castles of the landed aristocracy or the artificial world of the gentry. The bulk of the urban population, which numbered slightly over three million in 1910, was formed by the petty bourgeoisie: artisans, servants, small shopkeepers, small entrepreneurs and employees in the catering and transport services made up this stratum and mushroomed in towns and villages. The social distance to the upper, the gentleman (*uri*) classes was unbridgeable, but the petty bourgoisie remained open to mobility from below. If a contemporary Hungarian talked about 'the people', he had precisely this group in mind, and to move up to their ranks was the utmost a worker or a farmer could dream of. The largest class in Hungary was made up of the peasants, many of whom had to struggle for survival because their holdings were too small. The 1,280,000 smallholders (54 per cent of the landowners) owned 6 per cent of the arable land. All in all, the group comprised ten million people. The two million agrarian proletariat were the lowest class. They had emerged from feudalism without land and had to make a living seeking employment during the harvest periods. Together with the smallholders, whose plots tended to decrease even further as a result of hereditary divisions, this stratum was the main reservoir of the *emigrés* (two million Hungarians left for the United States alone). The main domestic migration process led millions of villagers into the expanding industrial centres; by the end of the nineteenth century Hungary's working class amounted to three million people (15 per cent of the total population) (Gergély & Száz, 1978, p. 106).

The Breakup of the Habsburg Monarchy

The political culture and the political traditions that had developed during the second half of the nineteenth century have left a lasting imprint on

Hungarian society and politics. Indeed, some basic behavioural patterns have survived until this day. Of course, the main political issues and concerns of Dualist Hungary were different. One of the cornerstones in the precarious equilibrium between Austria and Hungary was strict constitutionality. For the governing liberals (Szabadelvű Párt), who stood for a loyal attitude *vis-à-vis* Austria, the problem was to keep the critics of the Compromise under control. Moreover, the state was in the hands of the socially dominant class of landed aristocrats. Forty-four per cent of the government members under Dualism were noblemen; of fifteen premiers only two were of bourgeois origin; 50 per cent of the civil servants and three-quarters of the local administrators were aristocrats (Wandruszka-Urbanitsch, 1980, p. 473). Therefore, the state apparatus and above all the parliament had to be protected from the influx of competitors for political power. Suffrage was limited to the proprietors' class through a strict census. Between 1848 and 1913 only about 800,000 people (27 per cent of the adult population) were entitled to vote. In addition to the legal restrictions, the government resorted to manipulating election results via vote purchasing and administrative interference.

For the ordinary people, politics was the pastime of the gentlemen and not very meaningful for their own difficult lives. However, precisely because of the suffrage restrictions that produced a socially homogeneous stock of deputies, the Hungarian parliament proved to be a much more independent and viable forum and a counterweight against the government than the Imperial Council (Reichsrat) in the Austrian half of the Dual Monarchy. The opposition faction within the Liberal party itself was strong enough to withstand government attempts to paralyse the Parliament and the governing party actually lost the 1905 elections in spite of its extensive control possibilities. It became increasingly clear that the fragile coalition of interests that had kept the Monarchy and Hungarian society together was breaking apart. An extremist climate tending towards harsher methods of rule became more prominent. In 1906 the Trade Unions, that had existed since 1868, were suppressed, strikes were penalized and the so-called Whipping Post Act was passed, giving masters the right of corporal punishment over farmhands. The latter were also forbidden to quit their work without the permission of their employers. Yet, the old system only really collapsed with the military defeat of the Monarchy in 1918.

On 30 October 1918, the so-called 'Revolution of the Asters' broke out in Budapest, led by the long-standing opposition leader, Count Mihály Károlyi. The bourgeois republic that Károlyi tried to establish was doomed from the outset because the Allied Powers rejected all Hungarian demands for a reunification of the former territories of the Hungarian Crown. As a result of the founding of the successor states (Yugoslavia, Romania, Czechoslovakia), Hungary's territory had decreased from 325,000 square miles to 92,607 and her population from 20,900,000 to 7,800,000 with many Magyars living abroad, mainly in Romania and Czechoslovakia. The economic consequences of this dismemberment were a mixed blessing for Hungary. Paradoxically, the country gained in industrial strength because about 55 per cent of its industry had remained within the new borders, compared with only 41 per cent of the population. A gap opened, however, between the raw material resources and the manufacturing capacity; e.g. only 11 per cent of the iron ore and 15 per cent of the timber supply remained within the reach of New Hungary's industries, while she retained 80–90 per cent of the engineering and printing plants (Berend-Ránki, 1979, p. 111). Incidentally, this imbalance has continued to be a major constraint on economic policy up to the present. In the long run, the import of the vitally necessary raw materials has to be compensated for by exports. Therefore, a small country like Hungary has no alternative but to participate in international trade. This is why the economic policy of the ideologically widely different governments that Hungary had after World War I looks so strikingly similar.

The Károlyi government, a coalition between bourgeois and right-wing Social Democrats, faced an impossible situation: the economy was in shambles, the demobilized soldiers found no jobs, political radicalism was spreading and international pressure on Hungary was mounting. When the French Army summoned the government to hand over Magyar territories to the successor states (the 'Vyx note'), Károlyi's position became untenable. After negotiations with the Communist and leftist Social Democrat leaders who were still in prison at that time, the Károlyi Government resigned on 21 March 1919 and handed over power to a Communist-Social Democrat group under the leadership of the Communist party head Béla Kun. The rise of the left-wing workers' movement in Hungary had reached a temporary climax.

The Origins and Development of the Communist Party

The commander of the Austrian troops who marched into Buda in 1848 had called the Hungarian revolutionaries 'Communists'. Now, although Kossuth and his followers among the intellectuals and literati claimed allegiance to the principles of utopian socialism, they were—with the single exception of Mihály Táncsics, a genuine socialist—bourgeois radicals with strong social concerns who were appalled by the serious inequalities of Hungary's feudal society. 'We will not rest, until everyone gets his equal share from the basket of affluence' wrote Petőfi in one of his most famous poems ('Himnusz'). But both the formation of the working class and of a revolutionary Socialist ideology were still in an embryonic stage in the middle of the nineteenth century. In Hungary, the organization of the proletariat was hampered by the fact that workers were employed in small workshops spread all over the country and by the fact that literacy was an upper-class skill. The first labour leaders were either journeymen who returned to Hungary after having worked in West European countries or skilled workers who came to Hungary with a certain stock of organizational experience in the higher developed Western workers' movement. The first workers' organizations still bear the imprint of the guild system: their main goal was mutual assistance in emergency cases and the prevention of open conflict between proprietors and employees. The Buda-Pesti Munkásegylet (Workers' Association of Buda and Pest) formed in 1868 still conformed to this model. It responded to the aspirations of middle and lower middle class intellectuals like the writer Mór Jókai. However, a few days after this organization was set up the Általános Munkásegylet (General Workers' Association) was founded by workers who were interested in having an independent political instrument. Its programme was much more moderate than that of the First International, which demanded the complete destruction of the capitalist system. It was reformist-Lassalian; a left faction under Károly Farkas was excluded in 1870. The significance of the Általános Munkásegylet for the development of the Hungarian workers' movement lies in the establishment of ideological communication with the mainstream of European Socialism with its more advanced organizational and ideological patterns. This also meant the end of peaceful coexistence of workers and middle class, namely the state. While the Munkásegylet leaders had accepted state subsidies and royal donations during the early stages of the movement, the picture changed completely after strikes and demonstrations had spread in support of the Paris Commune (1871).

Genuine Marxism came to Hungary in the person of Léo Frankel, an associate of Karl Marx and a member of the Paris Public Council in 1871. After his extradition to Hungary, imprisonment and subsequent release in 1876, Frankel edited the Marxist *Arbeiter-Wochenchronik* together with trade union leader Antal Ihrlinger. The paper attempted to disseminate and popularize Marxist ideas. Preparations for the organization of a legal workers' party began in the second half of 1877. In contrast to Austria, Hungary's constitution did not guarantee the rights of assembly and association. As the Minister of the Interior had not permitted the holding of a socialist conference, Frankel called a 'Non-Voters Congress' because such a step was legal under the election law. The congress was held in April 1878 under strict police surveillance. Seventy-nine Budapest and twenty-five provincial delegates attended. The Congress set up a 'Non-Voters party' which for legal and organizational reasons consisted of three people (Frankel, Ihrlinger and Dr Zsigmond Csillag). A rival party, the Hungarian Workers' Party was founded on 10 June 1878, its members consisting mainly of Budapest intellectuals. In May 1880, both organizations merged to form the General Workers' Party of Hungary. As the authorities, obviously influenced by the abortive Bismarckian anti-socialist policy, had decided that it would be much easier to monitor a legal Socialist party, the General Workers' party responded in kind, emphasizing the legality of its demands put forth in its paper *Népszava* (*People's Voice*, still the trade union gazette in contemporary Hungary).

In spite of the depressing living and working conditions of the proletariat, strike activities were also relatively scarce and modest, albeit increasing steadily: In 1889 there were four strikes, in 1890 already thirty (Vincze, 1975, p. 42). The founding of the Second International (14 July, 1889) had a profound impact on the Hungarian Workers' movement. The first mass demonstration was held on 1 May 1896 with over 60,000 Budapest workers participating. The bourgeois papers were impressed, but registered the event with curiosity rather than anxiety (Gergély & Száz, 1978, p. 179). On 7 December 1890 the General Workers' party was renamed Social Democratic Party of Hungary (Magyar Szociál-Demokrata Párt, *MSzDP*), which represented primarily a semantic victory over the government that had embarked on a policy of social reform in order to curb worker unrest. The MSzDP adopted a much bolder standpoint than its predecessors had, pointing out in its 'Declaration of Principles' that it wanted to realize its program by making use of 'all means leading to the goal and corresponding to the natural sense of justice of the people' (*Népszava*, 14 December 1890). Like its predecessors, the MSzDP stood for the introduction of universal suffrage and basic political rights and freedoms. But overall, its programme had a much more internationalist and revolutionary tone than earlier documents that had emphasized legal activities and compromise. As a response to the problems of the rural proletariat the party stood for the transformation of state and Crown property, church land and large estates into co-operatives. This stance, however, did not reflect an analysis of the prevailing Hungarian situation, but was based as a matter of course on the international socialist doctrine, particularly Wilhelm Liebknecht's *Zur Grund- und Bodenfrage* (1874). But with the expansion of its perspective and the broadening of its social basis from the small group of skilled and educated workers to the millions of agricultural workers, small tenants and smallholders the movement had come into contact with the core problem of Hungarian society. It had spotted the real centre of power, the landed proprietors, and was beginning to jeopardize their rule.

In the nineties, several clashes occurred between local gendarmerie and demonstrators, especially in the central Danube–Theiss region which was hit especially hard by the agricultural crisis. Despite the miserable living conditions and the extreme poverty of the rural population, the party missed the chance to muster broad support because it stuck to dogmatic solutions, rejecting the distribution of land in favour of private farming (Vincze, 1875, p. 54). In 1896, a majority of MSzDP village organizations in the Great Plain left the party and demanded the parcelling out of large estates. Similar demands were advanced by the peasant mass movements after 1906. The MSzDP probably could not afford to sever its links with the internationalist socialist movement (and with Austrian and German Social Democracy in particular) and therefore considered their ideological position as binding. Since socialist parties defined themselves as workers' parties and not peasant parties, a certain *neglect of rural demands* was only too natural. Also, the party's social basis was in the large industries (mainly iron and machine industry) and, geographically, in Budapest. In the period immediately preceding World War I, the number of organized workers was about one hundred thousand, which meant that 10–15 per cent of the industrial proletariat were party members, of which 30 per cent worked in Budapest. The bulk of the blue collar party members were skilled workers (Erényi, 1975, p. 57). The Party was thus almost identical with the trade union organization.

It would be unjust to characterize the MSzDP as a dogmatist and sectarian group. It tried to win the support and the co-operation of the middle classes, the intelligentsia and the farmers by advancing the demand for universal suffrage. The party tried to promote bourgeois democracy as a first step on its path towards socialism. 'We are fully aware' wrote József Diner-Dénes, a leading party journalist, 'that it is the historical task of the Hungarian proletariat to transform feudal Hungary into a bourgeois-capitalist country' (Diner-Dénes, 1910, p. 51). But like most leftist parties the party was certainly an urban community, full of open or hidden contempt for what it regarded as the idiocy and the squalor of village life. When, under the impact of the growing rural unrest, several radical peasant parties were set up, the MSzDP reacted by drawing up a special agrarian programme. For the first time the slogan 'the land to those who till it' made its way into the party's rhetoric. But the version that was proclaimed in 1911 'almost completely disregarded the landed peasantry' (Erényi, 1975, p. 66) and reverted to the old empty formula of the 'co-operation of industrial workers and the agricultural proletariat'.

The majority of the 1911 Congress delegates spoke out against the distribution of the land to private farmers, and also against demands voiced by dissidents like the economist Jenő Varga and György Nisztor, the secretary of the Agricultural Workers Federation. The party found much more support in the ranks of the radical bourgeois intelligentsia and among the literati. For example, a group around the journalist Oszkár Jászi, favouring a bourgeois democracy with social priorities, collaborated with the MSzDP. One of Hungary's greatest poets Endre Ady made no bones about his leftist sympathies. György Lukács, Hungary's outstanding Marxist philosopher, began his career in bourgeois radical societies.

The MSzDP was the first modern party in Hungary. In contrast to the bourgeois concept of a notables' party, which defines the power and the significance of such a political community in terms of the leaders' status, the socialists tried to increase their political leverage by recruiting and mobilizing mass membership and partisans. The public presence of the masses became a salient criterion of a new definition for political success. But although the MSzDP was able to mobilize hundreds of thousands of demonstrators or strikers on several occasions, its real political influence was weak during the entire pre-war period. It was unable to become firmly rooted in the peasant masses, and social reality in Hungary was at variance with its Western ideological premises. In addition, the party was never able to develop revolutionary thrust. As one contemporary Hungarian observer remarked: 'behind the militant resolutions of the various congresses there lurked a policy ready for manoeuvre and compromise' (Erényi, 1975, p. 83). Like most of its sister parties in Europe, the MSzDP supported the Monarchy's entry into World War I, trading internationalism and pacifism for nationalist frenzy and belligerence. Only as the end of the war drew closer and the instances of opposition against the war and of social unrest multiplied, did the party become radical and primed for the revolution ahead.

The Emergence of the Hungarian Party of Communists
The success of the Bolshevik Revolution in Russia (October 1917) and its efforts to end the war had an immediate and profound impact on leftist movements all over Europe. In November 1917, Sándor Garbai, a member of the MSzDP leadership, compared the Russian Revolution to a well-stoked engine which had left St. Petersburg and to which every Social Democratic party should hitch its carriages. During 1918, hundreds of strikes erupted all over the country; the formation of workers' councils was demanded. *Oroszul beszélni* (to speak Russian) became a popular slogan indicating the willingness to follow the Russian example. The majority of the MSzDP leadership was

nevertheless hesitant to trade the German path to socialism for the Russian one and allied with the two left-wing bourgeois parties to establish a republican coalition government after the so-called 'Asters' Revolution of 1918. The success of the revolution was due to the almost total transfer of military authority to the soldiers' councils, which were, however, independent of the MSzDP and leaned towards the radical left (Milei, 1975, p. 107). But the adoption of the Russian-Soviet model was accepted only by a decisive change in the party's rank-and-file membership and its leading strata. During World War I about 500,000 Hungarians had been prisoners of war in Russia.

Some of them had participated in the armed uprising and the Bolsheviks hastily organized national branch units in order to speed up the revolutionary process in other European countries and thus ease the military pressure on the Russian Soviet state. On 24 March 1918, the Hungarian Group of the Russian Communist (Bolshevik) Party was formed under the leadership of Béla Kun, the son of a Jewish clerk and a part-time journalist of Transylvanian origin. After the signing of the Brest-Litovsk peace treaty with Germany (March 1918), the Hungarian prisoners of war were allowed to return home. The Hungarian section had established agitator schools in Moscow and Omsk and, by November 1918, some 500 Hungarians had been prepared for their future roles as party leaders in hastily organized crash courses. At the same time, efforts at mass indoctrination were undertaken. Kun arrived in Budapest on 17 November, determined to apply the Bolshevik experience to a Hungary in turmoil and decay.

As Kun's Leninism and MSzDP reformism proved to be incompatible, the Russians decided to establish a Marxist-Leninist Party. On 24 November, in a private apartment situated in Városmajor Street in Budapest's villa district of Buda, the Communist Party of Hungary was founded. Essentially, it was the result of a merger between Kun's followers and several Social-Democratic opposition groups. Of around twenty Central Committee members (the precise composition of this body is uncertain), eight represented the Russian line (Béla Kun, Ferenc Jancsik, Sándor Kellner, Ernő Pór, Erno Seidler, Károly Vántos and probably also György Nánassy, a young agitator-school graduate who was to become a police informer) (Kovrig, 1979, p. 27). The remainder were left-wing socialists and shop stewards (e.g. János Hirovski, Jenő László) and revolutionary socialists (like József Révai). They were young (aged twenty to forty), and most of them were of Jewish origin. More than half of them would die a violent death either as victims of Stalinism or of Hungarian anti-Bolshevism (Kovrig, 1979, p. 27).

The CPH adopted radicalist image from the start. 'Capitalism is ripe for its downfall' began the lead article of *Vörös Újság* (*Red Gazette*) that appeared first on 7 December 1918 and that attacked the Social Democrats vehemently for their alleged betrayal of the revolution. The MSzDP and the other coalition parties responded in kind by pointing at the non-Magyar, alien origin of the CPH's ideas. Indeed, not only had the ideas come from abroad, but also the necessary funds for revolutionary activities, mainly from Russia and Germany. The Party's influence was greatest among the unemployed, the crippled war veterans and the demobilized non-commissioned officers. The radical intelligentsia responded with enthusiasm to the revolutionary slogans, but was by and large, not willing to subject itself to strict Party discipline (Kovrig, 1979, p. 29). The philosopher and sociologist György Lukacs was a notable exception. By March 1919, according to the report of the Budapest prosecuting attorney, the party had recruited some ten to fifteen thousand members in Budapest and about twenty to twenty-five thousand in the provinces (Milei, 1975, p. 124).

The government decided to react to the communists' incessant attempts at inciting strikes and uprisings with a show of force. When shots were exchanged during a demonstration against the hostile tone of the socialist paper *Népszava* on 20 February 1919, the government ordered the communist leaders arrested. To counterbalance this move, a few conservative leaders who had violently attacked the concept of land reform were also interned. But it was too late to curb the inflamed political passions. Farm labourers took to seizing land and to looting in the villages, while workers' councils spread like wildfire all over the country. Although reality did not favour the communist objective of a proletarian dictatorship, the government was forced to enter into negotiations with the imprisoned communist leaders. The Vyx note eventually brought an end to the brief interlude of the left-centrist government in Hungary. 'Kun's small band of Bolsheviks grabbed for power in the name of their own laws of history' wrote a Western student of Hungarian communism (Kovrig, 1979, p. 37). 'With the birth of the Hungarian Communist movement, the greatest political force and organization of Hungarian history was launched on the road rich in struggles and achievements' runs the corresponding communist version (Milei, 1975, p. 125). In reality, the successes and failures of the Hungarian Soviet Republic were not due to the properties of communist ideology: they were largely attributable to the military situation. The failure of the communist experiment excluded the probability of a comeback for the Communist party until a favourable strategic situation materialized in 1944.

The Hungarian Soviet Republic

The note of 20 March, 1919 ultimatively requested the Hungarian government to hand over the territories that had been adjudicated to Romania,
Yugoslavia and Czechoslovakia. This ultimatum led to an upsurge of patriotic
feelings and to a temporary reunification of the left. The Social Democrats, in
whose hands power was placed by the unlucky Károlyi, invited the
Communists to participate in a new leftist government. Although the
government included only one Communist Commissar (Béla Kun himself),
the CPH actually dominated decision-making. This was due to the fact that
the programmes of both parties had far fewer differences than were later pro-
jected into them. The major disagreement between Communists and
Socialists and between the socialist centre and the left wing concerned foreign
policy: the success of the Hungarian Soviet Republic hinged on the solution
of the territorial question, by diplomatic or military means. The moderates
(the centrist social democrat and trade union leaders) and the radicals could
both advance good reasons for their respective standpoints. On the one hand,
the overwhelming military power of the *Entente* forces that backed
Hungary's enemies made successful military resistance improbable and
moderation in domestic policies advisable; on the other hand, the prospects
of an impending world revolution and a Soviet intervention on Hungary's
side gave hope to all those who favoured an all-out war and tried to prove
their loyalty to the Bolshevik cause by imitating Leninist policies, including
terror against the 'counter-revolutionaries'. But in the final analysis, differences were personal rather than ideological and communist and socialists
needed each other, because deep cleavages would have exposed serious weak-
nesses to external and internal enemies (Kenez 1971, 84). Alas, when it became
obvious that further military resistance was futile, the communists went into
exile on 1 August 1919, with, to their credit, long overdue social reforms, but
also with a record of extremely harsh measures such as requisitioning living
space for the proletariat and creating a climate of terror that worsened during
the last chaotic days of the regime. According to Hungarian sources, about
590 executions were carried out, many of them for counter-revolutionary
crimes (Kovrig, 1979, p. 52).

The significance of the Hungarian Soviet Republic for the further
development of socialism in Hungary lies in the symbolic aspects of this 133-
day interlude. For the Communist party, it is the epitome of cherished heroic
revolutionary traditions: 'The most beautiful pages of the history of the Communist Party tell of the Soviet Republic. The history of these 133 days belongs
to the traditions of the struggles in Hungary's rich past of which we will

always be proud, and which ensure for our people the love and sympathy of all progressive mankind' (Kirschner, 1975, p. 153). The lessons drawn from this event include the inability of bourgeois democracy to solve Hungary's problems and the unreliability of the Social Democrats (Kirschner, 1975, p. 145), but also the fact that it was impossible to apply Russian Bolshevism without adapting it to Hungarian circumstances. This refers especially to the agricultural policy of the Commissars, which 'failed to appease the peasants' hunger for land' (Kirschner, 1975, p. 173). For the anti-communists, the violent history of the Hungarian Soviet Republic is evocative of communist brutality, an attitude that silently passes over the fact that in 1919 Soviet Hungary Communists and Social Democrats were hardly distinguishable. In the eyes of many Hungarians, the failure of the Soviet Republic also discredited the bourgeois-democratic alternatives that had paved the way for the communist experiment.

Counter-revolution and Restoration

On 1 August 1919, the so-called Trade Union government took office under the premiership of Gyula Peidl. The majority of its members were liberal-minded trade union leaders who wanted to restore democracy and end the war. Yet the situation did not favour peace and democracy. When the Romanians occupied Budapest on 4 August 1919, anti-communist officers began to organize a 'White' army and a witch-hunt for communist sympathizers. When the Trade Union government resigned on 6 August, it was followed by a group of monarchist officers under István Friedrich, who were backed by the British and the Italians as well as by Archduke Joseph Habsburg. This government was unable to control the terror unleashed by officers' detachments all over Hungary and even contributed to it by issuing instructions for accelerated trials and stiff sentences for communists. White terror gained the dimensions of a nationwide pogrom, as many leading Communists had been Jews. According to Western estimates, about five thousand persons were executed and seventy-five thousand jailed for their activities during the Commune. Some hundred thousand went into exile, most of them not communists but socialist and liberal political activists and intellectuals as well as middle-class Jews (Kovrig, 1979, p. 74). The socialists remaining in Hungary had no choice but to dissociate themselves from the communists, reverting to their pre-war German programme and adopting a fierce anti-communist stance. This was the price they had to pay for readmission into politics. On 14 November 1919 Miklós Horthy, the commander of the White Army, rode into Budapest on a white horse—for him it was a 'sinful city' because of the two revolutions against the established order—and political power again reverted to the upper and upper middle classes. With the blessing of the *Entente*, a Christian Bloc government was assembled under Károly Huszár that included the Social Democrats (trade union leader Károly Peyer held the welfare portfolio) and even a few liberals. But essentially, the left had been emasculated and had to renounce any intention to oppose conservative restoration. The communists had lost all strength and its members and leaders were dispersed and decimated by executions, imprisonment or exile. The Diet passed a Law (III/1921) on the 'more effective protection of state and social order' that ruled out any communist activities in Hungary. Other laws reduced parliamentary authority by expanding the jurisdiction of the Head of State (Horthy), limited general suffrage, reintroduced corporal punishment and barred access to the universities for Jews. In spite of its heavy-handed policies, the Horthy regime met with growing acceptance both domestically and internationally. A modest land reform, distributing 13 per cent of the arable land, increased Horthy's popularity with the private peasant. The main asset of the regime was its effectiveness in maintaining law and order. The peoples in Europe were tired of war and revolution and longed for orderly reconstruction.

The exiled leadership of the Communist party, however, refused to see the changing of the tide and clung tenaciously to its old dogmas. Kun and Lukács tried to preserve the revolutionary and extremist spirit of the Hungarian Soviet Republic, still hoping for their early return in the wake of a world revolution. Meanwhile, the Soviet Bolsheviks had abandoned this idea and Lenin himself had the ultra-leftist Hungarians in mind when he castigated leftist extremism in his *Left-Wing Communism: An Infantile Disorder of Communism*. Lenin also referred to Kun's enunciations as *les bêtises de* Béla Kun. The Communist attempts to re-entrenchment on Hungarian soil were, by and large, a failure. Several illegal organizations were set up and immediately destroyed by the police. A cover party, the Socialist Workers' Party of Hungary, set up in 1924, was too weak to gather the necessary number of signatures for nominating candidates in the parliamentary election campaign.

The popularity of the leftist opposition among the workers increased as a result of the austerity measures under Premier István Bethlen. Bethlen had concluded a secret agreement with trade union leader Peyer, in which he had won the aquiescence of the MSzDP by guaranteeing the right to exist of workers' organizations in exchange for the promise not to set up trade union organizations for public servants, the railway personnel and the rural proletariat. There was widespread indignation about this agreement and it had repercussions in the Socialist International as well. It is difficult to imagine how Bethlen and a responsible socialist leadership could have acted otherwise in the circumstances. The war and the ensuing territorial redistribution had thoroughly disoriented an economy that had prospered in a market of fifty million people. The existing industrial surplus capacity could not be used because the successor states isolated themselves with high customs barriers. Thus, the giant Hungarian mills, that had once worked for the whole Monarchy, had to close down one after the other. The export of grain was both impossible and imperative. Hungary found itself in a vicious circle as a result of the breakup of the Dual Monarchy. An austerity policy entailing heavy social costs was the only option for the defeated countries of World War I. The vicious circle was temporarily broken by the negotiation of a foreign loan that involved League of Nations' supervision of the country's finances (1924).

By 1930, a favourable trade balance had been reached. In 1938, the industrial production was 38 per cent higher than in 1913. Bauxite mining, tin and aluminium production had begun and several large industrial complexes (e.g. the Izzó, Weiss Manfred, MOM and Gamma Works) which are still the backbone of Hungarian heavy industry had been established. However, these results were achieved at the expense of a substantial foreign debt, which went hand in hand with a growing economic dependence on Germany. In the second half of the 1930s, 50 per cent of Hungary's foreign trade was with the new and rapidly developing military and economic superpower—Nazi Germany. Hungary's two-class social system had been left practically untouched by political and economic change. The 'gentleman middle class' was the main pillar of the Horthy regime, a class that was still totally isolated from the masses of small peasants, agricultural workers and urban proletarians. Rural overpopulation could not be relieved by migration to the cities because the austerity policies of the twenties had resulted in high unemployment, partly spilling over into the middle class. The writer Gyula Oláh had christened Hungary the 'country of three million beggars'. An expanding state sector that provided the coveted status of a uniform (postman, policeman, railwayman, etc.) mitigated the impact of the economic crisis on the middle class and reinforced their supportive attitude. The grievances of the industrial proletariat were assuaged by social security schemes.

In this situation the Hungarian communists had to rely on the Communist International rather than on domestic forces as their main source of strength. Its influence among the unemployed workers never went beyond a figure of some thousand. The party leadership engaged in bickering over ideological nuances, their political activity consisted mainly of organizational work for the Comintern (thus, the General Secretary Elect Mátyás Rákosi was dispatched to Italy; B. Kun himself was put in charge of the Comintern Balcan Secretariat in 1929). Co-operation with the Social Democrats was excluded because of the current Comintern policy which branded them as 'Social Fascists' and because of their violent anti-communism within the MSzDP. When the spectre of fascism had become a tangible reality and had begun to annihilate the workers' movement in its entirety, the Comintern tried to correct its earlier tactical mistake by coining its 1933 'popular front' slogan. But this move came too late.

Bethlen's regime had not exactly been benevolent towards the opposition. Under his successor Gyula Gömbös (1932–36) the regime moved closer to overt fascism. Using Mussolini's Italy as a model, Gömbös' goal was to construct a corporatist *führer* state which would have meant the end of the independent workers' movement. The MSzDP was still the party of the industrial proletariat. However, with the increasing German orientation in Hungarian politics and economics, the Hungarian Nazi Party, the Arrow Cross (*Nyilasok*) advanced rapidly, and in the 1939 elections, took the majority of the workers' vote. The Social Democrats, anxious to survive amidst a general mood of increasing militancy and anti-Semitism, moved to the right. It voted for the militarization programme in the Diet and even put pressure on its Jewish leaders to resign and to disappear from the public eye.

To make matters worse, the hard core of the Moscow-based communist leadership had fallen victim to the Great Purge. Of the party's leadership, of the survivors of the Commune and founders of the party, almost everybody had been executed by the end of the Second Purge in 1939. Kun himself died on 30 November 1939 in Butyrka Prison, presumably executed. The Home party had been dismantled in 1936, its members instructed to join the trade unions and the MSzDP, and to wait for further orders. A provisional Central Committee had been set up in Prague. With the German occupation of Czechoslovakia, this body had to cease operating and the Hungarian Communist party had once again become defunct. Its main activity consisted in issuing periodicals in which the Comintern general line was reiterated. Nevertheless, the party was able to elaborate a new platform on agrarian policy: now, it stood for a land reform that would turn over the land to those who were tilling it. Obviously, its overall weakness had forced the party to make this tactical concession. Hungary's social composition clearly illustrates the potential radicalism of her countryfolk. In the thirties there were two million peasants of which 500,000 were farm-hands who had no land at all; 1,600,000 were smallholders with farms under ten acres (10 per cent of the arable land); over one million smallholders and medium landowners with farms ranging between ten and forty hectares held 21 per cent of the land; the rest (350,000 people) were the rural upper class (the *kulaks* in communist parlance) who as a group possessed 26 per cent of the land. The proportion of estate owners with more than 500 acres was 1 per cent, yet they held 43 per cent of the total farm area (Pintér, 1876, p. 226). However, unallied with a strong political group, the Communist party had no political influence in the villages, as it was in complete disarray. The political significance of the party was clearly a function of international developments, as was demonstrated by subsequent events.

Hungary During the Second World War

Following Hitler's ascent to power, Germany's economic and political influence had grown incessantly. Hungary eventually became Germany's military ally after Hitler had restored the last Romanian territories to it. In 1941 Hungarian units participated in the campaign against Yugoslavia and on 27 June 1941, war was declared on the Soviet Union. The Communist party immediately reacted with slogans that called for a separate peace and 'not a single soldier for Hitler'. This time, its slogans tied in with a general intellectual ferment that had been triggered by Hungary's wartime alliance with Germany. Premier Pál Teleki's suicide, in protest against the violation of Hungarian territory by the Wehrmacht came as a shock to those who were not willing to link Hungary's fate to Germany's war. In 1942 the communists set up the Hungarian Historical Memorial Committee (Magyar Történelmi Emlékbizottság) which was joined by many prominent personalities from political, cultural and intellectual circles (e.g. the Smallholder party leaders E. Bajcsy-Zsilinski and Zoltán Tildy, the writer Gyula Illyés and the historian Gyula Szekfű). The party organization itself suffered from repeated waves of arrests. However, the party could claim a number of sympathizers in other parties, such as the MSzDP leaders György Marosán and Antal Szakasits and the prominent Smallholders István Dobi and Endre Bajcsy-Zsilinski. Yet the opposition parties refrained from openly opposing a government which had succeeded in maintaining greater internal freedom than in the rest of occupied Europe. When the communists tried to turn the Memorial Committee into a weapon of political struggle against the government headed by László Bárdossy and later Miklós Kállay, some of its members (e.g. Bajcsy-Zsilinski) who were primarily interested in Hungary's withdrawal from the war left the Committee. Further development, however, forced the opposition to draw closer together. The Second Hungarian Army was annihilated during the battle on the Don in January 1943. The 40,000 casualties, 70,000 wounded and numerous prisoners had a profound impact on both the Hungarian population and its leaders. The 'Hungarian Stalingrad' made it clear that Hungary must leave the Axis. The many peace feelers put out towards the West did not lead to the conclusion of a separate peace, the East–West wartime alliance was still intact. When the Germans realized that their ally was faltering, they occupied Hungary on 19 March 1944 and upon the proclamation of an armistice by Horthy on 15 October 1944, installed a quisling government under the right-wing officer and Arrow Cross leader Ferenc Szálasi.

The CPH, which had followed the tactics of hibernating in other parties or setting up camouflage organizations, realized that its hour had struck. With the Soviet army rapidly advancing in the East and Hitler's military coalition breaking apart, with the Germans and their Hungarian puppets forcing the country into a last-minute war effort through terror and repression, the idea of a neutral Hungary had become illusory. As the Western allies were not willing to violate the agreements on the partition of Europe, Hungary's only option lay in siding with the Soviets. The party began partisan activities in the shrinking German-occupied territory; army generals, together with tens of thousands of Hungarian soldiers, defected to the Soviet side. All in all, 2,500 partisans are reported to have been active during the last year of the war (Kovrig, 1969, p. 149).

The Road to Takeover (1944–7)

During Anglo-Soviet negotiations in October 1944, Churchill had offered Stalin a shared responsibility in terms of a fifty-fifty influence in Hungary. The United States recognized the 'more direct interests of the SU' in this area (Us DoSt, 1955, p. 242). In spite of the formal consensus that was reached at the Teheran, Yalta, and Potsdam Conferences, containing a Soviet pledge to establish democratic and freely elected governments in the East European countries, Stalin did not hesitate to employ non-democratic methods once he was confident of Western non-intervention. The representatives of the CPH therefore had a dominant position in the local and central organizations that emerged in the wake of the advancing Red army. On 21 December 1944, a Hungarian National Independence Front was formed in Debrecen consisting of delegates from the CPH, the MSzDP, the National Peasant party, the Independent Smallholders' party, the Party of Field Workers and Citizens, the Citizens' Democratic party and the (communist-sponsored) free trade unions. In addition, nineteen independents participated, some of which were communist sympathizers. Thus, of the 230 members of the Debrecen Assembly, the CPH could count on the support of about 30 per cent of the delegates, but in reality the party's influence extended much farther. In fact, its succeeded in including into the Debrecen programme the demand for Hungary's participation in the Soviet war effort, a policy which was probably resented by a majority of the delegates.

Soviet and communist violence, itself a reaction to the atrocities of the Germans and the repression under Hungarian fascism and Nazism, could not be combatted effectively or even criticized by the opposition parties. The Soviets and their extension, the CPH, were in effective control right from the start. Their march to power had many facets. In January 1945, under the aegis of the communist Minister of Agriculture, Imre Nagy, the much-heralded land reform was carried out. This reform eliminated the large estate-owner and made the smallholder the dominant social figure in the village. Communist party membership began to climb swiftly. As before, the workers in the industries concentrated in and around Budapest proved to be the social stronghold of the CPH. In autumn 1945, the party had a peasant membership of some 150,000 members. But the overwhelming majority of Hungarian peasants streamed into the peasant parties. In the elections of 4 November 1945, in what was probably the only free election ever held in Hungary, the Smallholder party obtained 57 per cent of the vote and 245 Diet mandates out of 409. The CPH received 17 per cent (seventy seats), the MSzDP 17.4 per cent (sixty-nine seats). The more leftist-radical peasant party, the National Peasant party, got twenty-three seats and the Citizens' Democratic party two. The defeat of the CPH, which had reunited its domestic and Soviet branches in February 1945, was obvious. The party was confused by this serious setback. Under the undisputed leadership of the Muscovites, under the protection and assistance of the Red army, a middle-of-the-road policy had been worked out that was militant enough to suit the radicals and moderate enough to be palatable for the Hungarian voter. The failure at the November elections was a blow that was hard to take. 'The extent of the political ignorance and the gullibility of the working masses became numerically measurable,' commented a contemporary communist author (Ságvári, 1975, p. 304). Others blame the CPH leaders for having neglected the antifascist potential among the petty bourgeois strata and for the concentration on the Smallholders' left wing. 'The strengthening of the Smallholders party's right wing was a direct consequence of the position taken by the leftist parties', wrote a party journalist in a commentary on Gyula Kállai's memoirs (*Népszabadság*, 7 June 1984). The victory of the 'bourgeois' Smallholder party, however, did not necessarily mean the victory of middle class Hungary. There seems to have been a radical potential in several non–communist parties that was inadequately reflected in their leadership's policies (Gáti, 1971, p. 358). However, it seems highly unlikely that the Hungarians would have embraced communist radicalism in 1945, whatever the gullibility or the effect of anti-Soviet feelings may have been.

Faced with a strong opposition in the Diet, the CPH embarked on a policy of attrition (the notorious 'salami tactics'). This included tactical alliances with the left wings in the Smallholder and Social Democratic parties, the uncovering of 'conspiracies' (such as the 'Hungarian Community' a group that allegedly wanted to restore Horthyism and was said to be sponsored by the United States), the utilization of Soviet dominance to secure strongholds in the government (like the Ministry of the Interior), and the purge of anti-communists from the state apparatus (which was linked to a campaign to reduce redundancy for economic reasons). But the gradual loss of popular trust in the Smallholder party was probably due to the demonstrated political impotence of their leaders. Once it had become obvious that the West was not willing to intervene, the Smallholders with their pronounced pro-Western standpoint lost their political leverage. Finally, when Ferenc Nagy, the leader of the Hungarian Smallholder party was personally attacked and accused by the CPH of criminal activities in connection with the 'Hungarian Community' plot, he chose to stay abroad. His example was followed by many other prominent opposition leaders. This event, however, was nothing more than the end point of a long process involving the systematic destruction of domestic opposition to communist rule.

The government was reshuffled in June 1947. The elections on 5 September 1947 were the final step in the takeover process. The elections had been carefully staged and orchestrated by the CPH. The Minister of the Interior, L. Rajk, had prepared a new electoral law, that disfranchised many among the anti-communist opposition. In a majority of constituencies, the screening committees applied the discriminatory clauses of the new law, refusing to register 'reactionary' voters. The CPH displayed remarkable moderation in its electoral platform. The voters were promised a 'Third Road' Hungarian Socialism. In addition, the so-called 'blue slips', issued to voters who declared they would vote outside of their constituency, are reported to have been misused by officials in the Ministry of the Interior in order to increase the CPH vote. Communist sympathizers are reported to have been transported in Soviet army trucks from one polling station to the next (Kovrig, 1979, p. 218). The official election results showed 22.3 per cent for the CPH, 8.3 per cent for the National Peasant party and 14.9 per cent for the Social Democrats. The main opposition force, the Smallholder party, obtained 15.4 per cent, which reflected its disintegration as a result of its own helplessness and the establishment of rival opposition groups. Communist historiography describes this process as follows: '[The elections] were characterized by the strengthening of the working class power and by the destruction of the counter-revolutionary forces. The reaction had left the Smallholder party, because this party had stopped to give them shelter' (Nemes, 1960, p. 250). All in all, the Communist-led coalition took 60.8 per cent of the total vote. Communist vote concentrated in five urban out of sixteen electoral districts. Reportedly, only 40 per cent of the land reform beneficiaries supported the CPH. Thus, the communist takeover in 1947 signified not only the final step of Hungary's inclusion into the Soviet power sphere but also a continuation of the town–village gradient, this time in the form of a subjugation of the village under the industrial centres.

Developmental Periods in Regime History

All divisions into periods are to a certain extent arbitrary. They depend on a decision concerning the length of the time period under survey and on a judgement on the relevance of the aspects selected. Moreover, much will depend on which developmental goals are ascribed to the process. Thus, the most widely accepted periodization of regime development in Communist Hungary presupposes a dialectical triad consisting of Stalinism, the anti-Stalinist antithesis of the 1956 insurrection and Kádárism as the synthesis. However, while the 1956 revolution was undoubtedly a major turning point, this approach neglects certain long-term trends in Hungarian social and economic development and overemphasizes political phenomena. The political excesses of the Rákosi regime and its deep ideological commitment contrast sharply with the brief de-Stalinization and anti-Stalinist interludes as well a with the present regime's pragmatism, so that most observers have been prompted to explain regime development in political and ideological terms, breaking up regime history into handy time units: Totalitarianism (1947-53). The New Course and Revolution (1953-56 , Repression and Consolidation (1956-62), Decompression (1962-8), Liberalization (1968-72), Recentralization (1972-7), NEM Reinvigoration (1977 onwards).

In the light of Hungary's historical predicament, its high dependence on world markets, Rákosiism can be understood as a basically economic strategy designed to decrease dependence through a policy of self-sufficiency and autarky. The failure of this strategem paved the way to the alternative option of Kádárism, which as an economic strategy aims at making Hungary stronger and independent by harnessing the pull of the world market. This higher-independence-via-interdependence scheme appears as the logical response to the fact that the internal dynamics of the Hungarian economy cannot supply the necessary thrust to break with the traditional security-orientated and anti-competitive habits. As a social strategy, Kádárism means the full acceptance and integration of the peasant and a continuous closing of the social distance between town and village. The Hungarian peasant had been both a pariah and the main producer of surplus value for centuries; Rákosi's policy of financing industrial development through the exploitation of the farmers was no historical novelty. It was only during the sixties that the Hungarian peasants began to emancipate themselves and began to alter irreversibly their economic, social and political status. Last but not least, communism in Hungary can be seen as a specific incarnation of industrialism. The limited and delayed industrialization in the nineteenth century had provided the economic and political background for radical modernization, which in its initial phase took the form of a war between industrial cities against traditional agricultural producers. This war was terminated through a peace treaty proclaimed in 1962 (the official adoption of Alliance policy). However, the war against nature, that Hungary is waging together with all industrial nations, is likely to continue for an indefinite period of time; the prospects for a peace treaty or even an armistice are dim.

Thus, the forty years of socialism in Hungary should be reviewed from a broader historical perspective. Party policy undoubtedly brought about a radical transformation of the Hungarian society. The policy makers were operating in specific societal contexts and under specific historical constraints. Even the Rákosiites remained prisoners of historical processes in spite of their seeming arbitrariness. A *longue durée* perspective can provide criteria for the long-term significance of political events and can help to explain party policy as a response to secular changes in the deep structure of society.

Stalinism in Hungary

The founding of Cominform (September 1947) that had closed the ranks of Stalin's allies in Eastern Europe in the face of the incipient Cold War, signalled the end of moderate policies and ushered in a period of uniformity in Soviet East Europe. As 'American Imperialism' had become the main threat in the eyes of the USSR, all parties and groups suspected of disloyalty *vis-à-vis* the Soviet Union were wiped out. The last independent party, the MSzDP, merged with the CPH under the pressure of the communists and of its own left wing led by György Marosán on 12 June 1948 after a purge of rightist members and leaders. The new party adopted the name of Hungarian Workers' party (Magyar Dolgozók Pártja) and was completely dominated by its communist parent. Thus, the communists were free to launch their ambitious plan to turn Hungary into an 'iron and steel country'. The nationalization of all enterprises employing more than 100 workers was followed by the introduction of a Soviet-styled command economy which reflected Soviet defence priorities rather than Hungarian consumer needs. Huge steelmills (like the one at Sztalinváros which, incidentally, had been planned by the Horthy government as early as 1943) were set up in economically unfavourable locations, without giving any consideration to the availability of skilled labour and raw materials. Simultaneously, and against the advice and the protest of the moderate Minister of Agriculture Imre Nagy, the party waged a battle against the private peasant (kulak) who was treated as a class enemy. They were pressured to join the collective farms (*termelőszövetség, TSz*) through ever-increasing tax burdens and compulsory delivery quotas at artificially low prices. The Hungarian peasant reacted to this campaign with stubborn resistance; in 1953, the proportion of co-operative fields was still as low as 20.3 per cent, of the arable land. The party could nevertheless claim its crash industrialization policy had been very successful: national income had grown, the industrial proletariat had reached an impressive number (682,108 in 1954) and full employment had been obtained. On the other hand, the standard of living had declined drastically, product quality had dipped and in view of the growing popular disaffection the party felt obliged to resort to terrorist methods. The Constitution that was proclaimed on 20 August 1949, the traditional St Stephen's day, was a reflection of the social and political changes as well as the goals and policies of the HWP, e.g. by excluding all those who did not belong to the category of 'working people' from the exercise of the rights granted in the document. Thus, the Constitution duly recorded a situation in which the regime was engaged in an all-out battle against actual or imagined enemies: the bourgeoisie, the *kulaks*, the churches, in other words, most of the people. Hungarian Stalinism was characterized by the slogan 'Those who are not with us are against us'.

The party itself was centralized and practically ruled by the General Secretary, Mátyás Rákosi. When Yugoslavia's defiance threw Stalin into a veritable hysteria and purges were arranged in the satellite countries in order to uncover 'Titoists' and demonstrate the magnitude of the threat, Rákosi took the opportunity to eliminate his potential rivals within the party. The most spectacular case was the trial of László Rajk, a popular home communist, a participant in the Spanish Civil War and the Minister of the Interior until

August 1948. Rajk was forced to 'admit' under torture that he had been an informer for the Horthyist police, had betrayed his comrades in Spain, had acted as a spy for the United States and French intelligence services and had conspired with Tito to overthrow the regime and to restore capitalism in Hungary. Allegedly, it was his friend János Kádár who had persuaded him to admit the correctness of the trumped-up charges 'for the sake of the Party' (Shawcross, 1974, p. 66). The revolution devoured many of its own children. Among those who vanished into Stalinist prisons were J. Kádár, Gy. Kállai and other prominent Communists who were to play an important part in the establishment of a post-Stalinist Hungary after 1956. But the terrorist regime actually engulfed all parts of the population. About 4,000 former Social Democratic functionaries had been arrested by 1950 and the overall number of people arrested, imprisoned in labour camps and exiled internally is reported to have been 150,000 or 1.5 per cent of the population (Váli, 1961, p. 64). AVH (secret police) terror succeeded in intimidating the populace into submission. The elections on 7 May 1953, held on the basis of a uniform national ticket ended with 98.2 per cent of the voters 'endorsing' HWP policies. But this stability and unity proved to be only superficial.

The New Course

When Stalin's death in March 1953 had ushered in the 'thaw', a period of cautious liberalization in the Soviet Union, the East European communists soon found themselves a state of uncertainty. The first cracks in the monolith had appeared and popular resentment against Stalinism was expressed in a series of strikes and disturbances. Pressured by the new leaders in Moscow and in order to soothe people's feelings, Rákosi grudgingly acknowledged some of his mistakes. Imre Nagy, the moderate Muscovite, became Premier. On 28 June 1953, the Central Committee criticized Rákosi and his 'Personality Cult' and adopted a program of reforms (June Resolutions), calling for a greater emphasis on light and consumer industries and an alleviation of the private peasant's burdens. Collectivized peasants were allowed to relinquish membership in the agricultural co-operatives. As a result, the peasants began to leave the TSz in large numbers (according to official figures approximately 130,000 out of a total of 380,000 by December 1953) (Simon, 1975, p. 363), and the workers' living standard rose by approximately 15 per cent in 1954. Nagy also tried to democratize the party by introducing secret balloting and he attempted to remedy the distortions of the personality cult by lifting discriminations against 'class enemies' and emphasizing legality. The reforms, however created their own problems: the revamping of investment patterns caused inflationary pressures, increased the country's foreign debt and lowered productivity; the stimulation of private activity aroused the suspicion of many party leaders who saw the party monopoly jeopardized. In these circumstances Rákosi, who had retained the General Secretaryship of the party, was able to wage a successful war of obstruction against the reformers around I. Nagy. The eventual outcome of this tug of war was decided in Moscow. After Nagy's main protector Premier Malenkov was forced to resign on 8 February 1955, in connection with a new policy to stop the disintegrative tendencies inherent in the New Course, the HWP Central Committee expelled Nagy from the party under the charge of having pursued 'rightist, opportunist policies... factionalist methods'. He was also accused of 'clericalism' and 'nepotism'. Four days later, he lost all of his state offices, including his university teaching post. Nagy's New Course had never constituted a consistent set of policies and had been blocked from its very inception, but it certainly contained a dangerously disruptive element which was duly reinforced by a Radio Free Europe propaganda campaign haranguing Hungarians to exploit the possibilities of the New Course (Kovrig, 1979, p. 280), thus bringing grist to the mill of the conservatives. Post-1956 Hungarian historiography places the blame for the failure to implement the June Resolutions on both Nagy's 'rightist policies' and the 'revival of leftist sectarian policies' (Zsilák, 1975, p. 348).

October 1956

When the Soviet party committed itself fully to a de-Stalinization policy at its twentieth Congress (February 1956), Rákosi's position became untenable. The domestic opposition, which had made deep inroads into the party, began to employ what could be called 'reverse salami tactics': using Aesopian language and couching its demands in the official party jargon, it advocated an increasing number of policy changes that would have grave consequences not only for the Stalinist system still prevailing in Hungary but also for socialism in Hungary. As was to be expected, university students and intellectuals were generally the most vociferous groups. Their views found publicity in a discussion forum called the Petőfi Circle. Authorized by the party as a safety valve, the Petőfi Circle attracted thousands of people, including dissident communists like György Lukács, Géza Losonczy and Imre Nagy himself. In one of the discussions, the writer Tibor Déry declared: 'The real trouble is not the personality cult, dogmatism, or the lack of democracy, it is the lack of freedom.' When Rákosi wanted to break the opposition's back by proposing a return to terrorist methods, Moscow intervened. Anastas Mikoyan came to

Budapest and ordered Rákosi's dismissal and the election of another Stalinist, Ernő Gerő, as party head. The Soviets were obviously keen for a compromise solution because neither Rákosi nor Nagy seemed acceptable to
them. Gerő, who took office on 18 July 1956, tried in vain to stem the tide of
increasingly more radical demands that were further encouraged by the
developments in Poland where the 'Polish Nagy', Władysław Gomułka
offered a credible prospect for a free and prosperous Poland. The rehabilita-
tion and the public reburial of prominent victims of Stalinism were turned
into open demonstrations against the regime. The pressure to bring Nagy to
the top again became so great that Gerő reluctantly approved his readmit-
tance to the party on 13 October 1956. A psychological threshold was
crossed during a discussion in Győr on 16 October, when, for the first time,
the withdrawal of Soviet troops was demanded. Undoubtedly, the example
of Austria that had declared its neutrality about a year before loomed large
over all pertinent discussions.

The actual revolutionary process began with the election of a new
Executive Committee in the Writers' Union on 17 September 1956, in
which the official candidates were defeated. The process of party disintegration gained momentum when student assemblies adopted resolutions
following Gomulka's return to leadership on 19 October. The first of these
meetings took place in Szeged on 20 October; the most important assembly
was held on 22 October at the Budapest Technical University. The resolution that was adopted unanimously by around 5,000 students contained
sixteen points:

 (1) withdrawal of Soviet forces;
 (2) elections in the CPH by secret ballot;
 (3) dismissal of Stalinists from party positions and Nagy's reinstatement;
 (4) public trial of M. Farkas [Rákosi's henchman] and his accomplices;
 (5) multiparty general elections;
 (6) full equality in Hungarian-Soviet relations;
 (7) reorganization of economic life by experts;
 (8) publication of foreign trade agreements;
 (9) revision of work norms in industry;
(10) readjustment of the agricultural delivery system;
(11) release of political prisoners;
(12) full freedom of opinion and of the press;
(13) removal of the Stalin statue;
(14) readoption of the Kossuth coat-of-arms;
(15) expression of solidarity with Poland;

(16) convocation of a youth parliament; deposition of a wreath before the statue of General Bem [a hero of the 1830 Polish and 1848 Hungarian revolutions].

The last demand proved to be the spark that ignited what was to become the Hungarian Revolution—(namely Counter-revolution). The Petőfi Circle, together with student organizations, managed to assemble a huge crowd of peaceful demonstrators in the afternoon of 23 October. The demonstration had originally been prohibited, but the order was rescinded at 2.23 p.m. Demonstrators were gathering peacefully at other places in Budapest, too. All in all, the crowd amounted to hundreds of thousands of demonstrators, calling for Nagy's reinstatement as Premier and shouting anti-Soviet slogans. A helpless and confused Gerő tried to defuse the situation and save the party's face by warning of 'enemies of the people' who allegedly were attempting to 'rock the power of the working class, destroy the worker–peasant alliance, undermine the leading role of the working class. . . . and heap abuse on the Soviet Union'. But people had learned to link this type of ideological jargon with Stalinist tyranny and the result of Gerő's speech was an escalation of revolutionary passions. Violence started when panicky AVH men fired on the unarmed crowd that had assembled in front of the radio headquarters, demanding that the sixteen points be broadcast. Army detachments that were dispatched there handed over their weapons to the crowd. During the same night, other groups tore down the huge statue of Stalin, a symbol of Soviet domination. The following morning, the Central Committee decided to call in Soviet troops because it had become obvious that, with the exception of the AVH forces there were no armed units that could be depended on to back the regime. The Soviet military action was limited both in scope and effect and the rebels, equipped with arms from Army depots, were able to force the Soviets to withdraw from Budapest, giving the revolutionaries a dangerous illusion of military superiority and victory.

Meanwhile, on 24 October, Nagy was appointed Premier, and one day later upon the arrival of two emissaries from Moscow (Mikoyan and M. Suslov) Kádár was made General Secretary of the party, Nagy promised to establish a government 'on the broadest national foundations', called for an armistice and declared a general amnesty for the armed revolutionaries. Kádár was less conciliatory in tone; like Gerő, he warned of a relapse into capitalism and Horthyite fascism, but at the same time promised that relations with the Soviet Union would be restored 'in a spirit of complete equality'. The disintegration of the previous political organization went hand in hand with the formation of new and independent organizations. The

Trade Union Central Council had freed itself from party tutelage and encouraged the workers to elect workers' councils, the pre-1949 parties set up founding committees. With the Soviet withdrawal, the 'Revolutionary Councils' (commanding insurgent groups) and the 'National Guard' (under Defence Minister Pál Maleter) became the real locus of power. The revolutionary groups, by no means an organized or coherent force, began to play a game of nerves with the Soviets. There was no organization that could co-ordinate or aggregate escalating demands. The revolutionary process had gone completely out of hand.

On 27 October, a People's Patriotic Government was formed that included two former Smallholder leaders, Béla Kovács and Zoltán Tildy, the erstwhile head of state. The revolutionaries, however, were not satisfied. 'We do not recognize the present government' wrote *Függetlenség* (*Independence*), the paper of the Hungarian Revolutionary Committee on 30 October. This Committee was led by István Dudás, a national communist and a victim of the Rákosi era. 'Russians Go Home' ran another headline in the same edition. Thereupon, a multiparty system was established on 30 October. Mikoyan and Suslov had been dispatched to Budapest on another troubleshooting mission, and on 31 October Mikoyan negotiated with Tildy on the withdrawal of Hungary from the Warsaw Pact, the restoration of a multiparty system, the preparation of free elections and the immediate recall of Soviet forces. The overall anti-communist atmosphere in Budapest and in the country in general together with the climate of violence following street fights in Budapest also led to atrocities against communists. On 30 October, bands of insurgents attacked the party headquarters and lynched the AVO men who had sought refuge there (the AVH had been renamed the AVO in 1953). All in all, some 300 communists were murdered. Under the headline 'People's Judgement on Republic Square' *Függetlenség* applauded these sinister aspects of the struggle for freedom on 1 November 1956.

The most decisive stage of the revolution was reached on the same day when I. Nagy, upon receiving news that fresh Soviet army units had crossed the Hungarian frontier, and after fruitless negotiations with the Soviet ambassador Y. Andropov, decided to withdraw from the Warsaw Pact. Nagy notified the United Nations, asking the four Great Powers to recognize Hungary's neutrality. By the morning of 2 November, Soviet armoured divisions had reached the outskirts of Budapest. Imre Nagy, in a radio message that captured the gloomy atmosphere of despair that had seized the triumphant revolutionaries, said:

This is Imre Nagy speaking, the President of the Council of Ministers of the Hungarian People's Republic. Today at daybreak Soviet troops attacked our capital with the obvious intention of overthrowing the legal democratic Hungarian government. Our troops are in combat. The government is at its post. I notify the people of our country and the entire world of this fact.

At the same time, Kádár, who had restyled the Party into a Hungarian Socialist Workers' Party (Magyar Szocialista Munkáspárt) split with the Nagy Government and changed sides. Faced with the dilemma of becoming a realistic traitor or an irrational hero, he opted for the former. The military defeat of the rebels was swift and complete. Within ten days the last traces of military resistance were stamped out. The Revolutionary Worker–Peasant Government that had been formed in the Soviet border town of Uzhgorod came to Budapest on 4 November in the wake of Soviet troops to rule a country in shambles and a society in total disarray. Twenty-five thousand people had been killed, 150,000 injured, 200,000 had left the country. The downfall of the revolution that had eventually turned into a veritable war between nations had left only frustration, despair and sullen bitterness.

Controversial Issues in Historiography
The October war in Hungary was the most serious crisis in Eastern Europe since the establishment of Marxist regimes in this region. The political significance of the event is recognized by communist and non-communist historiography alike. While the revolutionaries were branded as 'counter-revolutionaries' bent on re-establishing the pre-communist order in the official government version 'Counter-revolutionary Forces in the October Events in Hungary' published by the Information Bureau of the Council of Ministers, Budapest, 1975, Western sources tended indiscriminately to hail all participants as 'freedom fighters'. Looking back upon the events, with the benefit of greater distance and less personal involvement, there have been more recent attempts to untangle a complex and confused situation. Still, a few hotly disputed issues have remained. They concern:

(1) The scope of the revolution and the backing that the revolutionary groups enjoyed. It is a fact that there existed no master plan drawn up by sinister conspiratorial forces. The revolution followed the law of spontaneity if nothing else. The revolutionaries had no common positive model for a future Hungary. There was consensus only in the negative, i.e. that the Soviets must leave the country and that the communist power system must be dismantled. As far as social backing for the insurgents is concerned, they were able to recruit 14 per cent of the professionals, 13

per cent of the industrial workers, 20 per cent of the students, 6 per cent of the peasants and 2 per cent of the white-collar workers. Most of them were young (Kovrig, 1979, p. 310). It is true that the insurgents' bands also attracted people who most certainly did not deserve the lofty title of a 'freedom fighter'. It is also true that among the political groups that were sprouting amidst the general turmoil and chaos, there were also groups with explicit monarchist and fascist tendencies. On the other hand, the communist allegation about Cardinal Mindszenty (who had been released from prison on 31 October) having demanded the restitution of church property is probably false. Anyway, in his famous speech of 3 November, he called for religious freedom, but recognized the historical change since 1945. In its 3 November edition, the catholic newspaper *A Szív* (The Heart) actually categorically rejected any demands for the restitution of church land. As far as the support for the communists is concerned, it was evaluated by György Lukács, who had been Minister of Culture in the Nagy Government, as follows:

> Communism in Hungary has been totally disgraced. Collected around the party will probably be small groups of progressive intellectuals, writers and a few young people. The workers will prefer to follow the Social Democrats. In free elections the Communists will obtain 5 per cent of the vote, 10 per cent at the most [*Nowa Kultura*, 2 December 1956].

(2) Soviet strategy: most Western authors see Mikoyan's promise to withdraw Soviet troops and the ensuing withdrawal after the first intervention as a purely tactical move. However, this view understates the confusion and hesitation prevailing in Soviet command centres. The Soviet military certainly had plans for a second and this time decisive strike in store because it was imperative to keep this option open. The picture of military operations was somewhat contradictory. While some Soviet trops were pulling out of Budapest, others were entering the country. The Soviet upper limit of tolerance was reached when it became obvious that the Nagy government wished to leave the Warsaw Pact, for this would have meant the disruption of the entire post-World War II security strategy. Nagy, in a radio broadcast on the evening of Wednesday 31 October, had declared Hungary a neutral country (*Népszabadság*, 2 November). In an interview to English and American journalists he declared on the same day 'Hungary has the alternative to leave the Warsaw Pact individually without breaking up the entire alliance and we will press this position energetically' (*Magyar Nemzet*, 1 November 1956).

(3) Western involvement: contrary to communist allegations there is no con-

vincing proof of direct military interference or Western military supplies to the insurgents. However, the fatal role played by RFE encouragement—raising hopes for an American military intervention—is very obvious. As a result of Soviet intervention and American non-intervention, most Hungarians began to adopt a pragmatic attitude towards both super-powers: they had to live with Soviet occupation and give up their illusions about the United States as an unselfish champion of human rights.

'Normalization' à la Hongroise; the Origins of the Alliance Policy

When János Kádár returned to Budapest on 7 November 1956, he headed a practically non-existing party in a country that was ravaged by civil war and that was united in its bitter opposition against the Russian invaders and all those who had taken their side. A few years later, Kádár had become the most popular leader in Eastern Europe, a political miracle which is still a source of perplexity for many observers.

The first years of Kádár's rule were characterized by a show of force under the cover of Soviet bayonets. The stubborn resistance of the workers' councils was broken by disbanding the workers' guard units and creating a Workers' Militia under the leadership of former AVO officers in February 1957. The few remaining workers' councils that had constituted a veritable counter-government and had effectively applied the strike weapon were dissolved in November 1957. Summary proceedings wiped out the last traces of resistance. According to estimates, 20,000 people were arrested, 2,000 executed and many thousand deported to the Soviet Union (Kovrig, 1979, p. 318). A purge that was directed both against the Nagyists and the old Stalinist guard was carried out in the party and state apparatus. In order to symbolize a fresh start, the party had, already in the October days, assumed the name HSWP. Reconstructing the party was an incredibly difficult task, as the new leadership had to face not only the overt hostility of the population and the bitter opposition of the Nagy group, but also the profound distrust of the Rákosiites and of most of the proliberation veterans. This battle on two fronts led to the exclusion of a number of high-ranking Stalinists and to the destruction of the Nagy group. Following a new Soviet verbal attack on the Yugoslavs, Nagy, who had taken refuge in the Yugoslav embassy and had been promised safe conduct, was arrested by Soviet troops on 22 November 1956 and transported to Romania. He and three of his followers were executed in June 1958 (apparently against Kádár's wish) and a number of other leading Nagyites received prison sentences. Several thousand party members who had been active during the Nagy government were expelled from the party as 'revisionists', namely 'nationalists'. Simultaneously, Kádár followed a policy of step by step economic reform. The Rákosi-type steel-eater command economy had been discarded but economic recovery was painfully slow, although by mid-1957 industrial production had reached its pre-revolution level. The stimulus had come from outside, via Soviet credits and a fuller integration into COMECON that provided Hungary access to a guaranteed market and to vitally necessary raw materials.

Serious party efforts to reconcile the peasant with communist rule only began after the 1956 events. The abolition of compulsory deliveries was followed by a new collectivization drive, as a solution to Hungary's agricultural problems. In mid-1957 the proportion of Tsz members in the total agricultural labour force stood at 6.1 per cent and the number of private farms had reached the 1949 level. Finally, after much debate in the party a collectivization campaign was launched in January 1959 which, by and large, desisted from using open coercion, relying instead on fiscal incentives and persuasion. By 1962, the collective sector had reached a peak of 75 per cent of the agricultural work-force. The economic side of this political victory was, however, less brilliant because the newly collectivized peasantry refused to work during official hours, preferring to cultivate their private plots instead, and as a result production stagnated at pre-war levels and family incomes declined. During this difficult period, only massive state support saved Hungary's socialist agriculture, but it was an investment that would bear fruit: The modernization of the underdeveloped, obsolescent agriculture was a major precondition for prosperity and social stability. Politically, the party had firmly committed itself to a policy relying on co-operation with the populace rather than coercion. After the completion of collectivization and with the backing of the CPSU's Twenty-Second Congress's anti-Stalin thrust, Kádár formulated this policy in his famous slogan, 'Whereas the Rákosiites used to say that those who are not with us are against us, we say those who are not against us are with us' (*Népszabadság*, 21 January 1962). Kádár's *Szövetségi politika* (Alliance Policy), an illegitimate child of the revolution, had been born.

The Alliance Policy received official sanction on the HSWP's Eighth Congress (20–4 November 1962). The new policy entailed a radical breach with past Stalinist practices and the promise of a gradual liberalization for the future. Inner-party democracy was emphasized (e.g. through the reintroduction of the secret vote). Amnesties were granted to counter-revolutionaries; a final amnesty was proclaimed in March 1963. Increasingly, non-party specialists were recruited for leadership positions in the state and economic apparatus. Political loyalty ceased to be the sole criterion for leadership selection. Clearly, Kádár was heading towards a reconciliation with the people who had totally rejected him as a quisling in 1956.

Hungary in the Age of Economism

1963 is a watershed year in the history of communist Hungary. Up to this time, the official creed was that Hungary's economic problems had a political solution irrespective of the economic and social costs. Since approximately 1963, with the first tangible successes of the Alliance Policy, the party has favoured an economic solution to political problems, thus assigning the economic system an uncontested priority. As had occurred in the other East European countries (notably Czechoslovakia), it had become clear in Hungary that the traditional command economy had become obsolete and unviable. Hungary's position as a small country with an insufficient raw material base was particularly precarious. No government could, in the long run, afford to neglect the structural characteristics of the Hungarian economic system. Thus, in December 1963, a Central Committee plenum entrusted Rezső Nyers, a former printer who had risen to the position of Minister of Finance, with the task of elaborating a programme for economic reform. Nyers' report was submitted in November 1965, and in May 1966 the Plenum approved the transition to a new system of economic guidance. Jenő Fock, a fervent partisan of the reform, became Premier in April 1967 and Hungary's New Economic Mechanism (*Új Gazdasági Mechanizmus*) went into operation as of 1 January 1968. The enterprises were freed from petty plan tutelage and during the first three reform years significant progress was achieved. The foreign trade balance turned positive and a boom in agricultural and consumer good production filled the hitherto empty shelves. This 'economic miracle', however, created its own problems, the contours of which have become visible since the early seventies. The investment and consumption boom led to excessive imports of Western technology and consumer goods and the volume of uncompleted investments grew steadily. Simultaneously, sharp differentials in the income structure appeared. All of this called for countermeasures, and in spite of a cautious recentralization the long-term objectives of the reform were never abandoned.

The year 1975 was another turning point. In January 1975, Hungary, which had hitherto been relatively sheltered from the oil crisis by Soviet energy supplies at a favourable price, concluded a new Trade Agreement that dramatically worsened its terms of trade. By 1983, Hungary had incurred a loss equivalent to its entire annual GNP over a period of ten years. This called not only for a careful husbandry of investment resources and a drastic increase in productivity, but also meant a temporary abandonment of growth objectives. The general policy became one of weathering the storm while seeking to develop internal resources. Since the end of the 1970s, private production and the service trades have received unprecedented encouragement, triggering a boom in private entrepreneurship. On the whole, the party has this time managed to keep the economic and social consequences under control.

Probably the main achievement of this period is the modernization of agriculture. Hand in hand with a drastic decline in agricultural employment due to the massive investments in large production units and the import of Western harvesting and processing technology, agricultural production reached a level which makes Hungary self-sufficient in major agricultural products and a net agricultural exporter. In addition a unique form of cooperation was found between the private and the socialized sectors of agricultural production, an arrangement that supplies around 30 per cent of the total agricultural output, provides employment and private activity for a large part of the population and is nevertheless monitored by the government. Hungary's peasants, once free horsemen, but who had lived in slavery for long centuries, are now beginning to reap the fruits of a millenium spent in drudgery, suppression, poverty, wartime devastation and revolutions.

2 The Political System

Between Dogmatism and Revisionism: Party Development since 1945

From Liberation to Takeover

When the Hungarian Comintern agents who had spent the war in Moscow came to Hungary in the wake of the Soviet troops, they found a party in shambles. It numbered about thousand members and most of its leaders had been imprisoned or executed following futile attempts to topple the pro-German governments. Party reconstruction was handled by the Muscovites (Rákosi, Farkas, Gerő, Kossa, I. Nagy, Révai and Vas) and directed from Moscow itself. The home communists, who had eagerly awaited the liberation (Apró, Horváth, Kádár, Péter, Rajk and others), accepted Moscow's policies without reservation, although the wisdom of some of the personnel decisions was questionable. Farkas for example had been a member of the Czech party and had little insight into the Hungarian situation. However, factional cleavages did not emerge because the most urgent task in this period was the forging of a mass party that could stand the electoral test. Therefore, the leadership had to relax ideological requirements for admission into the party, trading doctrinaire purity for mass influence. As a result, membership figures reached 220,000 in July and 500,000 in September 1945.

The November 1945 electoral defeat was a severe setback for the party, and the temporary decrease in membership indicated a widespread bandwagon mentality among the rank and file members. At its Third Congress (29 September–1 October 1946) the party had 653,300 members (6.7 per cent of the population). Membership composition conformed to the role of a proletarian vanguard that the party had carved out for itself: 42.6 per cent of its members were workers, 39.4 per cent peasants, 4.8 per cent intellectuals and 13.3 per cent others. However, as a consequence of the merger with the Social Democratic Party, these proportions changed drastically. At the time of the first Joint Congress (12 June 1948) peasant representation in the Party of Hungarian Workers had decreased to 18.2 per cent, while the proportion of white-collar workers and others had jumped to 37.5 per cent. The former Communists outnumbered former Social Democrats in all important party organs. Of the fourteen Politburo members nine were Communists and five Social Democrats. Rákosi became General Secretary and the Social Democrat Szakasíts was given the largely ceremonial position of Party President (Kovrig, 1979, p. 153).

The Cult of Personality (1948–53)

During 1948 Hungary was shaken by large-scale purges that were to restore the 'proper social balance'. In 1949 out of a party membership of 880,717, 49.3 per cent were industrial and agricultural workers, 13.4 per cent peasants, 4 per cent intellectuals and 33.5 per cent white-collar workers and others. The drastic decrease in the percentage of farmers was due to the collectivization campaign, which had turned the party to its new tasks of hunting down and destroying the 'class enemies'. A huge army of grassroots activists, trusties and informers penetrated the entire social fabric and took root in each institution and agency, even in individual apartment buildings. At the party apex Rákosi had succeeded in turning the apparatus into his personal instrument. Emulating his idol Stalin, he had staffed the top party bodies with individuals who owed loyalty and allegiance to him personally. Under the sole master, Gerő and Farkas occupied the second hierarchical echelon, being responsible for the economy, defence and security respectively. The fourth in the top leadership quadrangle was the party ideologist Révai, who was assigned the task of Sovietizing Hungarian cultural life. In order to remain the undisputed leader, Rákosi set out to annihilate every actual or potential opposition. His main strike was directed at the home communists and the Spanish Civil War veterans, or the 'Westerners' in general. They were selected as suitable victims to demonstrate the reality of a Titoist–Western conspiracy in a series of show trials. In 1950 most former Social Democratic leaders were purged. When, in November 1951 46.4 per cent of the middle and lower party leaders were replaced by a young guard that owed their careers to Rákosi, the whole party was virtually in his hands. The mechanism of power becomes obvious in an analysis of the career paths of the new recruits: in 1963, 38 per cent of the party members were active workers by their current profession but 59 per cent by their original occupation, while the figures for white-collar workers were 38.8 per cent and 13.2 per cent respectively. This means that the party was a major channel of social mobility for the more ambitious young workers. Around 60,000 workers were made enterprise managers during the 1949–53 period. Thus, Rákosi did not have to enforce obedience within the party. He could rely on the ambitions and on the anxieties of his protégés, who were strongly opposed to change because this could mean the end of their careers.

The New Course and Temporary Restoration (1953-6)

The New Course in Hungary was triggered in Moscow. The Stalinist system of personal power survived in several East European countries. In Hungary, power was dualized but remained asymmetric: Imre Nagy, who emerged as the spokesman of liberal policies, became Premier and a member of the Politburo and wielded influence in the revitalized Patriotic People's Front, but Rákosi still dominated the Politburo. The most prominent victims of the first round of destalinization were Farkas and Révai. The Third Congress of the Hungarian Workers' Party (24–30 May 1954) was preceded by secret party elections in which only 55.1 per cent of the former leaders were re-elected. But the extent to which Rákosi still dominated the party is demonstrated by the fact that among the nine-member Politburo elected by the Central Committee only one, namely Imre Nagy himself, was not a follower of Rákosi. Imre Nagy's popularity was higher among the non-party masses than within the party itself. That the Hungarian party leaders during this period were figures in a chess game played in Moscow was proved by Nagy's demotion on 14 April 1955, which followed Malenkov's downfall. Farkas, who had sided with Nagy not because he shared his liberal convictions but for opportunistic reasons, also lost his party offices.

Destalinization, Disintegration and Resurrection (1956-7)

Rákosi fell because of the Soviet leadership's apprehensions of repetition of the anti-Soviet riots in the Polish town of Poznań in June 1956. For the first time in the post-war history of the party, it had to react to popular moods and had lost its role as an active force. The basically Stalinist power system, which was a hierarchically structured, centralized apparatus with clear loyalties and command lines was ill-adapted to a situation in which it had lost its leadership and faced conflicting and openly anti-party demands voiced by the non-party public. Decomposition was the natural consequence. During the uprising, the party continued its organized existence only at the top level: on 28 October 1956, the Central Committee dissolved and placed power in the hands of an extraordinary Presidium chaired by Kádár. Gerő, Hegedűs and other Stalinist leaders followed Rákosi into exile in the USSR. After the defeat of the insurrection, four people (Kádár, Apró, Kossa and Münnich) set out to form a new party on 6 November 1956. To all appearances, Kádár was aware of the fact that he had to seek reconciliation with the populace in the long run, but the prevailing situation gave him no other chance than to mold a new party out of old Stalinists. The party that on 1 December 1956 had 37,818

members, mainly consisted of pre-1945 veterans and Rákosiites who had
hibernated during the uprising. Thus, among the 227,420 members reported
on 1 April 1957, only 10 per cent had been recruited after October 1956.
Embroiled in a two-front battle against the Rákosiites and the 'revisionist
Nagy–Losonczy group', Kádár's main strength lay in the trust that the Soviet
leaders put in him. He was therefore able to exclude from the party a large
bloc of leftist leaders (such as Gerő, Ács, Bata and Hegedűs) that had been
contaminated by their close co-operation with Rákosi. When, in January
1957, József Révai returned from the USSR to lead the dogmatist counterattack that sought to re-establish the old order, the failure of the Soviet 'anti-
party group' that had tried to dethrone Khrushchev came just in time. By
June 1957 Kádár's line had found a majority in the top organs of the
Hungarian party.

The Central Committee elected at the extraordinary party conference (27–
29 June 1957) consisted mainly of newcomers. Fifteen out of its fifty-three
members had been members of the 1954 Central Committee, eighteen had
been in the Central Committee elected in 1951, and ten had been elected both
in 1951 and 1954. In the 11-member Politburo, Kádár could claim a majority
of six Kádárites (including himself) and the only remnant from the Rákosi
period was D. Nemes, one of Rákosi's ideologists. The cosmetic purpose
behind the composition of the top-level party organs was to create the image
of a truly Hungarian people's government. There were only two Muscovites
in the Politburo and, much in contrast to the times of Rákosi, almost no Jews.
But the rank and file membership composition tells a different story: 85.2 per
cent of the entire membership had been in the pre-1956 Party. Obviously, this
type of continuity was the price Kádár had to pay to dispose of an army of
experienced and reliable party soldiers. Party strength increased slowly. At the
time of the Seventh Congress (30 November–5 December 1959) membership
stood at 402,456. Sixty per cent of the members were workers and 14 per cent
working peasants according to their original occupation, which meant that
the social composition of the new party did not differ very much from that of
its predecessor. Kádár had adopted a gradualist line, trying to eliminate
Stalinist leaders step by step and replacing them by individuals who had been
purged under Rákosi. The 1961 CPSU Congress provided the basis for a more
resolute attack against the dogmatist wing: Stalinists like I. Dögei and K. Kiss
were purged, and Rákosi himself excluded from the party. The purge also
encompassed the judiciary and the security forces, which had been strongholds of the hardliners. Yet the danger of a conservative restoration was still
far from being eliminated.

On 12 December 1962, the former left-wing Social Democratic leader

Gy. Marosán was relieved of his party offices because he had allied himself with the hardliners in an anti-Kádár plot. However, the Eighth Congress (20–4 November 1962) was a turning point in party history. The top party organs were packed with loyal followers of the new course: Gáspár, Komócsin and Szirmai rose to the Politburo and among the new Secretaries was R. Nyers, a former printer who, due to his ambition and his talent, had made it to Minister of Finance and who was to become the *spiritus rector* of the economic reform. The rise in overall membership (in August 1962 the figure was 511,965) documented the fact that the party as a whole was about to dissociate itself from the past. But at the same time, the course taken by Kádár—the Eighth Congress had proclaimed the Alliance Policy—had become relatively immune against the vicissitudes of political change in Moscow. Khrushchev's removal in October 1964 and the more conservative general line taken by his successor L. I. Brezhnev had remarkably little impact on the political climate in Hungary. The Eighth Congress had introduced important changes in the party rules: the call for vigilance against class enemies and the ban on admission against former 'exploiters' were dropped together with the concept of 'working peasants'. The silent funeral of class struggle terminology was an important symbolic victory for the new line. Dissenting views were encouraged within the party as long as a binding decision had not been taken. Elections were to be held by secret ballot. All this indicated a high degree of confidence and self-assertion within the Kádár group.

The Reform Period (1968–85)

Probably the most important step taken by the Hungarian reformers was the decision to revamp the centralist economic system. Reacting to popular discontent over emergency measures taken in 1965, a Central Committee plenum in May 1966 set the stage for NEM that was to go afloat on 1 January 1968. In a last-minute effort, the conservative faction had tried to prevent what they saw as a threat to the leading role of the party. Their defeat in the debate and the initial success of the reform silenced the anti-Kádár opposition and gave Kádár an opportunity to co-opt more reformers to the top party organs (Aczél, Benke and Németh). However, the price of NEM—increasing social inequalities—fuelled left-wing criticism once more. Reacting to strong trade union pressure, a November 1972 CC plenum decreed a wage increase for 1.3 million workers. Moreover, a resolution censured 'certain party organizations' for allowing open dissent. The following year witnessed another wage increase for workers and Aczél's and Nyers's removal from the Secretariat. Stiffer tax provisions were introduced to curb the profit opportunities of the rising new middle classes and a group of dissident sociologists lost party membership, as well as their jobs. The 'Workers' Opposition' was able to put brakes on the reform because it was backed by a broad coalition of those forces that saw their interests endangered by NEM: managers of big industrial enterprises who felt threatened by the burgeoning small and private enterprises that could offer better wage and work conditions, thus syphoning off the more efficient and better-trained workers; the ministerial bureaucracy whose activities became more and more questionable with increasing enterprise autonomy. The conservative faction that had viewed the introduction of the reform with fundamentalist distrust, were joined by Kádárites who were motivated by a sincere concern about the social goals and the identity of the party (like B. Biszku) or by local activists who were exposed to the direct onslaught of grass-roots criticism. But the fact that no viable alternative was available, apart from trying to correct some irritating aspects of the reform, left its essence untouched.

The new leaders that joined the Politburo at the Eleventh Congress (17–22 March 1975) were cautious reformers and technocrats like Gy. Lázár (who also took premiership from the ailing J. Fock). Losonczi's elevation to Politburo membership signalled an increased importance of foreign relations, since the former agricultural laborer had been Chairman of the Presidential Council since 1967. The conservative backswing ended in 1977 with the lifting of most restrictions. The reform efforts received new thrust; B. Biszku's fall from the Secretariat at the April 1978 CC plenum symbolized this new departure. Now K. Németh was given the important jurisdiction over the personnel (cadre) department. Deputy Premier F. Havasi, a technocrat, was charged with the promotion of economic reform and the erstwhile Minister of Justice M. Korom with the political control of the armed forces. The ensuing Twelfth Congress (24–7 March 1980) rubberstamped Biszku's fall and endorsed the reinvigoration of NEM. The improvement of the dramatically lopsided balance of payments received top priority, which implied a program of zero-growth and austerity.

The Thirteenth Congress

The Thirteenth Congress of the HSWP opened in Budapest on 25 March 1985 and lasted four days. In conformity with the expectations of foreign and Hungarian observers, it did not bring spectacular changes. The general policy line that had been initiated in the 1960s and that solidly stabilized itself in default of other realistic alternatives was reinforced. However, the Congress was characterized by an unusual degree of candour and open criticism.

Obviously, the party leadership tried to learn from its past unsuccessful practice, which consisted of explaining existing difficulties away and muzzling criticism. The documents issued by the Congress and the contributions made by the delegates mirror the problems of contemporary Hungarian society, the party's hopes and anxieties as well as the spectrum of tactical approaches represented in the party. The main social problems as perceived by the party were the declining birthrate, the lagging quality of the health services and above all the inequalities that had surfaced during the process of economic reform. Against the background of these developments, General Secretary J. Kádár said in his report to the Congress:

The CC is convinced of the fact that our people are politically mature. We trust in them. And it is sure that it will be able, under the party's principled and spiritual direction, with the support of the state and other executive agencies, to unfold creative work, to strengthen order and discipline, to eliminate those phenomena which are diametrically opposed to our social goals [*NSz*, 26 March, 1985].

That Kádár's main concern was less the unreliability of the populace than the conduct of party members in public, was revealed by a passage in his closing speech:

During the past four-five years with the problems intensifying, some unqualified critics, who were trying to blow up our problems and were stimulated by imperialist propaganda, used the public forums to quibble and fuss over the efforts of our people and society in an aggressive way. And it became ever more frequent that their views were not rejected in public, but that these extremist opinions were condemned only later, in the corridors. But we have to stand for our truth under all circumstances and at any time. We have to represent our policies publicly and courageously. [*NSz*, 29 March, 1985].

There are thus creeping apprehensions about the party losing its striking capacity should the appearance of unity disappear. The Congress documents are full of admonitions to the effect that a maximal degree of critical discussion be tolerated until a binding decision has been passed and that after this point a rigorous discipline be enforced. The general consensus prevailing in the party concerning the future of the Alliance Policy and of economic and social reform is procedural rather than substantial: isolated aspects of the reform policies may be legitimately attacked and criticized in public, but the formation of consistent opposition platforms remains an anathema. The torments and the frustration of broad strata within the party are reflected in K. Grósz's speech. Grósz, the First Secretary of the influential Budapest Party Committee is labelled a 'hardliner' in the West (e.g. RFER Hungarian SR, 27

April 1985). While drawing a generally positive picture of the achievements during the past years. Grósz also castigated serious shortcomings:

The trust in the party is strong. Our population sees the results of our economic buildup. They see our efforts. At the same time, social tensions are mounting. The political patience of the population has decreased, one can feel anxieties and insecurity about the future. Because of these factors the mood of the population in the capital is contradictory. Our most important task is to renew political support through spiritual change and resolute action [*NSz*, 26 March 1985].

But like all other leading personalities who took the Congress rostrum Grósz did not fail to express his full endorsement to the process of economic reform. By voicing his apprehensions about the possible consequences of the grave housing problem, the increased financial burdens on young couples and the deterioration of the technical intelligentsia's standard of living, Grósz responded to the pressure he was exposed to in his own party's organization.

The further course of the reform is also a matter of generational change. The new Politburo was staffed by three newcomers, two of which (Grósz, István Szabó) belong to the 'winning generation' that was born between 1920 and 1930. Grósz was co-opted because he heads the biggest party organization in the country (220,000 members or one-quarter of the total membership) and István Szabó's election is tantamount to an increase in the political profile of agriculture. The only generational change in the politburo is linked to the elevation of Csaba Hámori, the Secretary of the youth movement, KISZ. Hámori is thirty-seven, while the ousted members of the PB were hardly older than the three newcomers. The three new incumbents of the Secretariat positions (J. Berecz, Dr I. Horváth, Dr L. Pál) also come from the 1920–30 generation. Change was more pronounced in the Central Committee. One-quarter (twenty-six) of the members of the new CC were elected for the first time, which is a higher proportion than five years ago, when 21 per cent were newcomers.

East European party congresses are an opportunity for the CPSU to give a public evaluation of the performance of the party concerned. The Soviet observer of the Thirteenth Congress was G. Romanov, Politburo member and Secretary of the Leningrad Party Committee. In his appraisal of the Hungarian reform, Romanov said that 'its results have contributed to the strengthening of the Hungarian socialist society and its has speeded up economic and social development'. As a counterweight, he added a cautious warning:

The national interests of the socialist states cannot be reliably safeguarded other than by paying heed to the instruction of Lenin and several generations of revolutionaries, by strengthening our whole community and by basing ourselves on the traditions of proletarian and Socialist internationalism [*NSz*, 27 March, 1985].

Thus, Romanov fell in line with the general rhetoric of the Congress, which was rich in symbolic assurances for many different standpoints, attempted to reopen policy options, but simultaneously proclaimed muddling-through as the official policy line. This is certainly a sign of political maturity and realism, since at present the only option seems to be to weather the storm. As Kádár put it, quoting the poet Imre Madách: 'Man is born to struggle and to trust'.

The Hungarian Socialist Workers' Party: Structure and Functions

According to its 1985 rules, the HSWP is the 'revolutionary vanguard of the working class' which 'organizes and guides the people in their struggle to construct a Socialist society'. Its final goal is the establishment of communism. Any individual over eighteen years of age who embraces the Marxist-Leninist ideals, subscribes to the party's policies, displays high moral qualities and is ready to participate regularly in the work of a basic organization can join the HSWP if he is recommended by two party members.

The party is a mass movement cast into a strict hierarchical and centralized framework. The organizational principle of 'democratic centralism', combining centralist authority with democratic procedures and initiative from below, results in a topheavy organization in which power and information are unevenly distributed. Lower party organizations are strictly subordinated to the higher bodies and only the members of the CC are entitled to 'be informed about all important questions' (Point 16 of the rules).

Party bodies are formed through a series of indirect elections from the grass-roots level to the apex. Through its members in enterprises, state and social institutions, the party can enforce any decision and control its implementation. Although the party membership requirement for leading positions has been watered down by a steadily increasing number of exceptions, elite recruitment is still the key to Party power. And although the party has withdrawn from many decision-making areas and its presence has become less visible, it is still monitoring all political processes, ready to re-assume direct control in the case of emergency.

Of its 25,402 basic organizations, 9,456 (37.2 per cent) exist in state authorities, institutions and the armed forces, and 7.686 (30.2 per cent) in industrial and 3,819 (15 per cent) in agricultural enterprises, thus revealing significant differences in the degree of Party penetration, recruitment priorities and career patterns. Depending on the number of communists in a particular enterprise or institution, various representative bodies are elected by the party members working in them (e.g. if there are more than 200 communists, a party committee has to be elected). At the next higher level, the County organizations are formed. The party Congress, which is convened every five years, is composed of delegates elected at the County level by the County Party Conference (which also elects the members of the County Committee). According to a 1979 decision of the Political Bureau, all Party organizations with a membership exceeding 1,500 Communists are entitled to dispatch their delegations to the Congress directly. Thus, forty-seven delegates to the Thirteenth Congress were elected by the party conferences of twenty-six big industrial firms, the party organizations of the Ministry of the Interior and the Hungarian People's Army. The Congress is primarily used as a sounding board for the mid-term policies elaborated by the bodies occupying the top positions in the hierarchy: the Political Bureau and the Central Committee, namely their respective administrative apparatuses. Intensive grass-roots discussion of the guidelines that are published before each Congress may stimulate activities among the rank and file members. As the Thirteenth Congress showed, this forum can also be used as a communication device to direct the attention of the central leadership to the problems of specific regions, social strata or institutions. The composition of the Congress, however, is not representative of that of the party at large, let alone the population. Thirty per cent of the delegates to the Thirteenth Congress were workers and farmers, 23.1 per cent were functionaries working in the party or in social organizations, 24.9 per cent held leading executive and administrative positions and 8.4 per cent were employees. Twenty-seven per cent of the delegates were women. The Congress was primarily an assembly of the more energetic and experienced middle-aged generations: while only 15.8 per cent of the delegates were younger than 30 years, 74 per cent belonged to the thirty to sixty group.

The Central Committee is, properly speaking, the Party parliament. Its ordinary meetings take place once every three months. It is composed of the representatives of all groups and institutions that are accorded political significance and influence. The 105-member CC elected at the Thirteenth Congress was composed as shown in Table 2.1.

The CC is primarily a forum of the party regional and central apparatus. Almost 40 per cent of its members represent this group, while other relevant social and political groupings can claim equal but much smaller shares of the

Table 2.1 The Composition of the CC, 1985

Representation of	(%)
Party central apparatus	16.1
Regional party	11.4
Central state administration	11.4
Retired party and state functionaries	8.5
Workers and employees	8.5
Trade unions	5.7
Enterprise directors	4.7
Collective farm chairmen	4.7
Mass organizations	4.7
Military, militia	4.7
Party institutions	3.8
Science, culture, education	3.8
Radio and television	2.8
Foreign policy, international relations	2.8
Diet deputies	2.8
Co-operatives	1.9
Regional state administration	0.9

Women: 11 per cent
Re-election 24.7 per cent

Source: own calculations

CC seats. The CC apparatus is the real locus of power. Here, all important
decisions affecting party members and the whole society are prepared,
elaborated, and their implementation controlled. The eight secretaries are in
charge of specific policy targets. J. Kádár and his deputy K. Németh have a
general jurisdiction in all matters handled by the Secretariat. The secretaries
have made their party careers in their field of specialization: The average age
of the secretaries is 58.3 years, and half of them are between fifty and fifty-six.
Their education, their experience and their age characterize them as middle-
aged technocrats who tend to give pragmatic and especially economic considerations precedence over ideological commitment.

The Political Bureau, which is also formed by the CC, functions as a kind
of party government. It can be called an embyronic version of the CC in that
all major groups and tendencies represented in the CC can claim a 'Politburo'
seat. Thus, the thirteen-member Politburo elected at the Thirteenth Congress includes spokesmen of the economic reform and industrialists like
F. Havasi and G. Lázár, representatives of agriculture like I. Szabó and
P. Losonczi and ideologists like M. Óvári. The two ex-officio members of this

body are K. Grósz and Cs. Hámori, representing the influential Budapest Party organization and the youth organization KISZ, respectively. The Thirteenth Congress also made K. Németh, Kádár's long-standing aide, who had shouldered an increasing workload to exonerate the ageing Party leader, his formal deputy. Obviously, he is scheduled to act as the transitional party leader after Kádár. In 1985 the Politburo is an all-male body. The average age of its members is fifty-nine years. Five are workers by social origin, two are peasants, two former teachers and three belong to the technical intelligentsia. Seven members have university education and 69 per cent represent the politically dominant 1920–30 generation.

The CC also elects the Central Control Committee, which is to 'promote the political, organizational, spiritual and practical unity of the party, to educate the party members, to monitor their political conduct, their allegiance to the party and their moral fibre, and to struggle against all forms of anti-party factional activities'. In addition to its task of setting and implementing the moral standards of the party, it decides on complaints filed against party members and audits the financial management of party affairs. According to the report of its chairman, A. Gyenes, 28,739 party members (3.4 per cent of the total membership) were subjected to party penalties between 1980 and 1985. A relatively small number of members, namely 7,639 (0.9 per cent) individuals were excluded from the party, 17,591 (2 per cent) names were cancelled from the files and 19,188 individuals (2.2 per cent) had resigned their membership. Among those disciplined were party officials who had tried to suppress criticism (304 cases) and who had 'violated Socialist property' by engaging in speculation, black market deals and other illegal machinations (more than 5,000 cases) (A MSzMP XIII, Kongresszusa, 10, p. 150). In contrast to the Stalinist practice, exclusion or resignation from membership is not tantamount to the annihilation of one's civil existence. The party is interested in recruiting politically active citizens, who are capable of convincing agitation for the party's goals. It is not interested in promoting careerists and opportunists, although the existence of this problem cannot be denied (*NSz*, 27 February 1985). The Central Control Committee report also singled out several long-standing problems of internal party life such as insufficient consultation preceding the making of decisions, violations of the norms of socialist morality and a failure to reach youth and certain intellectual strata. Recruitment is still guided by statistical considerations and not by paying regard to the recruits' motivations (A MSzMP XIII. Kongresszus, p. 126).

Party careers are frequently tied to rising educational qualifications. The party's own educational institutions are to supply future leaders with the necessary ideological, scientific and organizational skills. During the past five years, 152 party members earned their doctorate at the Budapest Political College.

In addition to its decision-making and organizational role, the party also engages in large-scale propaganda activities. Close to three million people were reached by party propaganda and agitation activities during the 1981–4 period (A MSzMP XIII. Kongresszusa, p. 14).

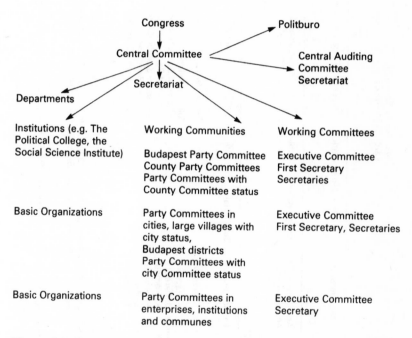

Figure 2.1 The Organizational Structure of the HSWP

		First Secretary		
	Secretary	Secretary	Secretary	
Party and Mass Organization Department	Administration Department	Propaganda and Education Department	Economic Policy Department	Accounting and Services

Figure 2.2 The Structure of the County Committee Apparatus

First Secretary
János Kádár (73)

First Deputy Secretary
Károly Németh (63)

Secretaries of the CC

Miklós Óvári	Mátyás Szürös	Dr István Horváth	János Berecz	Ferenc Havasi	Dr Lénárd Pál

CC Bureau   *Departments of the CC*

Party and Mass Organization	Accounting and Services	Foreign Affairs	Public Administration	Agitation and Propaganda	Economic Policy	Science, Education and Culture

Head: *Department Heads*

Miklós Óvári	István Petrovski	László Karakas	Géza Kótai	Péter Varga	Ernő Varga	László Lakatos	Katalin Radics

Committees and Working Groups: *Chairman*

Economic Policy Committee	F. Havasi
Agitation and Propaganda Committee	J. Berecz
Working Group on Party Building	K. Németh
Economic Working Group	F. Havasi
Working Group on Educational Policy	L. Pál
Youth Committee	K. Németh

Central Party Institutions   *Head*

Political College	
Institute of Social Sciences	József Szabó
Institute of Party History	György Aczél
Társadalmi Szemle (CC theoretical monthly)	István Huszár
Pártélet (*Party Life*)	V. Benke
Népszabadság (CC daily)	Sándor Lakatos
	(to be appointed)

The HSWP Political Bureau (1985)

János Kádár (73), Károly Németh (63), Károly Grósz (55), Csaba Hámori (37), Sándor Gáspár (63), István Szabó (61), György Aczél (68), Ferenc Havasi (56), György Lázár (61), Miklós Óvári (60), Pál Losonczi (60), István Sárlos (64), László Marothy (43)

Figure 2.3 The Structure of the Central Committee Apparatus, 1985. (*Source*: *NSZ*, 29 March 1985.)

The Rank and File Members

The social and economic changes during the past decades are also reflected in the party membership's composition. Since the Twelfth Congress, the total number of party members has grown by 7.3 per cent, to reach 870,992 (8.1 per cent of the population). Economic modernization has led to a decline of the proportion of workers and peasants in favour of the white-collar group as well as to a sharp increase in educational levels. The unfavourable age structure of the population makes itself felt in a higher average age of the party members and a steadily increasing proportion of pensioners (see Table 2.2). Due to the party's age structure the number and the influence of the pre-liberation veterans is declining while the proportion of those who joined the party after the 1956 uprising has already reached 80.3 per cent.

Political Generations

In the history of the Hungarian Communist Party we can distinguish between 'winning' and 'losing' generations. The most successful generation was the one born betwen 1920 and 1929: in 1970 they occupied more than 50 per cent of the leadership positions in the economic and adminstrative systems. They left little room for the following age group which moved into only 17 per cent of the positions at the same time (Illés, 1981, p. 51). This can be explained by the general features in the biographies of the former. At the time of the liberation, the 1921-30 generation was too young to have been involved to any significant extent in the authoritarian and fascist regimes but old enough to engage in the political reconstruction of Hungary after the Second World War. They could fully profit from the expansion of educational facilities. Career motives as well as sincere beliefs in the viability of a communist solution made them staunch followers of the regime. Their identity was linked to the achievements they reached or envisaged through the most creative period in their lives. The rapid increase in leadership positions and the generational gap caused by wartime losses offered them the unique opportunities to rise to the top of the administrative hierarchies at an early age. On the other hand, most of them never rose high enough to enter the top leadership circle that after 1956 was to shoulder personal responsibility for the crimes of the Rákosi regime. Yet they also remained faithful to the *ancien régime* in October 1956 because they could hardly expect the new order to treat them as favourably as did the Stalinist system. Nevertheless, they were able to profit from the post-1956 normalization and became a consolidated ruling class, held together by common experiences, personal ties and common convictions.

Table 2.2 The Social Composition of the HSWP (%)

	Jan. 1975	Jan. 1980	Jan. 1985
Present occupation			
Active manual workers		28.6	27.4
on pension		7.9	8.1
Agricultural workers in collective farms	n.a.	4.9	4.5
Foremen in industry		7.0	7.1
Foremen in collective farms		1.4	1.5
All foremen	6.1	8.4	8.6
Active intellectuals		34.3	33.5
Intellectuals on pension	n.a.	6.7	8.9
All intellectuals	40.0	41.0	42.4
Others	8.4	7.4	7.2
Original occupation			
Workers	59.2	62.4	62.3
Farmers	13.0	10.8	8.9
Intellectuals	8.9	9.2	10.2
Employees	16.3	16.1	17.0
Other	2.4	1.0	0.8
No original occupation	0.2	0.5	0.8
Age structure (years)			
18–21		0.3	0.4
22–26		3.8	3.0
27–29		5.1	4.1
30–39		25.5	26.0
40–49	n.a.	26.0	25.5
50–59		23.9	23.0
over 60		14.8	18.0
average		45.5	46.9
Length of membership			
Before 1944	1.1	0.8	0.5
1944–45		7.4	5.3
1956–48		8.6	5.3
1949–56		9.2	8.6
1957–70	n.a.	42.3	35.3
1971–79		31.7	28.2
after 1979		—	16.8

Table 2.2 (*cont.*)

	Jan. 1975*	Jan. 1980	Jan. 1985
Educational level			
Unfinished basic	—	11.5	7.9
Basic	—	25.4	21.5
Unfinished basic and basic combined	55.4	36.9	28.4
High school	33.8	28.9	31.6
Special secondary school	—	16.6	17.7
University, college	10.8	17.4	21.0
Candidates or doctors of science	—	0.2	0.3
Women	32	28.3	30.5

* New members since 1970.
Source: Az MSzMp Központi Bizottságának előzetes jelentése a XIII Kongresszue küldötteinek.

The 1930–9 generation had a vastly different fate. Too young to be active in politics during the first phase of Stalinism, they started their career in 1953 at a time when the expansion of the bureaucracies had reached its climax. After 1953, job opportunities were rapidly decreasing under the impact of policies designed to eliminate bureaucratic overmanning while at the same time universities and colleges could not cope with the increasing demand for higher education to which they responded by a downgrading in curricular quality. The frustrations of the 'successor generation' explain why so many among them defected from Hungary (80,000 individuals as compared to 30,000 from the 1920–9 age group between 1 January 1956 and 1 January 1960; Illés, 1981, p. 53).

Between 1956 and 1958 the administrative bureaucracies were reduced by about 100,000 positions. University graduates had no chance of being accepted into leadership positions directly without previous professional experience. This biased the recruitment system in favour of the 1920–30 generation and to the detriment of the young. The latter are Hungary's 'lost generation', one that is alienated because it was kept from realizing its potential.

The following generation's chances happened to improve because of the thrust that was provided by the NEM which needed fresh people unaffected by the Stalinist past. The lifting of the employment stop for young graduates catered to the expectations of the 'NEM-generation'. The generational flux in and out of the party follows this general pattern.

Table 2.3 Age Groups in the Central Committee (%)

Year of birth	pre-1900	1901–10	1911–20	1921–30	1931–40	after 1941
9th Congress (1966)	6.9	13.9	27.7	51.5	–	–
10th Congress (1970)	3.9	10.7	25.2	58.3	1.3	–
11th Congress (1975)	1.6	7.3	19.5	62.6	4.9	4.1
12th Congress (1980)	0.8	5.6	13.6	62.4	12.0	5.6

Note: the 1985 figures were not yet available at the time of writing (July 1985).
Source: Illes, 1981, p. 55.

The Hungarian Communist Youth League (Magyar Kommunista Ifjúsági Szövetség, KISz)

As in other Communist countries, the young generations are organized in mass movements that form a pyramid capped by the party. In Hungary 98 per cent of the six to fourteen age group are members of the Young Pioneers (Úttörők), an organization that does little more than provide them with uniforms and familiarize them with the symbols of communist power. The youth organization designed to embrace the higher age brackets (fourteen to twenty-eight years) is much more selective. In 1985 KISZ membership stood at 913,000 (38 per cent of the eligible age group), with clear recruitment priorities in the various social strata.

One can conclude that the officially assigned functions are performed inadequately by the Youth League. According to several CC decisions, the KISZ has the task to instil the proper ideological values in the young generation, to mobilize them for participation in the political institutions and in social activities, especially voluntary summer labour camps. KISZ is also the authorized spokesman for the young in the highest party echelons; according to the unofficial rules that govern the composition of the Politburo, the KISZ Secretary is one of the ex-officio members of this body. From the perspective of KISZ members themselves, however, the organization is primarily seen as a career device. The recruitment figures unambiguously reflect the still existing linkage between higher education, political involvement and career. A good KISZ record helps in the highly

Table 2.4 Proportion of Organized Youth,
by Social Stratum

Working youths	26.6%
Skilled workers, secondary school students	71.8%
University and college students	65.8%
Women	46.7%

Source: A MSzMPKB előzetes jelentése . . .

competitive admission procedure to the universities and it certainly does not hamper one's chances to occupy higher adminstrative positions. For the relatively small group of KISZ leaders—9.9 per cent of the KISZ members are simultaneously party members—the organization serves as a training ground for their future party career. Organizational, debating, agitation and leadership skills may be acquired during the innumerable meetings and discussion forums organized by KISZ. The fact that KISZ is the Party's main leadership recruitment channel and that the 'Party for the young' is recognized by the party rules explains why party decisions are binding on the KISZ and its sub-organizations.

The Constitutional Arrangement

History of Constitutional Developments

The first major documents defining the distribution of power and the main institutions in the medieval Hungarian state were the Golden Bull (1222) and the Tripartitum (1514). On the basis of these and later legal enactments, Hungary's form of government was a representative feudal monarchy, in which the King and the nobility jointly exercised the right of legislation. Hungary's state law preserved numerous elements of feudalism up to 1945. But there were also a series of attempts at modernizing the country's constitutional life. Thus, after 1790 several constitutional proposals modelled after the revolutionary French Constitution were formulated. Two authors actually were executed (József Hajnoczi, István Martinovics) because their constitutional drafts threatened the *ancien régime*. The revolution of 1848–9 was the first breakthrough of bourgeois constitutionalism, proclaiming the institutions of popular representation, responsible government, a national army and fundamental rights. Conversely, feudal traditions like *sociage, robot* and the ecclesiastical tithe were abolished along with the tax privileges of the nobility.

However, due to the short duration of the revolutionary Hungarian state, a charter-constitution did not materialize. In contrast to the Austrian part of the monarchy, the 1867 Compromise was not linked to the enactment of a Constitution in Hungary. Constitutional principles were embodied in several pieces of legislation. The 1918 Revolution of the Asters did not produce a comprehensive Constitutional document either. But its successor, the short-lived Hungarian Soviet Republic, passed a Constitution in order to underline a new departure and a radical breach with the past (23 June 1919). Modelled after the 1918 RSFSR Constitution, this document laid down the fundamentals of proletarian state organization, the election system, basic rights and duties of the workers as well as those of the nations and nationalities and disposed of the basic principles of budgetary law. The Horthy regime returned to the tradition of unwritten constitutions, re-establishing the pre-1918 state structure with the exception of royal power, which was replaced by the institution of the Regent (*Kormányzó*). Legally, the Hungarian monarchy was abolished only by Law I/1946, which introduced a parliamentary republican system of government. The same law also proclaimed 'natural and inalienable rights' of the citizens, including the right to work and to live in dignity. The constitutional follow-up after the communist takeover took two years. At its First Congress in June 1948, the Hungarian Workers' Party decided to 'lay down the fundamental changes in the state, the economy and the society'. The Council of Ministers established a Drafting Committee on 29 May 1949, which submitted a Constitutional project to the Council of Ministers on 5 August 1949. This short preparation time can be explained by the fact that the framers of the Hungarian constitution could draw on a rich body of already existing people's democratic constitutions (Heinrich, 1980, p. 232). M. Rákosi wanted to produce an advanced constitution, thus underlining his role as 'Stalin's most faithful disciple' in the all-out competition for the USSR's grace.

The Constitution was enacted on 20 August 1949 to make the new national holiday coincide with the traditional St Stephen's day. Although the document tries to emulate the 1936 Soviet Constitution, it does not record socialist achievements, but is much more programmatic in character. Nevertheless, the basic features of the 1949 Constitution have been preserved until this day. Technically, the 1949 Constitution is still in force, but it has undergone a series of far-reaching revisions. The most important amendments were passed in 1950, 1953, 1954, 1972, 1975 and 1983. In contrast to all other amendments, the 1972 reform was all-embracing in that it changed all chapters of the Constitution. The 1972 document is much more pragmatic and less programmatic than its predecessor, laying down the achievements of the Kádár group and providing a constitutional basis for the Alliance Policy, e.g. by replacing the category of 'workers', who alone were entitled to full citizen status in 1949 with the term 'citizens'. The 1972 text was amended several times: in 1975 the mandate of the Diet and local council deputies, of the Supreme Court Chairman as well as the Chief Prosecutor were uniformly extended to five years to make this period compatible with the five-year plans. The 1975 reform established a single election day for the Diet and the local council elections. The 1983 amendment brought significant changes in the election procedure and in the composition of the Council of Ministers. The districts (*járás*) were abolished as units of territorial administration and a Constitutional Law Council charged with the function of constitutional review was set up.

The Constitution of 1949 (1972)

The main political motive underlying the 1972 constitutional reform was the need of the Kádár leadership group to document their breach with the Stalinist past and to signal the end of the normalization period following the 1956 uprising. Although many of the suggestions submitted by the leading constitutional lawyers were rejected, the 1972 text is legally much more meaningful than its predecessor. As Socialist constitutions do not take the rights of the individual, but the real situation of classes and groups as their point of departure, the 1972 Hungarian Constitution does, as a rule, not entitle individuals to use legal remedies against a violation of its provisions. The rights granted to individuals and groups are to be understood as a solemn self-obligation of the government to safeguard the former in political practice.

Prior to 1983 the Hungarian constitutional system had followed the traditional practice of other socialist systems which consisted in entrusting a plethora of institutions with the task of constitutional review and safeguarding legality. Thus, the Constitution obliged the Diet, the Presidential Council, the C.o.M., the local councils, the courts, the Procuracy and the Hungarian People's Republic as a whole to safeguard constitutionality, the legal order and the rights of the citizens. After much discussion among lawyers and politicians, a constitutional amendment (Law I/1983) established a Constitutional Law Council that has the function of monitoring constitutional life in Hungary, noting possible violations of the Constitution and initiating procedures to eliminate normative acts that are at variance with the

Constitution. The Constitutional Law Council is a fifteen-member body elected by the Diet from among its members and other personalities in public life. Currently, eleven of its members are lawyers of high professional standing, such as the former Minister of Justice, Dr Mihály Korom, who serves as the Chairman of the Council, the former Deputy Chairman of the Supreme Court, Dr György Gellért and the well known Professor of Constitutional Law, Dr Imre Takács. Among the other members are the Mayor of Budapest, Zoltán Szépvölgyi, the Chief Secretary of the National Union of Producers' Co-operatives and two factory directors.

As the Council has no sizeable apparatus of its own, it is dependent on reports and complaints that are filed with this body by the so-called 'authorized entities' (national state agencies, the heads of social and corporate organizations and the local councils). Once the Council has established a case of unconstitutionality it acts as a go-between, mediating between the agency that has filed the complaint and the state organ that has passed the unconstitutional law, decree or guideline. The composition and the mode of operation of this new institution suggest that it has to perform real functions and was not created for symbolic purposes alone. At the beginning of 1985, five cases had already been taken up by the Council. Since the principle of the unity of state power excludes the Western model of independent judicial review, a solution had to be found that would be in harmony with both general socialist legal doctrines and with the specific features of Hungarian political culture. Thus, the Council is expected to act as an agent of the Diet, subordinated and responsible to this supreme organ of state power. At the same time, it must use its authority to bargain for a solution that is acceptable to all interested agencies. The Council may therefore suspend unconstitutional acts, but may not repeal them. As the debate in the Diet showed, the introduction of the Council was regarded as a further step in the development of a socialist *Rechtsstaat* (rule of law) in Hungary (*NSz*, 13 April 1984). Nevertheless, the principle of denying individual citizens direct access to the constitutional review system was upheld. If the individual's constitutional rights are violated by individual acts of state authorities, he can employ the normal procedural remedies including judicial review of administrative acts. His case will be reviewed by the Constitutional Council only if it was based on an unconstitutional norm and if an 'authorized entity' is ready to file a complaint with the Council.

In establishing the Constitutional Law Council, the Hungarian political leadership primarily responded to the demands of the constitutional lawyers. But it was also interested in promoting 'legality from above' in order to upgrade the impact of laws in their implementation process. The major problem area lies in the ministerial guidelines, which often distort the political intention of laws particularly in the field of economic reforms. The debate centring around the Constitutional Law Council shows the main characteristics of the Hungarian constitutional system: access to the decision-making arenas is granted to those interest groups who can claim the support of an officially authorized agency. On the other hand, there is a considerable degree of pluralism and even conflict among these agencies and bargaining is an essential part of almost all political decisions. The final arbiter is the party's CC which must be consulted and gives final decisions in all cases of major political significance. Thus, although petty party tutelage over state agencies has been overcome, it is still doubtful whether the party's role is in keeping with the fundamental principle of party leadership in the Hungarian Constitution. 'The Marxist–Leninist Party of the Working Class is the leading force of society' (§ 3 Const.).

In contrast to other socialist constitutions, the Hungarian document defines the party as the focus and motivator of social forces. Thus, it is the incarnation of the unity principle, which is complemented by institutional pluralism. Yet the wording of the Constitution leaves ample room for political development. Most of its provisions are of a dynamic and not of a prohibitive character, calling for affirmative action in lieu of checks on governmental activity. This fact and the lack of institutional autonomy makes the maintenance of stability and orderly procedure a task of the political and social configurations themselves. In fact, Hungary's *Rechtsstaat* has been safe-guarded by the post-1956 consensus to mutually respect the vested rights of social groups and political factions. This state of affairs explains the virtual absence of large-scale and general abuses of the law, the kid-glove handling of most conflicts, but also the isolated instances of arbitrariness against individuals who have overstepped the boundaries of the 'tolerated'.

The Elections: Planned Participation

Chapter VIII of the Constitution contains the 'Fundamental Principles of the Elections'. In 1983 a constitutional amendment paved the way for the intro-duction of a new election system that promises more electoral participation and differs in several respects from the traditional Soviet model. Prior to 1967 Hungary had adopted a procedure according to which the voter could cast his vote either for or against an entire list of candidates. In 1967 individual election districts were introduced which made the nomination of more than one candidate for the same seat possible. In the four elections that have been held under this system, there has been a number of multiple candidate races, both in parliamentary and local council elections.

Table 2.5 Elections to the Diet

	1967	1971	1975	1980
No. of seats	349	352	352	352
No. of unopposed candidates	340	303	318	337
No. of double candidacies	9(2.57%)	48(13.6%)	34(9.6%)	15(4.26%)
No. of triple candidacies		1(0.2%)		

Source: various issues of *Magyar Nemzet.*

In the local council elections multi-candidate races took place in 4.2 per cent of the election districts in 1971 and in 3 per cent of the cases in 1980 (Demszky, 1984, p. 27). The nomination of candidates was placed in the hands of voters' meetings held in each electoral district. These meetings were organized by the PPF, which also proposed the candidates. A candidate was considered nominated if 33.3 per cent of those present cast their vote for him. In the case of multiple candidacies, the choice at the primaries and on election day was between personalities and not between competing programmes.

In an attempt to promote or resuscitate voters' participation, the new electoral law makes multiple candidate races obligatory for each election district. In order to avoid creating 'winners' and 'losers' the candidates not elected serve as substitutes for the elected deputies if they have received at least 25 per cent of the vote. The most incisive change is the introduction of a National Nominating List, on the basis of which 10 per cent of the Diet deputies—around 30–35 prominent personalities—are elected. This novelty was justified by PB member Mihály Korom on the grounds that

important interests demand the representation of leading personalities from that policy, society, culture, science, the churches and the non-party partners of our Alliance Policy . . . The character of their work, the province of their activities go far beyond the boundaries of their electoral districts . . . [*Nsz*, 23 December 1983].

Candidates on the national ticket are elected by a simple majority; their seats are added to the 352 seats going to the successful candidates from the constituencies. The purpose of this national ticket is clearly to minimize the risk for prominent personalities in the nomination and election processes as well as to symbolize national unity under the Alliance Policy. Under the new system the Hungarian voter is issued with three voting slips: one for the National Nominating List, one for his national election constituency and one for the elections to the local council.

All candidates must subscribe to the PPF programme, which is identical to that of the party. In the 1985 election campaign, seventy-eight independent (i.e. non-PPF) candidates were nominated by the pre-election meetings; eventually, thirty-four of them were elected Diet deputies. Two well known dissidents (László Rajk and Gáspár Miklós Tamás) also tried to get their names on the ballot, but—allegedly due to the machinations of the Patriotic People's Front—failed to reach the required share of the votes at the pre-election meeting (*NSz*, 29 June 1985, RFER Hungarian SR, 16 May 1985).

During the 1985 election campaign, about 1,500,000 citizens participated in the 42,500 local council and 719 parliamentary nominating meetings. For the 352 Diet seats, there were fifty triple and four quadruple candidacies (15.4 per cent, 0.9 per cent). For the 42,734 local council seats, there were 2,345 triple and eighty-seven quadruple candidacies (5.4 per cent, 0.2 per cent). The elections produced several unexpected results. In forty-two electoral districts by-elections had to be held because none of the candidates reached the necessary quorum. Several prominent candidates were defeated; the most spectacular victims were the former Premier J. Fock and CC member I. Huszár. By-elections could not be held in one electoral district (district No. 5 in Zala County) since out of the three nominees, only one accepted his nomination. As in the case of three local council electoral districts, elections were adjourned.

The abstention rates are strikingly high by East European standards. For the first time since 1947, the regime treated active suffrage as a right and not a duty of its citizens. For the party leadership the 1985 election was a bold step towards more democracy. On the other side of the political spectrum the opposition has criticized the new election system as 'openly anti-democratic' and serving the interests of big business, which can create parliamentary lobbies that increase their political leverage in the fierce competition for subsidies (nomination proposals were indeed advanced by enterprises at the electors' meetings). The decrease in the proportion of multiple candidacies in past elections was attributed to the lack of tangible differences between the candidates' political views and programme (Demsky, 1984, p. 28). While the

Table 2.6 Main Results of the 1985 Elections (percentages)

	Participation	Valid votes	Invalid votes	Vote against elected candidates
8 June 1985				
National list (35 seats)	94	99.2	0.8	0.8
Diet deputies in electoral districts (352)	93.9	94.6	5.4	1.2*
Local council deputies (42,734 seats)	93.9	95.4	4.6	1.1
22 June 1985 (by-elections in 41 Diet and 846 local council electoral districts)				
Diet deputies	83.0	98.8	1.2	1.2
Local council deputies	73.9	98.3	1.7	1.4

* Several prominent candidates were elected in a close contest (50–60% of the vote)
Source: NSz, 10 June 1985 and 24 June 1985.

latter is undoubtedly true, the new electoral law is a serious attempt at increasing citizen participation, a safety valve for the social tensions which have been building up in the last decade. As far as the role of lobbies is concerned, big business, just like other interest groups, will try to make inroads into the representative assemblies by using its political weight during the nomination process. Interest groups, however, cannot obtain political leverage through elections in Hungary and the composition of the assembly reflects the political weight of social forces and not vice versa.

The Diet: from Rubber Stamp to Interest Articulation

The Hungarian Diet (Országgyűles—National Assembly) is a Soviet-type parliament whose deputies are elected directly and do not give up their original occupations during their terms, thus providing for—as the constitutional doctrine has it—a direct input of practical production and local experience into political decision-making at the national level. According to the Constitution, the Diet is the supreme organ of state power. The top organs of the functional state divisions are elected, guided, controlled and subordinated to it: the C.o.M., the Supreme Court and the Chief Prosecutor. Thus, the Diet caps a multi-tiered structure of general representative bodies (the Councils) and administrative agencies, which are subordinated to the councils on the appropriate level.

According to the Constitution, the Diet performs the most important state functions: it enacts the laws, passes the important state functions, approves the five year plans and the annual budget, approves the programme of the government and elects the Council of Ministers, the Supreme Court Chairman, the Chief Prosecutor and the Constitutional Law Council (§ 19 Const.). Yet since it assembles only three or four times a year for a period never exceeding a few days, the plenary sessions used to be hardly more than rubber stamp procedures to adopt programmes elaborated, sanctioned and introduced by party and state executive bodies. The composition of parliament is meant to reflect the political weight of the social groups and to underline the representative character of the Diet.

The deputies to the Diet perform their parliamentary activities in four different roles: as contributors to plenary discussions, as members of the County Groups (*megyei csoportok*), as members of the standing committees and as representatives of their constituencies. Politically, the committee activities are the most significant. 'One has to confess that here the real legislative work is done, so that the plenary session can deal with an already elaborated draft', says a deputy (*NSz*, 12 May 1984). The contributions to the plenary discussions concern mostly local problems and are an attempt at using the Diet's publicity to put pressure on the authorities in charge of the regional distribution of funds. The Hungarian Diet knows the institution of a question period. The Diet takes a vote on the answer of the executive questioned. In most cases, the vote consists of unanimous approval. Abstentions, negative votes or majority rejection of the answer used to be a rare exception (e.g. *NSz*, 19 October 1984). The deputies elected in one county form the County group that is to articulate and to represent the interests of a given region. As most counties have a mixed industrial–agricultural structure, the formulation of a uniform policy within the County group is difficult. As there were several predominantly agricultural regions, agriculture used to enjoy a relatively higher political leverage *vis-à-vis* industry on the level of the County group. Moreover, the cleavages within industry (above all between big and small industry) were more pronounced than within the agricultural camp. The June 1985 Plenum of the CC has taken a bold step towards an emancipation of the parliament from close party tutelage. The party directives spell out unambiguously that the Diet and its committees are to enjoy the right of deciding on the drafts and proposals administered to them (*NSz*, 1 July 1985). It remains to be seen to what extent the new deputies will be able to break the old traditions. Majority votes and, in exceptional cases, rejections of government drafts of low political significance seem to be possible in the post-1985 Diet.

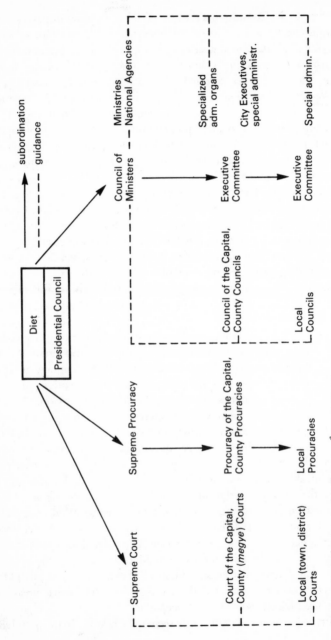

Figure 2.4 The Hungarian System of government

Table 2.7 The 1985–90 Diet

The 1985–90 Diet actual profession	Deputies from electoral districts (%) (N = 351)	Deputies on National List (N = 35)	Total (N = 386)
Industrial managers	17.0	—	15.5
Workers, employees	15.7	—	14.2
State and co-operative farm managers	13.1	—	11.9
Physicians, veterinarians	8.5	—	7.7
Foremen	8.3	—	7.5
Managers in the co-operative service sector	5.1	2.9	4.9
Council administrators	5.1	—	4.6
Educators	4.8	—	4.4
Local, regional party secretaries	4.3	—	3.9
Retired politicians	3.1	14.2	4.1
Scientists	2.3	8.5	2.8
Trade union functionaries	1.9	2.9	2.1
Mass media personnel	1.7	—	1.5
Artists	1.4	5.2	1.8
Central party functionaries	1.4	14.2	2.6
Central state officials	1.1	11.4	2.1
PPF functionaries	0.8	5.7	1.3
Functionaries of other mass organizations	1.1	5.7	1.5
Army commanders	1.1	—	1.0
Lawyers	0.9	—	0.7
Priests	0.5	17.1	2.0
Police officers	0.3	—	0.2
Chairmen of national minority associations	—	11.4	1.0

Original profession (all deputies, %)		*University degrees in*	
Workers	34.4	Economics	5.4
Farmers	4.1	Law	3.6
Intellectuals	46.3	Technology	15.0
Employees and other	15.0	Agriculture	16.5
Younger than 31 years	5.1	Medicine	8.8
Women	20.9	Pedagogy	9.8
University or college education	73.0	*First elected*	63.2
		Party members	77.0

Source: own calculations (errors due to rounding).

The bulk of parliamentary work is handled by the Standing Committees. The 1985 Diet convocation elected twelve committees: The Committees for Construction and Transport, for Defence, for Culture, for Industry, for Trade, for Foreign Affairs, for Agriculture, for Social and Health Affairs, for Infrastructural Development and Environmental Protection, for Planning and Budgeting, as well as the Defence and the Legal, Administrative and Judicial Committees. During the 1980–5 convocation, 221 out of 352 deputies were involved in committee work. The ten standing committees held around fifty meetings per year (*NSz*, 5 July 1981). Their main function is the discussion of draft laws that are usually introduced into parliament by the C.o.M. The draft is then discussed by the County groups and submitted to the Legal, Administrative and Judicial Committees and the appropriate specialized standing committees. Usually, discussion in the committees ends by proposing marginal changes in the draft text. However, sometimes drafts are rejected or withdrawn at this stage (Heinrich, 1980, p. 64). The committees are also active in the supervision of the implementation of laws. Hungarian sources criticize the inertia of the administrative strata to react to the suggestions and to the critical statements as well as the low frequency of interpellations arising from committee monitoring activities (*NSz*, 5 July 1981). Committee work is coordinated by the Diet Presidency, which consists of the Chairman and two Deputy Chairman and is aided by the small Diet Buro.

The activity of the deputies in the constituency consists of reporting on their parliamentary activities and of generally mediating between the citizens and the local authorities. Although deputies are not used as errand boys by the local population as in the American system, the deputy is seen as a trouble shooter for the solution of local and individual problems. Housing shortages and supply deficiencies occupy the top positions on the grievance list (*NSz*, 12 May 1981).

The Presidential Council

Due to the low frequency of the plenary meetings the bulk of legislative activity is performed by the Presidential Council, a twenty-one member body elected by each Diet convocation at its first session from among its members. In addition to its function as a substitute for the Diet (it is empowered to take any decision on behalf of the Diet when the latter is not in session, but it may not change the Constitution), it acts as a collective presidency, appointing important state functionaries, electing the professional judges, establishing and awarding orders and titles, exercising the right of amnesty and proclaiming a state of war, i.e. martial law. Thus, the Presidential Council is a combination of a 'small parliament' and a collective head of state. Although its substitutive jurisdiction is not unlimited and it can only pass law-decrees, parliamentary practice has somewhat blurred the boundaries between the competencies of the Diet and its substitute, giving flexibility and expediency precedence over abiding by strict procedural rules. Thus, in spite of the recurring criticism of constitutional lawyers, law-decrees still contain regulations affecting the fundamental rights of citizens and bypass the standing committees (Heinrich, 1980, p. 282, p. 301). The law-decrees enacted are approved at the following plenary session in a wholesale manner, without any discussion or suggestions for amendment. The membership composition of the Parliamentary Council corresponds to its political functions. The party core consists of J. Kádár and his deputy K. Németh, the Politburo members S. Gáspár and P. Losonczi (The Chairman of the Presidential Council, who acts as the formal head of state) and the CC members I. Katona (the Secretary of the Presidential Council) and Gy. Kállai (a long-standing PPF functionary). The other members of this body represent important social and political groups and institutions such as the churches, the national minorities, the mass media, women and the collective farms.

The Local Councils

Hungary's system of local councils, established in October 1950 to replace the traditional administration, underwent several far-reaching reforms aiming at increasing the councils' legal and financial autonomy. Under ever mounting budgetary pressures the efforts at streamlining the system led to a process of permanent centralization at the middle level to the detriment of the smaller communities.

According to the 1971 Council Act the council and its organs are 'the self-managing representative organs of socialist state organization, operating on the basis of democratic centralism and realizing the power of the people' (§ 2 Council Act). As of 1983, councils are elected in the communes (*község*), the cities and the districts of the capital. These councils, together with their executive departments, function as first-instance administrative authorities and handle practically all local affairs. Depending on the size and the importance of a local community, the local councils, the first echelon in the three-step hierarchy of the council system (if one includes the Diet at its apex) can be the council of a commune, a large commune (*nagyközség*), a large commune with city status, a city or a county city. The middle level is taken by the county councils, e.g. the Budapest County Council. Prior to 1983 councils had also been elected on the intermediate level of the region (*járás*) which were eliminated as a unit of territorial administration to render the system more effective and less costly. However, this relatively simple setup is complicated by the side-effects of administrative centralization. While in 1960 there were 3,151 communal councils, their number had shrunk to 1,381 in 1984 due to mergers between communal councils, the inclusion of communes in cities and above all, the setting up of joint communal councils (more than half of the communal councils are joint councils) for two or more communities. At the end of 1984, 1,576 satellite communities had no elected representative organ (Ádám, 1984, p. 149). Therefore, from 1985 special boards will be formed by the joint councils that will represent the interests of the satellite communities. These local boards (*elöljáróságok*) have a limited jurisdiction in regard to local affairs of the satellite community they represent but must be consulted before the Council takes a decision on certain issues.

Table 2.8 Membership and Social Composition of the Local Councils, 1980

Blue collar and foremen	34.6
Collective farmers, agricultural workers	16.2
Other (white collar, pensioners) professions	49.2
Party members	47.3
Women	33.8
Under 30 years of age	19.3

Source: *NSz*, 23 March 1985.
Note: $N = 59, 270$.

The Government Structure

The Council of Ministers

The general rule that administrative bureaucracies show a tendency to dominate representative bodies was confirmed by the Hungarian experience. Although according to the Constitution the C.o.M. is an executive organ subordinated and responsible to the Diet, it has become the most important focus of state life, a centre of information, operational decision-making and guidance. Established in 1949 following the Soviet model, the Hungarian C.o.M. quickly moved into a monopoly position in economic decision-making. Since its political significance is contingent on the significance that is ascribed to economic factors by the party, its position has become even more authoritative since the New Economic Mechanism had assigned priority to economics in 1968. The 1972 constitutional reform brought an *ex-post facto* recognition of the C.o.M's enhanced role. The 1949 constitutional formula, according to which it served as the highest organ of state administration, gave way to a new concept that makes it the task of the C.o.M. to 'guide, influence and control the entire construction of socialism' (Ádám, 1984, p. 140). The most important competency is still the elaboration and implementation of economic plans (§ 35 sec 1 e Const.). But its practical ubiquity and omnipotence is reflected in the role that empowers it to 'take any measure directly or through one of its members that falls into the purview of administration' (§ 40 sec 1 Const.). In spite of the decentralization tendencies since the early sixties that resulted in a more even distribution of economic, technical and legal know-how, the C.o.M. still consists of the country's largest and highest qualified brain trust. The Academy of Sciences and the Hungarian universities co-ordinate their research programmes with the C.o.M. and the priorities that are set for development by this body cannot be disregarded by any institution. As far as its capacities in the preparation and implementation of economic decisions are concerned it is second to no institution, including the party CC's specialized departments. As far as its relationship with the council system is concerned, it regularly fulfills its constitutional duty to report to the Diet and to respond to interpellations by individual deputies. But no elected body is in a position to encounter the concentrated expertise of the C.o.M's staff. In the words of the former CSA Chairman I. Huszár 'the analysis of the real decision-making practice shows that in general the most important decisions are taken via bargaining between departments . . . the decisive reason for this fact is that only they dispose of the so-called 'service knowledge', the knowledge of facts and data resulting from an insider position' (Huszár, 1984, p. 11). The C.o.M. is the spider in the information web, sifting and condensing consistent policy programmes from personal, departmental and national interests. These programmes are presented to the Diet in an elaborated and pure form which leaves the representative assembly practically no other choice than to accept them with only marginal changes. Moreover, the Diet and its Presidential Council are understaffed. In the years following 1968, a tendency to transfer functional departments from parliament to the C.o.M. has become apparent. Thus, in 1972, the P.C.'s Council department was dissolved and the guidance of the Council system placed under the jurisdiction of the C.o.M's Council Office alone. But there were also centralization processes designed to streamline the C.o.M. itself. In 1980 the industrial branch ministries were merged into one Ministry of Industry.

In 1985 the C.o.M. consisted of the Chairman (the Prime Minister), five deputy Prime Ministers, thirteen ministers as well as the Chairman of the

National Planning Authority and the Central Committee of People's Control.

In 1968, the institution of the State Secretaries that had existed under the post-1945 coalition system was revived. A number of State Secretaries head national agencies that work independently of ministries, like the CSO, the C.o.M.'s Information Office, the National Bank, the National Material and Price Office, the National Water Conservation Office, the State Office for Church Affairs, and the Council Office. The other State Secretaries serve as substitutes for one specific minister. The government as a whole is formed at the first session of each new Diet convocation. In off-election years personnel changes are made by the Presidential Council acting on behalf of the Diet and upon proposals advanced by the PPF Presidium. Of course, such top-level decisions are subject to party scrutiny and approval.

Local Government

While the councils function as legislatures and control institutions on their territory, the operative and organizational work is handled by their executive agencies: the executive committee, the council committees and the special administrative services. The status of the Executive Committee is characterized by the principle of dual subordination: it is guided, controlled and instructed by both the local council and the County executive committee. The council committees correspond to the Diet Standing Committees. The specialized administrative services are the Ministries' field organizations that are controlled certainly via the County executive committees.

The performance of local government is of primary importance for the quality of the citizen's daily life. All elementary schools, almost all middle schools, 90 per cent of the state-owned apartments, 90 per cent of the crèches and the kindergartens, 80 per cent of the hospital beds and 70 per cent of the libraries, theatres and educational centres are run by the local administrators. The functioning of local government is mainly dependent on the availability of financial resources for local budgets. Council spending is financed from several sources: grants (*dotáció*), local taxes and credits. The local budgets are also fed from the profits of institutions belonging to the council and from 'material' (non-money) transfers. The most recent trend is to conclude co-operation agreements with enterprises in the council's territory that finance infrastructural investments servicing both partners (e.g. kindergartens). In many cases, enterprises expect the councils to grant them certain privileges (e.g. the exemption from administrative fines) in exchange for providing investment funds. For this and for other reasons, the councils must try to increase their financial self-sufficiency. However, increasing local financial autonomy is not a consistently rational strategy because the central grants that are distributed via the national budgets to the counties (*megye*) and then redistributed by the county councils, have assumed the role of a stopgap that complements other local council income to cover the bare minimum of expenses. Therefore, an increase of local income in practice means a corresponding decrease in central grants.

Table 2.9 Council Income Sources (%)

	1971	1976	1981
Local taxes	13	13	7
Patrimonial income	6	12	28
Credits	12	8	10
Central grants	49	56	46
Material transfers	20	11	9

Source: Társadalmi Szemle, 1983, no. 7, p. 57.

In spite of the intention of the political leadership to free the local councils from central tutelage, council autonomy has only grown at the middle level. Before 1971 (the passing of a new Council Act), a city council chairman had to struggle for a 'soft plan' and for more funds from all levels including the Planning Authority and the Ministry of Finance. Now, his point of reference is the county. It can be safely assumed that one of the main motivations for the 1971 reform of local government was the need to exonerate the central financial authorities by reinforcing the county 'filter' and thus reducing the number of bargaining partners. Nevertheless, the situation did not change for the local councils. The centralism of the national agencies in Budapest was replaced by the centralism of the county councils. This 'new centralism' exists in practice and can hardly be traced in relevant legislation. Thus, most grants are given without strings attached. Theoretically, a grant for building apartments can be re-allotted by the local councils for the financing of infrastructural investments. Yet, due to the overall lack of funds, the system of central priority-setting (*megpántlikázás*) has managed to persist. In this system, the county officials act as go-betweens, conveying and pressing ministerial priorities *vis-à-vis* the peripheral councils.

The county council leaders know that their chances of increasing their territory's share in the national budget rise if they emphasize centrally set priorities. Moreover, they do not expect to meet much resistance with the local executive personnel because the latter are heavily dependent on the highest level. Their salary, premises, the awarding of distinctions, the enforcement of discipline, their service classification and their annual leave schedules are regulated and decided by the county administration. Incidentally, this fact renders the principle of dual subordination a fiction. In the case of political conflict, the county executive will always be in a more powerful position than the local council chairman. The local leaders face a dilemma, being caught between the Scylla of centrally set priorities and the Charybdis of financial starvation. Obviously, a viable solution, albeit with limited possibilities, is seen in the encouragement of local initiatives. In 1983, the total value of local income generated by voluntary social work (such as the construction of kindergartens, environmental protection etc.) was 7.5 billion ft, which compares very favourably to the sum of 5 billion ft invested by the councils during the same period (*TSz*, 1983, no. 7, p. 51).

Mass Organizations

Socialist societies are permeated by a plethora of organizations to safeguard the inclusion and the participation of all individuals and social groups in the fulfilment of national programmes. They are to tap motivational resources, mobilize support, organize contributions and monitor social processes. The most important social organizations in Hungary are the HSWP, the Communist Youth League (KISZ), the PPF, the trade-unions, the Hungarian Red Cross, the Collective Farm Union, the Unions of Small Artisans and Retailers, the residents' committees articulating the interests of people living on one block or housing area, the Workers' Militia, the Bar Chambers and the churches.

The Patriotic People's Front

The historical forerunners of the PPF, namely the March Front, the Historical Memorial Committee and the Hungarian Front came into being as pre-governmental organizations that were based on the consensus of anti-fascist groups struggling for a new and different Hungary after the war. Today, the PPF is a mass movement that according to the 1972 Constitution has the task to 'galvanize the social forces in the interest of the complete construction of socialism, the solution of political, economic and cultural problems and to participate in the election and the work of elected organs of popular representation' (§ 4 sec 2 Const.). The PPF has no individual members, but operates through around 130,000 grass-root committees that are elected by the local citizens (*lakossági gyülés*). At the apex the Congress, the National Council, the National Presidency and the National Secretariat are integrated into the system of central political decision-making. The most important PPF activity is the organization of elections. The nomination of candidates for Diet seats, for the 40,000 positions of council deputies and for the 13,000 lay judges is handled by the appropriate PPF committees. Candidacy proposals for the positions of the Diet Chairman, the members of the Presidential Council, the C.o.M., the Chairman of the Supreme Court and the Chief Prosecutor are formally introduced by the PPF Presidency. But the PPF also regularly participates in the discussion of draft laws and issues declarations on current policy. Thus, its main function is that of a transmission belt between party and government on the one hand and the citizens on the other. In its programme and its activities it tries to emphasize topics that symbolize national unity and the necessity to integrate marginal groups into the texture of Hungarian society. Thus, the Eighth Congress in March 1981 gave top priority to topics like women's and youth problems, the care of the aged, family protection, church politics, the integration of gypsies, minority rights, mass sports, culture and education. Although there is a policy to make committee membership composition as representative of the population as possible, the actual recruitment procedures distort this intention somewhat.

Table 2.10 Percentage Membership in the PPF Committees, 1981

Workers	26.2	
Collective farmers	21.4	
Intelligentsia	14.7	
White collar	21.3	
Women	34.3	(1985: 37.3)
Under 30 years of age	21.6	(1985: 23.6)
Over 50	27.8	
Party members	34.2	(1985: 35.5)

Source: A Hazafias Népfront VII Kongresszusa, 14–15 March 1981, Hazafias Népfront Országos Tanácsa, Budapest, 1981: p. 13; *NSz*, 23 March 1985.

The PPF is an umbrella organization capping a multitude of suborganizations that are to represent and articulate the needs of particular sectors of Hungarian society. Due to the specific social and political patterns that have emerged in Hungary, the Hungarian Women and the Nationality Associations (the Democratic Unions of Hungarian Southern Slavs, Hungarian-

Germans, Hungarian-Romanians, and Hungarian-Slovaks) have shown considerable activity and political presence in recent years.

The Trade Unions

The Hungarian Constitution distinguishes the PPF and the trade unions from other social organizations by according constitutional status to them. According to its § 4 sect 3, the trade unions defend and strengthen the power of the people and protect and represent the interests of the workers. Ensuing legislation has regulated the role of the trade unions in detail. The extent of their participation and co-determination rights are indeed impressive: they must be consulted in questions of enterprise planning, their consent is required in most issues concerning work organization and safety, wage and premium determination, and they decide on the distribution of the enterprise cultural and social funds, e.g. on the granting of social fringe benefits and the issuing of sanatorium vouchers. Enterprise policy is handled by a troika consisting of the enterprise director, the party secretary and the TU secretary. In the case of unresolvable conflicts between the trade union standpoint and the management a compromise is sought in higher-level bodies. But in most cases, economic necessities enforce a uniform policy. On the national level, the trade unions enjoy broad consultation rights and they are represented in the top decision-making organs. The heyday of the trade union-led 'workers' opposition' was the period between 1972 and 1977 when it succeeded in temporarily reversing economic reform policies.

The Hungarian trade unions have around 4.4 million members (96 per cent of all active earners). There are more than 7,800 grass-roots organizations. The nineteen branch trade unions employ about 460,000 elected functionaries. The trade unions run 3,000 houses of culture and over 5,000 libraries as well as a widespread network of recreational facilities.

The System of Party Rule: the Interlocking Directorates

In spite of the fact that the party under Kádár has withdrawn to the commanding heights of the policy, the economy and the society, its rule via the control of the leadership positions has remained undisputed. Conversely, the fact that a specific state, economic or social position is held by a high-ranking party functionary gives the former a special political significance. In 1985, the incumbents of the most important positions were as shown in Table 2.11.

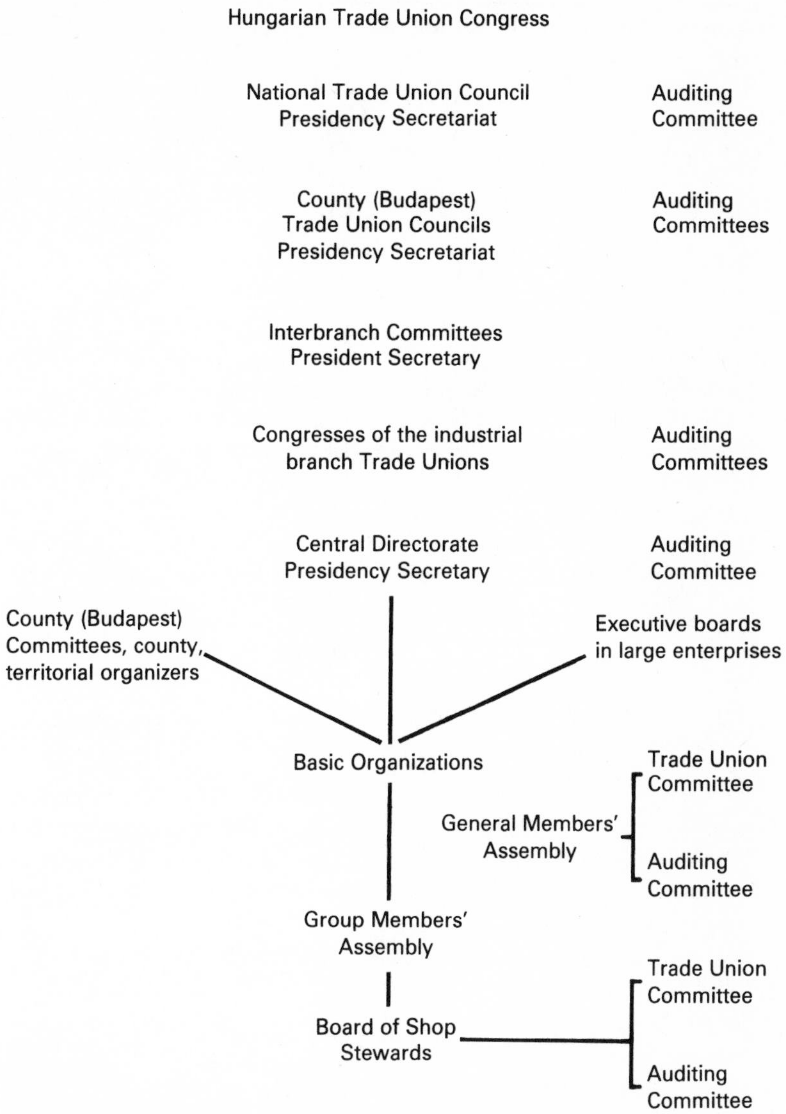

Hungarian Trade Union Congress

National Trade Union Council
Presidency Secretariat

Auditing
Committee

County (Budapest)
Trade Union Councils
Presidency Secretariat

Auditing
Committees

Interbranch Committees
President Secretary

Congresses of the industrial
branch Trade Unions

Auditing
Committees

Central Directorate
Presidency Secretary

Auditing
Committee

County (Budapest)
Committees, county,
territorial organizers

Executive boards
in large enterprises

Basic Organizations

Trade Union
Committee

General Members'
Assembly

Auditing
Committee

Group Members'
Assembly

Board of Shop
Stewards

Trade Union
Committee

Auditing
Committee

Figure 2.5 The Structure of the Hungarian Trade Union Movement

Table 2.11 Overlapping holding of principal elite positions

Council of Ministers (Government)

Chairman	György Lázár	PB
Deputy Chairman	Dr László Marothy	PB
Members	Lajos Czinege	CC
Dr Judit Csehák	CC	
Lajos Faluvégi	CC	
József Marjai	CC	

Ministers

Domestic Trade	Dr Zoltán Juhár	
Interior	János Kamara	CC
Health	Dr László Medve	
Construction and City Development	László Somogyi	
Defence	István Oláh	CC
Justice	Dr Imre Markója	
Industry	Dr László Kapolyi	
Traffic	Dr Lajos Urbán	
Foreign Trade	Péter Veress	CC
Foreign Affairs	Dr Péter Várkonyi	CC
Agriculture and Food	Jenő Váncsa	CC
Education	Dr Béla Köpeczi	
Finance	Dr István Hetényi	
Chairman of the State Planning Authority	Lajos Faluvégi	CC
Chairman of the Central Committee of People's Control	József Szakali	CC

Party Representation: PB—10.5 per cent; CC—57.9 per cent

Presidential Council

Chairman	Pál Losonczi	PB
Deputy Chairmen	Sándor Gáspár	PB
	Dr Rezső Trautmann	
Secretary	Imre Katona	CC
Members	Sándor Barcs	
	Dr Tibor Bartha	
	Mrs Géza Bánáti	
	Imre Biró	
	Mrs Lajos Duschek	
	Mrs Teréz Michelisz Krémer	
	Dr Marin Mandity	
	László Nánási	

Table 2.11 (*cont.*)

Károly Németh	PB
Géza Szalai	
János Szentágothai	
Dr Miklós Vida	
Dr János Eleki	
Dr István Gajdócsi	
Mrs Sándor Horváth	
János Kádár	PB
Gyula Kállai	CC

Party Representation: PB—19.0 per cent; CC—28.5 per cent

Diet Standing Committees

Only two out of the twelve committee chairmen are members of the top leadership group: Mátyás Szűrős (Committee for Foreign Policy) and Rezső Nyers (Trade Committee). Szűrős is PB member and Secretary for Foreign Policy in the CC; Nyers, the architect of the 1968 New Economic Mechanism, is a CC member.

Constitutional Law Council

Of the fifteen members, only the Chairman, the former Minister of Justice, Dr Mihály Korom, is a CC member.

Mass organizations and other important functions

Chief Secretary of the National TU Council	Tibor Baranyai	CC
Chairman of the PPF	Gyula Kállai	CC
Secretary of the PPF	Imre Pozsgay	CC
Chairman of the National Union of Co-operatives	István Szlamenicky	CC
Chairman of the Diet	István Sarlós	PB
Chairman of the National Union of the Agricultural Producers' Co-operatives (Collective Farms)	István Szabó	PB
Deputy Minister of Defence	Ferenc Kárpáti	CC
Hungarian Ambassador in Moscow	Sándor Rajnai	CC

Political Dissent: 'Her Majesty's Tolerated' Opposition?

The way in which societies deal with deviant behaviour is dependent on a complex configuration of situational constraints, traditional patterns, the possibilities for learning and innovation and the beliefs and orientations resulting from these factors. In spite of its relative underdevelopment, pre-1947 Hungary had known long periods of intellectual freedom which was by no means inferior to that enjoyed by its Western neighbours. Yet, freedom of opinion in dualist Hungary (1867–1918) was by and large limited to Budapest alone. Only the country's industrial and cultural centre could provide the necessary human and infrastructural resources necessary for intellectual pluralism: social strata with a sufficiently high level of education, newspapers, people who bought and read them and a functioning court system. In the villages complaints, grievances, dissatisfaction and deprivation had no chance to be articulated and cast into consistent ideologies that were within the intellectual grasp of the rural population: a system of personal rule and feudal power managed to preserve the middle ages until the twentieth century. Even the aristocratic liberalism in the capital had clear limits, the most important being the fact that Hungary was a multinational empire under Magyar domination, so that most reform proposals sooner or later threatened to spill over into demands for minority rights, thus undermining the very basis of Magyar rule.

The failure of the first communist experiment in 1919 had dealt leftist ideas a heavy blow, but left-wing political radicalism, banned from the political scene, found an outlet in the sphere of the arts. In societies lacking the freedom of political expression the arts assume the role of a political forum: small wonder that the most outspoken critics of the social system under Horthy were writers and poets like Gyulla Illyés and Endre Ady. The majority of the Hungarian intelligentsia identified with the conservative or liberal-democratic camps (Lackó, 1981, p. 523). The years following the communist takeover and the elimination of political opposition silenced dissenting voices until they re-erupted in 1956. Needless to say, it was not the lack of opposition but the hopelessness and the futility of expressing organized protest that was characteristic of the Stalinist period. The 1956 uprising was preceded by intra-party dissent, which was raised mainly in discussion circles held under the auspices of a party that together with its units had lost much of its former strength. Again, literati assumed the role of the nation's spiritual leaders, chastising the abuses of Stalinism with less and less inhibition.

During and after the October 1956 days, communism was socially marginalized; the intelligentsia either left the country, fell victim to the eventual victors' wrath or remained in a deep alienation towards the new regime which was seen as a Soviet puppet government. Only in 1963, when internal liberalization and international recognition gained momentum, was the regime able to win over a few leading personalities of the Hungarian cultural scene into their camp (e.g. the writer Tibor Déry). Meanwhile social protest surfaced in the form of deviant behaviour by the young generation. For some time long hair, blue jeans and portable stereos symbolized protest and elicited corresponding reactions from the authorities, such as detaining youths who had participated in rock parties for 'indecent behaviour' or giving police-sponsored hair cuts. Yet, as social acceptance and general tolerance *vis-à-vis* deviance, and the openness of Hungarian society grew, the symbols of youthful protest lost their political significance.

While the party during the late sixties and early seventies was able to win popular support and to decrease former hostility, intra-party criticism mounted. In 1973, a group of sociologists and philosophers who had accused the Kádár leadership of having perverted the original Marxian ideas was expelled from the party. They had been disciples of György Lukács and formed the nucleus of the so-called Budapest School of Sociology. They were to become the hard core of future opposition movements. Due to the growing self-assurance of the regime and the skilful tactics of György Aczél, the party secretary responsible for cultural affairs, a broad opposition movement never did materialize. Many dissenters, like György Márkus, Ágnes Heller, Iván Szelényi, Miklós Haraszti, Ferenc Fehér and Mária Márkus have been allowed to settle in the West without having to sever relations with their home country. The group produced classical pieces of social criticism like M. Haraszti's *Piece Work* (*Darabbér*) or Konrád-Szelényi's *The Intellentsia on its Way to Class Power*. But their products were read in the West rather than by the Hungarian public. In contrast to other socialist states, Hungary makes the production and distribution of illegal publications subject to an administrative fine which is levied without a court trial. That there is a market for critical literature is evident from the fact that 'official' works like Antal Végh's essay, *Miért beteg a magyar football* (*Why Hungarian Soccer is Sick*) became bestsellers and quickly disappared from the shelves.

In recent years the dissident movement seems to have gained some strength. Several samizdat publications have appeared—*Beszélő (The Talker)*, *Tájékoztató (The Signpost)*, *Hírmondó (The Messenger) ABC Bulletin*—and there has been considerable spill-over and overlapping between the political opposition and the ecological and peace movements as well as the basic church communities advocating conscientious objection. Also, the attitude of the regime has hardened somewhat. Police harassment against leading dissidents has increased, their apartments searched for illegal literature, and publications prohibited, confiscated or their publication delayed. As of 1 September 1983, illegal publishers can be fined up to 10,000 fts. According to a report to the International Helsinki Federation for Human Rights (*Violations of the Helsinki Accord: Report From Hungary*, May 1983) prepared by leading dissenters, the regime discriminates against religious denominations, sentencing thirty to forty citizens annually for conscientious objection, violates the right to work by ordering the dismissal of signatories to protest resolutions and abridges the constitutional guarantee of freedom of the press by its own press regulations. The closing down of László Rajk's samizdat boutique (the owner is the son of L. Rajk who was executed in 1949) in May 1983 fits into the overall impression of a—at least temporarily—chillier climate.

The basic line of the government, however, has not changed. There is a principal commitment to continue the dialogue in order to prevent even deeper rifts. Already by 1969 the Central Committee had passed a resolution (the so-called Science-Policy Directive) stating the intention of the party to respect the freedom of science and artistic creation. The representatives of the regime, due to the ambiguous policies that have been pursued in dealing with recalcitrant intellectuals, have become disorientated and lack precisely defined boundaries that may not be overstepped. Many functionaries feel they have been edged into a defensive position. The Party Gazette *Népszabadság* expresses this widespread attitude by stating:

We can now feel in many instances that the categories of the 'tolerated' and the 'non-tolerated' have become blurred, in the first line because of the ideological vapidness that one can encounter in many fields. This in turn happens because instead of criticizing, arguing and enlightening positions are abandoned in favour of bourgeois philosophy and its value order. If we talk about a dialogue, then it is natural that we need a partner. It does not matter, that others, non-Marxists, can also freely voice their opinions and philosophies, directly or via artistic creation. But if we have condemned the political and ideological monologue pursued by Marxists, we should also reject a monologue under reversed premises. [*NSz*, 25 August, 1984.]

The lack of a consistent policy and strategy is also underlined by the fact that different representatives of the regime take different attitudes in dealing with the phenomenon of political dissent. Thus, when Deputy Minister of Culture Dezső Tóth (who does not enjoy a liberal reputation) had come under the heavy criticism of university students for his order to dismiss the editor-in-chief of the controversial monthly *Mozgó Világ (Moving World)*, he chose to go into the lion's den and confront about 800 disgruntled students of Budapest's Eötvös Loránd University in an open discussion at the end of October 1983. Tóth proved to be a flexible negotiator, and did not insist on the correctness of some of the authorities' past decisions (RAD/BR 16/Hungary, 3 February 1984).

As far as the intelligentsia at large is concerned, the prevailing mood seems to be a moderate reformism. For a majority of them, work and career conditions are more than acceptable. There is no general official censorship. For the mass media, which represent the highest degree of publicity and draw the highest degree of attention, a system of self-censorship prevents the discussion of certain topics. However, the party's commitment to create an autonomous sphere for science is a reality. The responsibility has been delegated to the research institutions and the individual researchers themselves. Official and opposition perceptions of the handling of the dissent problem in Hungary converge to an astonishing degree. In an essay on 'The Democratic Opposition in Hungary: Current Status and Expectations', Ferenc Köszeg assesses the state of affairs in the following way:

The existence of an opposition plays a great role in providing the Hungarian government with a favourable image in the international press. Naturally, many other issues that are much more important for the great majority of the Hungarian population play a part in creating this image—the liberal and pragmatic economic policies of the government, the relatively high living standards (which, by the way, the great majority of the population maintains only though immense efforts), the relatively free flow of information, the relative freedom to travel (although the Ministry of Interior can deprive virtually anybody of this any time), public security (maintained by a vastly inflated police force, which is beyond any public control), and the fact that the authorities more or less respect human rights.

Everyday violations of human rights—teenagers or gypsies beaten up by policemen, discontented or angry men being sentenced to imprisonment for 'subversive propaganda' or 'offences against the community'— are not covered by the world press, and even the Hungarian public is hardly aware of them. However, anyone who reads the papers carefully can know of the existence of the political opposition—at least anyone in Central Europe, and perhaps even in the West as well. When news about the opposition reaches the international press concerning a house search or an interrogation, on the next day everyone interested in Hungary is afraid of hearing news of arrests or legal proceedings. Yet, until now, nothing of that kind has taken place (and let us hope it never will). Readers are surprised to witness the liberal-mindedness of the Hungarian government again and again.

When dealing with persons they consider as 'dissidents' the authorities have so far never transgressed the limits of mere harassment, interference or causing damage. They attempt to curtail the activities of the oppositions by police actions and fines for offences. But in addition to these legal retaliations, they have resorted to harassment in public places which sometimes verges on assault and battery, and have interfered in the free practice of professions. [Violations of the Helsinki Accords, p. 18.]

At present, several major opposition groups have appeared on the Hungarian dissident scene. With their largely overlapping membership, they form a system of communicating pipes which is held together by a hard core consisting of the 'Budapest School' and the 'Democratic Opposition'. Their total potential must be assessed as relatively weak. While around 300 people signed a letter to the Presidential Council protesting the prosecution of the Czechoslovak Chartists in March 1977 and November 1979 (*Gegenstimmen*, 1982, nos. 10 and 18), the appeal to stop the construction of the Gabčikovo-Nagymaros Danube dam was signed by fewer than 10,000 people (*Kurier*, 24 February 1985). Thus, the hard core consists of about 300 individuals and the maximum reach of the movement is represented by the latter figure.

The Budapest School

Grouped around the erstwhile Premier under Rákosi, András Hegedűs, who after 1957 (his return from exile in the Soviet Union) led the Institute of Sociology of the Hungarian Academy of Sciences, the ideology of this movement draws heavily on György Lukács' return to original Marxism and on the ideas of the West European New Left. They feel that the original socialist ideas were distorted, especially in the Soviet Union during the Stalin era, but also by contemporary 'established Socialism' in Eastern Europe. They propose a new departure that would overcome the ossified socialist bureaucracy (Hegedűs & Márkus, 1974). In 1973, the Central Committee reacted with a statement that condemned these views as undermining the purity of Marxism–Leninism. As the document puts it:

> Allowing variety in research trends and schools becomes politically and ideologically dangerous if it results in the establishment of a conceptual political system whose tenor is to query, dissolve, or reject the theoretical system of Marxism–Leninism . . . An ideological concept of pluralized Marxism might lead to political pluralism and to a denial of the leading role of the Communist party and in the last analysis of that of the working class . . . Freedom of research postulates a high degree of political responsibility and consistent self-control. [*Magyar Filozofiai Szemle*, 1973, 1–2, translated in RFER *Hungarian Press Survey No. 2309*, 1 October 1973, p. 2.]

On the basis of this document András Hegedűs, Mihály Vajda and János Kis were excluded from the party and together with the non-party philosophers Mária and György Márkus lost their professional positions. The ideas of the 'Budapest School' are still present in the critical studies of young sociologists castigating the social inequalities in contemporary Hungary.

The 'Democratic Opposition'

This group formed around disgruntled intellectuals who had come, for one reason or the other, into conflict with the regime. Thus, György Krassó, an economist, was sentenced in 1957 for 'attempting to overthrow the people's democracy' and for 'theft', amnestied in 1963 and retried in 1964. Other leading members of the movement are Gábor Demsky (a sociologist and publisher), László Rajk and Ferenc Köszeg. The group has issued several samizdat periodicals whose publication was tolerated by the authorities for some time. Its main activity is directed at documenting illegal and unconstitutional acts of Hungarian authorities. In this connection the relatively unorganized movement also regards itself as the Hungarian National Group of the International Helsinki Federation. Therefore, it also keeps contact with similar groups in East European states and in the West. Among other things, it has issued appeals against the 1979 trial of the Charter 1977 members in Prague and for solidarity with the Polish people in January 1982, and it also protested against the arrests of Hungarian intellectuals in November 1982. In May 1983 it called attention to human rights violations in Hungary. It also issued a letter dated 3 November 1984 to Father Popiełuszko's church in Warsaw expressing commiseration and solidarity with the priest murdered by Polish State Security officers.

The 'Peace Group For Dialogue'

This group did not regard itself as a dissident grouping and sought co-operation with the Hungarian Peace Council; however, its concept of the equal responsibility of both East and West for the arms race ran counter to the official policy line and activities like the organization of peace camps and the participation in international peace conferences were severely hampered by the authorities. Eventually, the group dissolved itself because of the Peace Council's obstructive attitude but decided to carry on operations on an informal basis. Allegedly, its former leader F. Köszeg is now heading the official youth group of the Peace Council (Beszélő, 1984, p. 9).

The Young Writers' Circle 'József Attila'

This group started out as a section within the official Writers' Union and published the critical magazine *Mozgó Világ*. A conflict erupted when the cultural authorities decided to dismiss its editor-in-chief Ferenc Kulin from his position. This administrative interference drew strong objections from both members of the Young Writers' Circle and university students. A protest resolution was issued and the Deputy Minister of Cultural Affairs had to intervene in order to calm the situation.

The Foundation for Assistance to the Poor (SZETA)
This group is interconnected with the Budapest School. Its founder is Ottilia Solt, a sociologist. It came into conflict with the authorities when it wanted to stage a discussion forum on inequalities in Hungary in November 1984. The authorities felt that the topic was too sensitive to be discussed in Hungary (AFP, 22 November 1984).

The Jewish Group 'Shalom'
This small group appeared very recently, advancing demands to establish diplomatic relations with Israel and to preserve the Jewish heritage.

Hungarian Minority Spokesmen
Grouped around the samizdat periodical *ABC Bulletin*, a number of ethnic Hungarians who had lived in neighbouring countries and emigrated to Hungary monitor the situation of Hungarian minorities in Romania, Czechoslovakia and Yugoslavia. The best-known personalities among them are Gáspár Miklós Tamás, a writer and philosopher and the editor Károly Tóth who both left Romania and continued their critical activities in Hungary. The Hungarian poet István Csoori, who had written an introduction to a book by the spokesman of the Hungarian minority in Czechoslovakia, was prohibited from publishing anything political for an indefinite period of time (Hungarian SR/14, 29 November 1984). Although the group rejects nationalistic attitudes, certain elements of traditional Magyar nationalism cannot be denied.

There are several specific features of the Hungarian dissident scene. First, dissenters are marginalized, but unlike their counterparts in Czechoslovakia or in the Soviet Union they are not treated as political and social outcasts. Neither the opposition nor the authorities seem to be willing to stop the direct or indirect dialogue for good. Extremist attitudes are the exception on both sides. Neither are the boundaries between dissenters and intra-system reformers clear. Officially recognized writers like Gyula Illyés brand the suppression of the Hungarian minorities in the neighbouring countries as strongly as the 'real' opposition, and criticism of social inequality is a commonplace topic in 'official' sociology as well. Most dissidents started out as conformists and slowly dissociated themselves from their former 'normal' status. Apart from the New Leftist hard core of the movement, it has no clear and consistent ideological convictions. The ideological spectrum is almost fully covered: on the extreme left, members of the Budapest School like A. Heller and M. Vajda reject the bourgeois family and propagate communes and ideas such as those of the 'official dissident' economist Tibor Liska. Liska stands for 'right-wing' reforms enhancing the role of private capital, and is very popular among the opposition (and to be sure, among the reformers in the government as well). The older generation of Hungary's 'angry young men' are disillusioned Stalinists who have had to give up the ideals of their youth. They have preserved the basic syndrome of their Stalinist past, namely, an obsession with absolute truths going hand in hand with a black and white image of the world and the rejection of pragmatic approaches. The young generation's recruitment pool is a small but relatively vociferous unemployed intelligentsia. Most of them are graduates of the arts faculties or individuals planning for a scientific career in one of the research institutes. In contrast to the ample job supply for graduates with practical qualifications, the openings for theoreticians are scarce in Hungary. Thus, a widespread frustration and a feeling that society has no use for their talents has befallen precisely the group that has learned to express their feelings in public—the artists and the literati, who naturally assume the role of spokesmen for the whole alienated group. Thus, the traditional political significance of the arts has been preserved until today. On the other hand, their alienation is not total and it does not seem to be the outcome of generational conflict since most of the leading personalities are over thirty.

As far as the authorities' approach to the problem is concerned, the general attitude is an outcome of the traumatic 1956 experience. For both society and leadership, a violent resolution of social and political conflicts has been an anathema. The interest of most political leaders to preserve their image with the Western press is an additional motive. Therefore, open coercion is replaced by self-restraint, and 'soft' administrative methods. Occasionally, the interests of the opposition and the regime coincide, e.g. with the promotion of critical works on Hungarian Stalinism which makes the present regime appear in a better light. On the other hand, the failures of Kádárism, namely the high degree of inequality, the high level of social discontent and the increasing unemployment are grist to the mills of both dissidents and hardliners within the Party CC. The regime's reactions are diversified, depending on situational constraints and group allegiances. There are several topics that are taboo for public discussions, and any attempt to table such topics openly provokes instant reactions. Above all, this concerns the role of the Soviet Union, but also the relations with other East European countries. Therefore, an art exhibit in Budapest was closed on 30 January 1984, where one work was exposed that bore the caption 'Hungarian and Poles: Two Good Friends Who Fight And Drink Together' and 'We Fight Together, 1956–1981'. For similar reasons, the authorities reacted to American Vice-President George Bush's remarks about socialist states that 'introduced greater openness in their societies' and others that 'unfortunately follow the Soviet line' in September 1983 in Vienna (Cercle Diplomatique International, 1983, pp. 7–10, 13).

Hungary's precarious international position also explains the crackdown on the minority spokesmen and on some of the organizers of the protest movement against the joint Czechoslovak–Hungarian project of a Danube power station. Other touchy topics are the Nagy trial and the involvement of contemporary leaders in Stalinist abuses in general. Social inequality may be raised as a topic, but it is still dangerous to query the very basis of NEM, which relies on a philosophy of achieving higher productivity through increased inequalities. As far as the future of the opposition movement is concerned, much will depend on the future of NEM. Hitherto, a majority of Hungarian intellectuals, faced with the choice of adjusting or becoming marginalized, have opted for the first alternative. Their decision is made relatively easy by the consumption and career possibilities made available to them. In contrast to the period immediately preceding the October uprising, most people have too much to lose, no matter how high the level of social discontent may be. On the side of the rulers, most people realize that the concessions and small freedoms granted to the citizens are irrevocable and that a relapse into Stalinist coercion would trigger incalculable developments. Dissent, a minor problem in contemporary Hungary, could develop the capacity to foment large-scale resistance.

3 Between Feudalism and the Technotronic Age: Hungarian Society

Introduction

All societies are the result of a process of trial and error. Adaptation to the natural, social and political environment results in the emergence of patterns of institutions, of power and co-operation. The need for continuous adaptation in a changing world triggers new responses until a new state of temporary balance has been reached. For those groups who perceive a need to devise new patterns, the existing ones appear obsolete and doomed to decay, whereas those interested in maintaining the traditional way of life experience any attempt at changing it as a threat. Thus, when the Hungarian communists set out to radically revamp the whole society, conflicts between the 'progressive' and 'traditional' forces were inevitable. Rákosi's attempt at moulding a new society resulted in the creation of two societies that were bitterly opposed to each other. The communists drew their confidence from the feeling that they had to accomplish a mission entrusted to them by history. The other society, a majority of citizens, did not so much resent the basic ideological values (which they did not know anyhow) but did object to the brutal interference into personal life. Today, the picture has become blurred. It is no longer possible to identify the party with a radically innovative force and the rest of society with stubborn resistance. The party has become socialized and has embraced many 'old' values and patterns whereas the politicization of society under Rákosi has generated many 'new' features that are viewed with distrust, but can hardly be stopped from above. There are still two societies, each of them characterized by different structural properties. But the front lines no longer coincide with those of the political-ideological camps. They run through all provinces of the social fabric and mark developmental tendencies rather than distinctly separate subcultures. The Hungarian sociologist E. Hankiss has tried to describe these conflicting tendencies by the following characteristics:

(a) Diffuse unity versus differentiation and integration: the communist strategy was aiming at the destruction of the traditional hierarchical structures. It sought to replace the latter by strict uniformity. Yet, many of the traditional differentiations could not be eliminated; many were revived in a new form, and many new ones emerged. Today, the 'other society' tries to integrate the different cultural, religious, political and social tendencies by accepting and consciously preserving their specific properties.

(b) Verticality versus horizontality: the maintenance of hierarchical structures under communism since the Second World War was dictated by the need to control and implement the party's policies. Attempts at breaking vertical command lines culminated in the 1956 revolution. Since then, numerous initiatives to counter the official hierarchical structures by setting up horizontal channels of communication, have gone afloat within and outside the party, on national and regional levels and in the economic, social and political systems.

(c) Centralization from the above versus decentralization from below: the official society is run by the party headquarters. However, as the example of the second economy shows, the party's real domain can be compared to islands of control which are half immersed in a sea of grass-roots activities beyond its purview and monitoring capacity.

(d) Official versus inofficial public opinion: under Rákosi, all non-Marxist–Leninist views were discredited as 'reactionary'. This attitude has partly survived in the 'first', official society. But beneath the threadbare facade of unity all kinds of views and philosophies flourish in an atmosphere of semi-tolerance, which lends a kind of semi-legitimacy to non-official views and activities. Although the degree of officially permitted plural-ism is astonishingly high in Hungary, there are still topics which may not be discussed openly. The second, unofficial public opinion does not suffer from the same inhibitions. However, sometimes the relationship is reversed: officially published views, such as the critical analyses in the works of Hungarian sociologists are often much more radical than the popular evaluation of social problems (Hankiss, 1984, p. 25).

Thus, an in-depth analysis of contemporary Hungarian society must try to explain the complicated web of conflicting tendencies of phenomena that are in the public focus and of those that are hidden from the social vision, of social processes that are, or are not, amenable to political guidance. It is only following this complex background that statistical data become alive and meaningful.

Social Policy

The social policy of the Hungarian communists has undergone several decisive changes in response to the exigencies of a changing economic and social environment as well as to the consequences of their own strategies. One can clearly discern three phases:

(a) *The phase of reconstruction.* This period begins with the communist take-over and ends in the early fifties. Since about 40 per cent of the national income had to be earmarked for the reconstruction of wartime losses during this period (Szalai, 1981, p. 62), the ambitious communist goals to supply each citizen with work, educational, health, transport and other facilities had to be limited to a strategy of redistribution. The benefits and services that, according to the constitutional proclamations, were to accrue to all workers equally, were transferred from the market to the state sphere. The state offered them to the citizens as straight services and not as monetary fringe benefits. Consequently, personal incomes could be held at a very low level.

(b) *The phase of stagnation.* During the early fifties, the undisputed priority of industrialization and collectivization made a further deployment of the social services' network impossible. Funds and manpower were syphoned off from the 'unproductive' branches and channelled into heavy industry, thus causing a lowering of the general standard of living and a fallback in the quality of social services.

(c) *The phase of differentiation and (relative) decay.* When the limits of 'extensive' economic growth were reached at the end of the sixties, Hungary had to revive market mechanisms again. In social policy, the new economic strategies led to a rapid increase of monetary fringe benefits as well as to the completion of the social insurance net. While only 47 per cent of the citizens had been insured in 1950, practically the entire population (99 per cent) was insured in 1972 (Halay, 1980, p. 49). The new policies aiming at the improvement of the citizens' living standards led to an unprecedented expansion of social services. Now, 3–3.5 per cent of the national income is spent for health purposes (Halay, 1980, p. 51). Generally, 32 per cent of the national income is earmarked for social services. Since 1975, every Hungarian citizen is entitled to obtain free health care. The chances of a child getting a kindergarten or crèche place have risen to 88 per cent (with great regional disparities). The number of doctors and hospital beds has risen absolutely and relatively to reach and partly surpass the standard of Western industrial states (*Nsz*, 22 April 1982).

However, the existing social network has become insufficient for the rising quantitative and qualitative expectations. Moreover, the whole system needs a complete overhauling. In a literary sense, this is true of the hospital buildings, three-fourths of which are older than fifty years and one-third of which must be torn down and rebuilt from scratch. Most of the hospitals use outdated technical equipment (Halay, 1980, p. 51). Rising cost pressure calls for urgent countermeasures which have mainly been taken in the form of limiting the access to social services (e.g. by introducing priority criteria).

The higher emphasis on market-regulated processes has led to a greater differentiation in the services offered to the population. Under an ever-increasing budget pressure—at the end of the eighties there will be one old-age pensioner for each working citizen—centralization processes were initiated not only in general state administration, but also in education, health and other areas. The social service institutions left the smaller satellite communities and were concentrated in the regional centres. This process has increased the leeway for the heads of the newly created social service centres to distribute funds and manpower within their enlarged empires, thus promoting their qualitative differentiation. The unwanted consequence of the strategy to raise the efficiency of the system has led to a decrease of the life chances for the less mobile and less educated parts of the population. The young and mobile strata can follow the educational, health and other institutions more easily. Moreover, their network of friends and acquaintances usually includes people in leading positions (like chief surgeons and heads of pension authorities). Through their direct personal access their chances to obtain kindergarten places or hospital treatment of an above-average standard are much higher than those of the underprivileged strata. Hungarian sociologists correlate the relative decay of the system of social services with deteriorating mortality figures, increasing childhood neurosis and other negative social phenomena (Szalai, 1981, p. 65).

Thus, the MSzMP finds itself in a difficult situation. On the one hand, it remains firmly committed to its policy of equalization and on the other hand

Table 3.1 Opinions on whom the State should support

	1978	1980	1982
'Those who live in poorer, worse circumstances'	33	38	47
'Those who deserve it on account of their work and conduct'	50	45	40
'Nobody'	17	17	13

it has to cope with formidable budget and general economic constraints. The tacit bargain between party and population excludes visible cuts in the supply of public goods. The population has become used to a strong protective state. Polling results show that this attitude has become more pronounced during recent years. Asked which individuals the state should support, a panel of respondents answered as shown in Table 3.1.

The breakdown of the respondents by social classes shows that Hungary's skilled workers rely least of all on state support. However, even this 'enterprising' group welcomes the protective state by a high majority (see Table 3.2).

The strong demands voiced *vis-à-vis* the socialist state also reflect the higher risks created by the NEM and the deterioration of the overall economic situation. In addition, they reveal a propensity to trade higher living standards for central risk-taking.

Population

The twentieth century has witnessed a steady increase in Hungary's

Table 3.2 Opinions about State Support by Social Class

	'the poor'	'the deserving'	'nobody'
Leading positions			
1978	13	71	16
1982	39	52	9
Intellectuals			
1978	26	67	7
1982	36	51	13
Skilled workers			
1978	30	53	17
1982	35	50	15
Semi-skilled workers			
1978	28	52	20
1982	49	39	12
Unskilled workers			
1978	16	61	23
1982	51	39	10
Agricultural blue-collar workers			
1978	26	48	26
1982	50	39	11

Source: Angelusz & Tardos, 1983, p. 118.

Table 3.3 Population Trends, 1930–85

Year	Population	Time period	Real increase	Average annual increase
1930	8,659,109	1921–30	8.7	0.8
1941	9,361,109	1931–41	7.3	0.7
1949	9,204,799	1941–48	−1.2	−0.2
1960	9,961,044	1949–59	8.2	0.7
1970	10,322,000	1970–76	2.9	0.4
1980	10,709,550	1970–79	3.8	0.37
1985	10,659,000	1980–85	n.a.	n.a.

Source: Balint, 1983, p. 120, *StZsK*, 1984.

population since the 1920s, interrupted by several sharp oscillations during the twenties and the late-forties as well as a dramatic fall after the Second World War. Hungary's war losses amounted to 420,000 or about 4.5 per cent of her total population (Bálint, 1983, p. 121). Yet, as a reaction to these losses and despite the political turmoil prevailing during the late-forties, Hungary's population returned to a net growth in the period between 1949 and 1960 (see Table 3.3). In 1982, however, the trend was reversed. Live birth figures tell a similar story. Their decline in the twenties and thirties was due to a temporary social and economic crisis. The long-term trend clearly points downwards, which will result in consistent zero or even negative growth (see Table 3.4). This point was reached in 1983, when the mortality rate rose to 13.9 per 1,000 inhabitants.

As a zero population growth is apt to cause a deterioration in the age structure, and consequently a decline of the active earners, Hungary's budget planners face a serious problem. In 1985 the age cohorts were: children (0–14 yrs.) 21.6 per cent; young adults (15–29) 20.2 per cent; adults (30–59) 40.1 per cent; senior citizens (over 60) 18.0 per cent (Source: StZsK, 1984). There is a clear shift of the age groups towards the adult cohort. In 1980, children still accounted for 22 per cent and senior citizens for 17.0 per cent of the population (Bálint, 1983, p. 166).

The oscillations in the number of live births are partly a result of population, health, economic and other policies. In post-war Hungary we can distinguish between three policy phases that each set specific priorities for population policy. During 1946–53 the main goal was the improvement of the dramatically high rate of infant mortality. As a result of the decrease of live births, the government pursued an explicit population growth policy from 1953 onwards. The Eighth Party Congress reinforced this platform,

Table 3.4 Live Births, 1920–84

Year	Live births	Per 1,000 inhabitants
1920	249,458	31.4
1930	219,784	25.4
1941	177,047	19.9
1946	169,120	18.7
1947	187,316	20.6
1948	191,907	21.0
1952	185,820	19.6
1953	206,926	21.6
1954	223,347	23.0
1956	192,810	19.5
1957	167,202	17.0
1960	146,461	14.7
1962	130,053	12.9
1968	154,419	15.1
1970	151,819	14.7
1971	150,640	14.5
1973	156,224	15.0
1975	194,240	18.4
1976	185,405	17.5
1980	148,673	13.9
1981	142,890	13.3
1982	133,559	12.5
1983	127,553	11.9
1984	124,934	11.7

Source: Statisztikai Évkönvv 1967–1984, Stat. Havi Közlemévvek 1984/1.

issuing a strong warning against the dangers inherent in falling fertility rates (A MSzMP IX kongresszusának jegyzőkönyve, Budapest, 1967, p. 460). A Politburo decision of 11 February 1973 partly revised this all-out growth policy, defining an annual population increase of 0.16 and an average 2.16 children per family as a desirable standard (Bálint, 1983, p. 121).

Most developed industrial states have experienced a fall in their birth rates. However, when mortality rates surpassed the birth rate in 1983, Hungary's political leaders were faced with a challenge that they cannot ignore.

Hungary's population problem is generated by a unique configuration of interrelated factors. The fall of the birth rate can be explained by:

(a) *The housing situation*. On a country-wide average, young couples have to wait about six to seven years for an apartment. In Budapest, the situation is even more dramatic.

(b) *Female employment*. In 1984, 45.5 per cent of all active earners were women, and 81 per cent of all women in the eligible age brackets were employed. The rising proportion of female work corresponds to the needs of the planners who promoted industrial growth by the expansion of the labour factor as well as to the wishes of the families themselves who were interested in higher living standards or simply had no other choice because one wage did not suffice.

(c) *Abortion policies*. Prior to 1955, Hungary had very strict abortion regulations. The number of reported abortions was around 1,700 per year in the beginning of the 1950s; by 1955 it stood at 35,000 and at the end of the 1970s, it had reached 200,000. Between 1959 and 1973 the annual number of abortions surpassed the number of life births. In 1973, the government tried to revise this trend by passing stiffer abortion regulations. As a result, the number of reported abortions fell to an annual 100,000 and has stabilized at a slightly lower level ever since (Bálint, 1983, p. 124). It is questionable whether the figure of non-reported abortions has grown to a similar extent.

(d) *Infant mortality*. Between the wars, Hungary had one of the worst infant mortality records among European states. In 1940, 130 out of 1,000 babies died before their first birthday. In 1976, due to the dramatic improvement of medical facilities, this figure had been reduced to 30, and in 1979, to 24. In 1983 it was eventually down to 19.0, only to rise to 20.2 in the following year. Thus, Hungary had ceased to be a developing country in this respect, but it is still far away from the record of developed capitalist countries (e.g Norway with 9 per 1000 live births).

(e) *Divorces*. The pace of modernization and social transformation is reflected in the development of divorce rates. Currently, about 40 per cent of marriages end in separation. The lack of stability in marital relations contributed to the decreasing birth figures because most divorces concern childless couples (Cseh-Szombathy, 1984, p. 74). See Table 3.5.

(f) Temporary oscillations of the birth rate are caused by a change in the political situation. Thus, the birth rate sank significantly among intellectuals after 1956 and among farmers after 1959, when the collectivization drive was renewed (Tóth, 1983, p. 73). In addition to the temporary variations, the birth rate seems to be a function of geographical location and ethnic cultural origin as well. The deteriorating life birth record goes hand in hand with an increase in mortality rates. Life expectancy

Table 3.5 Divorces 1921–84

Year	Number of divorces	Divorces/ 1,000 marriages
1921	6,188	3.8
1930–31	4,926	2.6
1938	5,754	2.8
1948	11,058	5.3
1960	16,590	6.5
1970	22,841	8.4
1975	25,997	9.3
1976	27,075	9.6
1977	27,167	9.6
1978	28,407	10.1
1979	27,606	9.8
1980	27,797	9.9
1981	27,426	9.8
1982	28,687	10.3
1983	29,337	10.7
1984	27,000	9.9

Source: Statiszikai Évkönyv, 1982; *StZsK*, 1984.

rose steeply following the improvement of health conditions after 1954 but started to climb downward in the male category during the sixties. This fact is due to dramatically increasing mortality rates in the forty to sixty bracket. Also, the improvement of female life expectancy seems to have come to a standstill. Average life expectancy was 66.0 years for men and 73.4 years for women in the period from 1975 to 1981; in 1983, it was 65.6 and 73.5, respectively. The main social reasons for the failure to improve life expectancy are to be sought in the impact of diseases caused by civilization itself, in increased alcohol consumption and suicide rates, but also in a 'sleeper effect' of formerly incurable congenital diseases that led to high infant mortality before.

Stratifications in Hungarian Society

All classifications and taxonomies select a specific pattern out of an unlimited number of possibilities. Statistical categories, too, are highly selective and represent a specific viewpoint or cognitive interest. The 'official' structure of Hungarian society conforms to the ideological perspective of the party which sees itself as the builder of a classless society which is to be constructed through the expansion of the working class. According to the tenets of

Marxism–Leninism, classes differ from each other by their specific position in the process of production. The current practice of defining workers, peasants and intelligentsia as 'classes' implies not only that these groups live and work under different circumstances, but also that they are not (in contrast to the worker-capitalist dichotomy in capitalist societies), irreconcilably opposed to each other. In Hungary, the classification used in official statistical reporting is based on a decision of the party's CC taken in 1974. In this document, the party stated

The correct interpretation of the term 'working class' is always a principal question. Any definition has to take the relevant principles of Marxism–Leninism and the present state of society into account. The workers' class is to be defined on the basis of its position in production and in a wider, political sense. [A MSzMP határozatai és dokumentumai 1971–5, Bp 1978, p. 664.]

The Working Class

At present, the official definition of the category 'working class' embraces the following groups:

(a) blue-collar workers in state enterprises operating in the various economic branches (including agriculture and forestry);
(b) blue-collar workers in industrial, construction and service co-operatives;
(c) skilled workers, technicians and foremen (*közvetlen termelésirányítók*);
(d) pensioners from these occupations and persons who have transferred to other jobs but who originally came under the working class definition.

Lumping together agricultural and industrial workers corresponds to Hungarian general semantics (*munkás*—worker) but also serves the political purpose of inflating the ranks of the working class, thus supporting the party's claim to be building a socialist society. The development of the economically active part of the workers' class was suddenly interrupted after the Second World War when a large part of the blue-collar group (that in 1941 made up 53.6 per cent of the active earners) returned to their native villages to profit from the land reform. Thus, the proportion of the working class in the total economically active population fell to 37.6 per cent to reach 56.0 per cent only in 1980 (Bálint, 1980, p. 29). In 1984, this figure had declined to 55.7 per cent.

Within the working class, the industrial workers are the strongest group. Their number is decreasing in favour of the tertiary sector. The small group of foremen has remained fairly constant over a period of thirty years.

Table 3.6 The Hungarian Working Class, 1949–84 (%)

	1949	1960	1970	1980	1984
Economically active workers' class					
(blue-collar)	38.8	n.a.	56.5	n.a.	55.7
Industry	35.9	44.5	49.0	44.7	
Construction	4.2	9.5	9.8	10.0	
Other non-agricultural branches	33.4	29.3	28.0	34.6	
Agriculture, forestry, water economy	23.5	13.7	8.4	7.6	
Foremen	3.0	3.0	4.0	3.1	

Source: Balint, 1983, p. 39; *StZsK*, 1974.

The Collective Peasantry

The official statistical category of 'collective peasantry' includes the members of the collective farms and those individuals who are employed on the basis of a labour contract, irrespective of the kind of work they perform. The number of active earners in this category was decreasing rapidly as a result of the socialist industrialization process. In 1980, it had fallen to 606,700. In recent years, a slight rise in their proportion of the total set of active earners could be registered (1984: 648,200 or 14 per cent; *StZsK*, 1984). This fact is due to the absolute decrease of the economically active population and an increase in the sub-category of the non-manuals and workers in non-agricultural occupations. A restructuring of the traditional character of agricultural work has become visible; the trend goes towards an increasing complexity of technical, legal and economic skills needed for the operations of farms, but also towards the expansion of ancillary industries. In fact, the proportion of manual workers in non-agricultural occupations (like technicians and construction workers) was already as high as 41.5 per cent in 1980 (Bálint, 1983, p. 55). A second and related developmental characteristic of the collective peasantry is the fast rise of the 'employed' category to the detriment of the collective farm members themselves. During the period from 1973 to 1980, the proportion of manual workers who had contracted for work on a collective farm rose from 12 to 23.9 per cent. The proportion of employed foremen was 27.2 per cent in 1980 and is still rising. However, a more moderate rise can be expected for the future, because the main motive to change from 'member' to 'employed' status was the privileged position of the latter *vis-à-vis* the former with regard to labour law and social security legislation. Although this gradient has been leveled out by legislation passed in 1980, a number of motives to opt for employed status has still remained.

Above all, the employees work in occupations with a higher prestige. Besides, the simple labour contract is regarded as a lesser obligation and therefore a lesser obstacle to mobility, particularly by the young generation.

The White-Collar Stratum
Industrialization has generated not only the white-collar class, but also a large group of people who plan, supervise and guide production directly or indirectly. During the 1949–80 period, the number of people in white-collar occupations increased by 40.9 per cent, reaching a figure of 1,388,200 or 27.4 per cent of the active earners. If one includes the foremen, the percentage is 29.3 per cent. This means that Hungary has created a native intelligentsia that has been exposed to its significant life experiences after the war. The 'old' intelligentsia has retired. Only 2 per cent of those who had reached an age of twenty-five by 1945 are still active. As far as the internal composition of the white-collar group is concerned, there is a disproportion in favour of authority positions. The ratio of 'leaders' (*vezető*, i.e. heads of organizational units or departments) to executive personnel (*beosztott ügyintézo, beosztott ügyviteli dolgozó*) is 1:3.6. In other words there are too many chiefs and too few indians. All in all, there are 323,100 'bosses' in Hungary. A Hungarian sociologist comments on this phenomenon as follows:

One can conclude that the increase in leading and directing positions is not only a consequence of organizational necessities, but that the former are, so to speak, 'generated' as sources of income and prestige which in view of the magnitude of the phenomenon can no longer be regarded as normal. [Bálint, 1983, p. 71.]

The rise of bureaucracies was also a consequence of central planning. The dominant role of the 'productive branches' in socialist economies is reflected in their supply with administrative jobs as well: two-thirds of the additional

Table 3.7 White-collar Positions, by Economic Branches ('000)

Productive branches	1949	1973	1981
Industry	49.5	322.9	330.3
Construction	2.7	71.8	92.9
Agriculture	5.5	93.9	141.6
Transport	29.8	88.8	101.1
Commerce	28.2	142.3	162.8
All productive branches	125.6	719.7	827.7
Non-productive branches	213.6	499.5	571.5

Source: Balint, 1983, p. 75.

white-collar positions have been claimed by the primary and secondary sectors; 23.5 per cent by industry alone (see Table 3.7). However, the analysis of the activities performed in practice by the Hungarian white-collar stratum reveals that a majority of its members engages in bureaucratic work. As can be seen from the evidence in Table 3.8, administrators and economists experienced the most spectacular increase in numbers. This is a result of the changes following the introduction of NEM in 1968, which aimed at enhancing enterprise autonomy. This process in turn led to a transfer of economic and legal knowhow from the centre to the enterprises.

Table 3.8 White-collar Jobs

	1970	(%)	1980	(%)
Technicians	177.2	(15.9)	283.8	(20.5)
State administration, economists	90.5	(8.1)	349.5	(25.1)
Health, cultural work	267.2	(24.0)	359.4	(25.8)
Bookkeepers, accountants	577.9	(51.9)	359.8	(28.5)

Source: Balint, 1983, p. 76 and own calculations.

If one assumes that Hungary is a medium-developed country, it holds a top position in this group as far as the proportion of white-collar workers is concerned (the average is about 35 per cent for developed and between twenty-five and thirty for medium-developed countries). But Hungary can also boast a proud record concerning the educational level of her white-collar class. Already in 1973, two-thirds of them had high school diplomas, and in 1980 29 per cent were university graduates. However, if one takes real, not just formal qualification into account, the picture changes somewhat, since a large part of the university diplomas goes to students of correspondence and part-time evening courses (Kulcsár, 1984, p. 115).

Small Commodity Producers and Shopowners
In 1949, this stratum (including the small farmers) had been the largest population group in Hungary. It was the policy of the Hungarian communists to reduce this vast group of small proprietors as fast as possible and to turn them into dependent workers and employers. As a result of the new economic strategy private enterprise has mushroomed. A majority of private entrepreneurs pursues service activities. For example, there were 1,006 watchmakers, 4,273 engine fitters, 1,457 radio and tv technicians and 2,145 car mechanics in 1984 (at least according to the official figures that list holders of permits only; *StZsK*, 1984).

As far as the individual peasants are concerned, there were 63,000 independent farmers (including active family members) in 1980. They are a dying species. In 1980, every fourth one was over sixty years of age, and only 8.4 per cent of the individual peasants were younger than thirty years. Three-fifths are small or dwarf holders with the size of their holdings not exceeding three hectares (Bálint, 1983, p. 84).

Crosscutting Cleavages

The Village-City Gradient
In spite of the far-reaching social transformations that had been ushered in by the industrialization drive, the village is still present in the Hungarian mind. While it is true that urbanization has advanced at a fast pace and that the extreme grade between the industrialized region around Budapest and the countryside has gradually been reduced, there are still very few urban centres that would conform to Western standards. Only seven towns have a population exceeding 100,000 (Budapest and the county centres Debrecen, Győr, Miskolc, Pécs, Szeged and Székesfehérvár), the remaining towns have populations between 96,000 (Kecskemét) and 8,000 (Lenti). Even the bigger towns have a distinctly rural character: the city centre proper is usually formed by a few official buildings and is surrounded by a village-type settlement sprinkled by occasional modern multi-level apartment houses. Registration as a 'town' is not only a question of prestige, but one of access to financial means as well. This fact has certainly contributed to the inflation in the number of towns. It is also true that a majority of Hungarians work in non-agricultural professions. Yet, on the other hand, it is a fact that almost all workers have strong ties to the villages, either by virtue or their origin or by virtue of their place of work or permanent residence.

In 1949, only 31 per cent of the skilled and 42 per cent of the unskilled workers in industry were of peasant origin. In the mid-sixties these percentages had risen to 36 and 68, respectively (Kulcsár, 1984, p. 104). In

Table 3.9 Occupational Groups, by Place of Residence (%)

	Budapest	Towns	Villages
Workers	17.7	36.3	46.0
Collective peasantry	4.2	12.3	83.5
White-collar	33.1	41.1	25.8
Small commodity producers	12.8	26.9	60.3

Source: *NSz*, 23 November 1983

1979, 37 per cent of the unskilled and semi-skilled, 28 per cent of the skilled, 17 per cent of the white-collar workers and 9 per cent of the professionals had a parent working in agriculture (Akszentievics, 1983, p. 57). The percentage of active earners who had begun their working life in agriculture and had then transferred to non-agricultural jobs (intragenerational mobility) is already very low: in 1979, only 2 per cent of the unskilled or semi-skilled workers and 1 per cent of the white-collar workers had pursued this career path.

The high significance and the extent of the village lifestyle in contemporary Hungary is also revealed by the statistics on rural and urban residence. In 1985, 19.5 per cent of Hungary's population lived in Budapest, 36.9 per cent lived in the ninety-six towns, and 43.6 per cent in the 2,955 villages (*StZsK*, 1985). About one-half of Hungary's workers live in villages (*Nsz*, 23 November 1983). A majority of these workers with rural residence was employed in industry and construction (37 per cent), transport (7.6 per cent) and commerce (7.5 per cent) at the end of 1980. Only 32.8 per cent performed agricultural work. The distribution of the occupational groups to places of residence (Table 3.9) shows that all groups are affected by the village or small-town lifestyle. Undoubtedly, the new industrial society has made inroads into the traditional lifestyles. The character of agricultural work has changed under the impact of mechanization; new consumer habits, the creation of new opportunities and options have had a long lasting effect on social relations in the village communities. Work in heavy industries has added new attitudes to the traditional world outlook of the subsistence farmer. But the ties to the soil are still strong. Around 90 per cent of the village dwellers are involved in some way in agricultural production (*NSz*, 23 November 1983). More than half of Hungary's population pursues agricultural activities in addition to their main occupation. Of these, 2,600,000 hold non-agricultural jobs or are self-employed family members. Consequently, one can speak of an enmeshment of industrial and agricultural work which is certainly not typical of a highly specialized modern society. Beneath the industrial surface, the subsistence farmer who is ready to give up his industrial job and rely on his own resources in cases of emergency is still there.

In conformity with the political strategems Hungarian sociographic literature treats private plot and ancillary farming as a relic of the past which is bound to become obsolete. Yet, there are strong grounds to believe that the specific pattern of industrialization and social development in Hungary makes the maintenance of the present model imperative. The main reason that speaks for this assumption is that the rising expectations of the village consumer can only be met through additional sources of income provided by ancillary farming, which in turn is consuming most of the village dwellers' leisure time. Thus, the strict separation between work and leisure which is so characteristic for our industrial lifestyle is prevented in favour of a pattern which in many ways resembles the traditional model of agricultural production, where work conditions cannot be stipulated by a work contract, but are by and large dictated by the exigencies of climate, soil and environment as well as of the animal stock.

A major social consequence of the fact that working place and place of residence do not coincide for a large part of Hungary's active earners is the unusually high number of commuters and weekly or monthly lodgers. While the proportion of commuters was 13 per cent of all active earners in 1960, their numbers soared rapidly during the following years to break the 1,000,000 threshold in 1970. According to Hungarian sources, there were 1,047,000 commuters and weekly or monthly lodgers at the end of the 1970s (Bálint, 1983, p. 91; *NSz*, 4 April 1981). Western estimates had this figure at 1,300,000 in 1973 which was tantamount to claiming that 39.7 per cent of the male and 30 per cent of the female workers and employees were concerned (RFER Hungary, 4 June 1974). Budapest attracts 250,000 commuters from some 250 settlements, many of the former covering long distances. Commuting is significant in the industrial centres in the north of the country. A majority of commuters consists of young and skilled labourers who are attracted by better paid jobs. Thirty-five per cent of all commuters have journeys exceeding one hour each way and one in four is absent from home for twelve to fourteen hours daily (Fuchs-Demko, 1977, p. 466). Weekly or monthly commuting resulting in lodging at one's place of employment involves over 50,000 Hungarians (Enyedi, 1975, p. 96).

The rural-industrial enmeshment is also reflected in a high proportion of mixed peasant–worker households. Thus, in 1980, only 55 per cent of the collective farm households were purely 'rural', the rest was mixed (i.e. one spouse belonging to the worker or other occupational categories). The proportion of 'homogeneous' households was highest among unskilled or semi-skilled workers.

Young and Old Generations

Hungary is a young society. The quota of her working age population (fifteen to sixty-four years) is slightly higher than that in developed Western societies (around 66 per cent). In 1984, 41.8 per cent of the population was under thirty years of age. On the other hand, Hungary has also a relatively high percentage of citizens in the pension age. This is the result of the rapidly increasing quality of the health system but also of the relatively low pension age (fifty-five years for women and sixty for men). On 1 January, 1985 1,922,000 citizens had passed the age of sixty (18 per cent of the population). The life situation of young and older generations differs in all societies. Each of these groups encounters specific difficulties at a given moment. While the young seek entrance into a world which they want to transform according to their needs, the old seek to avoid the risk of change and expect society to take care of their needs. However, the numerical preponderance of the young causes a distortion of the dominant social perspective to the detriment of the elderly. Thus, a majority of respondents to a survey taken in 1982 designated the periods of beginning a career, founding a family, finding an apartment and raising children as the most difficult stages of the life cycle. In contrast to the trend experienced in developed Western societies, the care of the aged is not regarded as a duty of the state (or the market), but as one of the family (according to 82 per cent of the respondents). This result is indicative of the fact that village morality is still partly effective (a fact that can coexist with the dramatic increase in divorce rates). Only a small fraction of the Hungarians polled (7 per cent) found that there was 'excessive care for the aged', and that they lived 'too comfortably at the expense of the young'. Typical generational conflicts were expressed in answers like 'the old like to intrude into the lives of the young families' (70 per cent) or 'the older generation does not take notice of the necessity to surrender their position to the young' (40 per cent). Overall, the survey proved that a majority of Hungarians 'views the problems of old age with understanding and tolerance' (*NSz* 3 December 1983).

Although the intensity of intergenerational conflicts is mitigated by the continuity in traditional family relations and by paternalistic attitudes, which are still very strong, Hungary has not remained untouched by the problems generated by urbanization and the dissolution and atomization of the village clan and family system. And although Hungary's planned labour market reduces the unemployment risk to a considerable degree, the choice of an appropriate education, career paths, and of one's general future identity in adult life poses a serious problem for Hungarian youths. The graduates of technical schools have, with the exception of very few branches, few problems in finding jobs which are in line with their qualifications. Skilled workers are in high demand and an annual 50,000 young graduates are absorbed into the job market without visible difficulties. The graduates of technical high schools, numbering 25,000 per year are in a similarly favourable position. It is estimated that only around 25 per cent of them find jobs that do not match their qualifications. The greatest problems exist for graduates of some liberal arts and science university departments (especially in the theoretical disciplines) who find themselves to be overqualified for the average openings in industry and administration and cannot find employment in the country's few research institutions. This concerns about 100 to 220 young specialists per year (*NSz*, 22 December 1983). Job hunting is further complicated by the serious shortage of apartments. This problem is especially acute for young couples.

Male versus female

Traditional Hungary has defined itself as a male chauvinist society, with a higher status accorded to men, a strict separation of life and work spheres, and the dominance of male values camouflaged by 'chivalrous' manners. However, the real contribution of Hungary's women to the survival and development of Hungarian society through the ages is much more significant than it appears in the male perspective. In addition to running the household and rearing offspring women have actually worked on a par with men in agriculture. Socialist industrialization made full use of and is in fact unthinkable without the female labour potential. While in 1949 91 per cent of the men and 34.6 per cent of the women in the working age brackets were active earners, the respective percentages had almost levelled out by 1985 (84.4 per cent and 77.5 per cent). The distribution of working women over the economic sectors shows areas of female concentration and male preserves (see Table 3.10).

Table 3.10 Female Employment, by Economic Branches (%)

	1949	1960	1970	1975	1980
Industry	22.6	32.7	41.4	44.9	43.9
Construction	3.7	10.6	15.5	16.8	18.0
Transport and communication	10.2	17.4	22.5	23.7	24.4
Commerce	35.9	52.0	61.0	63.9	63.3
Other branches	43.0	45.1	57.4	60.4	59.6
Non-agricultural branches, total	28.7	33.9	42.4	45.4	n.a.
Agriculture, forestry, water economy	29.7	38.1	37.6	39.2	35.2
Total	29.2	35.5	41.2	44.0	43.4

Source: Balint, 1983, p. 143.

Some areas are indeed female-dominated, like the low-grade jobs in the textile industry, assembling jobs in canneries and jobs in the service sector (chemical cleaning, hairdressers, tailors, etc.). As for the white-collar group, women dominate the lower-profile desk jobs. Education and health protection have become typically female areas. Overall, about 59 per cent of the economically active female population are manual workers, and 41 per cent have white-collar jobs. The 'male' distribution is 80:20 which, however, does not mean that women are in an advantaged position. In spite of the good record with regard to technical education, women have not yet closed the gap with men in terms of technical qualification. Thus, 40 per cent of the university graduates are women, as opposed to 28 per cent from the technical schools (*NSz*, 25 September 1982). The progress achieved by women over a span of fifty years is illustrated by Table 3.11.

Table 3.11 Education Levels, by Sex and Age

	No school	Primary school	High school	Institution of higher learning
	10 years and older	15 years and older	18 years and older	25 years and older
Men				
1930	7.4	14.1	7.6	3.3
1941	5.2	16.1	7.0	2.8
1949	4.1	21.9	8.1	3.1
1960	2.6	34.5	11.6	4.5
1970	1.5	55.1	17.8	6.4
1973	1.3	59.9	19.6	6.9
1980	1.0	71.2	24.2	8.6
Women				
1930	11.1	11.8	2.1	0.3
1941	7.5	14.1	1.6	0.4
1949	5.5	19.5	3.3	0.5
1960	3.7	31.3	6.3	1.1
1970	2.3	48.0	13.5	2.3
1973	2.2	51.7	15.9	2.9
1980	1.7	61.7	22.4	4.8

Source: Balint, 1983, p. 140.

Rising qualifications have, however, not automatically led to a more equal distribution of jobs among the sexes. Although the Constitution of the HPR (1972) proclaimed that 'in the HPR women enjoy equal rights with men' and that the 'quality of rights is safeguarded by the provision of work openings and conditions in an appropriate manner' (§ 62 sect 1 and 2), the obstacles and prejudices still to be overcome are enormous. Thus the number of female party members has not yet crossed the 30 per cent threshold. The general rule is: the higher the level in the hierarchy, the fewer women there are. Of the party secretaries on all levels, only 11 per cent are women. The same applies to the leading positions in the state and the economy, where in 1980, the percentage of women in the higher echelons was 12.6 (*NSz*, 25 September 1982) and to agriculture, where in spite of the dramatically rising level of qualification—56 per cent of the women employed on collective farms hold high school diplomas—the chances to rise to a leading position are very low. Nine per cent of these positions are occupied by women and only thirteen out of 1,300 co-operative farms are administered by female directors. 'Besides the higher workload of women in families and households, views devaluing the female sex still play a significant role' concludes the party daily mournfully (*NSz*, 27 September 1984). The struggle for more equality is still a vexing problem for a movement that draws much of its energy and motivation out of its historical mission to level out social differences.

Social Equality—Promise and Reality

The leftist parties have considered the erasure of differences between classes and groups, the abolition of privileges and the equalization of opportunity for all as their primary goal. Hungary's pre-communist society was extremely unequal in terms of the distribution of income and wealth, class and status prerogatives and access to political and economic power. According to the ideological tenets of Marxism–Leninism, the abolition of classes would lead to equality. The Hungarian experience proved that the first step—dismantling the privileges of the higher classes and dividing up national wealth more justly—provided no long-term solution of the problem. As a Hungarian sociologist comments:

> Our social experience has proved that such a policy is utopian. Despite every effort at social levelling various latent inequalities re-emerged. At the same time, such policies often involved the limitation of 'genuine' equality ... It appears that if private ownership of the means of production is replaced by collective ownership, some types of inequality are eliminated, some others remain, and some new sorts of inequality emerge in social life. [Kolosi & Wnuk-Lipiński, 1983, p. 3].

The glaring disparities between word and deed, between the equalitarian self-image of the party and the emergence of a new privileged *classe politique* was the main factor that sparked the uprising of 1956. The extreme sensitivity given by the Kádár administration towards the equality issue shows that Hungary's current leaders are aware of the problems of social and political significance. However, the exigencies of economic modernization and above all, the professed creed of the Kádárites to respect vested rights, limit the possibilities for a considerable reduction of old and new inequalities. Yet, the main problem is probably not so much the continuing existence of inequalities and disparities, but rather, their high visibility. Wealth is openly displayed in contemporary Hungary and it exists side by side with distressing poverty.

Income Differentials

In 1984, average income was 4,800 ft/month (*Magyar Hírlap*, 15 September 1984). At the same time, Hungary has set the official income poverty level at 2,500 ft per month. Five per cent of the economically active population earn ten times the monthly average. According to Western calculations, 28 per cent of the population had an income below the established minimum. The haves are a motley group including doctors, lawyers, engineers, literati, party apparatchiki, bureaucrats, private artisans, collective farmers and business contractors. Many of Hungary's new rich have profited from the short-comings of the supply system and from the expanding legal opportunities for private entrepreneurship. Some earn higher incomes from illegal activities such as profiteering on the black market. On the other side of the spectrum, Hungary's poor are a mixed bunch too. Most of them are old age pensioners, or single mothers, unskilled female white-collar workers and people living in sublet rooms.

According to the most recent available official data, income differentials have been consistently levelling out over the past few years. Minimal and maximal incomes seem to have been redistributed towards the middle (see Table 3.12). Hungarian sociology classifies 15 per cent of the population as being 'multi handicapped' by their life circumstances (Kulcsár, 1984, p. 120).

Table 3.12 Income Groups, 1978–82

Forints per month	1978	1980	1982
2,000 and lower	3.0	1.3	1.7
2,001–4,000	20.0	23.9	23.0
4,001–5,000	22.1	25.3	23.5
5,001–6,000	19.3	16.1	17.3
6,001–7,000	9.8	9.3	10.2
7,001–8,000	7.8	5.2	5.4
8,001–10,000	4.7	3.6	4.3
10,001–12,000	2.6	2.2	2.2

Source: *NSz*, 30 May 1984.

The contradictory findings are due to the use of different statistical categories. While the Western estimate probably considers extra-legal sources of income as well, the Central Statistical Authority's reports rely on declared income. Graduated taxation precludes monthly incomes over 40,000 fts. However, taxation cannot curb the growth of unofficial and illegal incomes. Official Hungarian sources do not deny the existence of millionaires (e.g. *Élét és Irodalom*, 7 September 1984) but point out that Hungary's nabobs are 'poor rich' compared with the luxury and leisure classes in the West.

Poverty in contemporary Hungary has long been the topic of sociological studies. One general conclusion from these analyses is that poverty is concentrated in the backward regions of the country (especially in the Szabolcs-Szatmár, Somogy and Baranya counties). These regions are characterized by the lack of suitable work opportunities and the lack of infrastructural amenities (water supply, transport, social services, etc.). The inhabitants of these territories have to commute to distant urban centres in order to escape the vicious circle of unemployment, poverty and lack of work motivation (Orolin, 1980, p. 142). It appears that the two main poverty groups are families with more than three children and old age pensioners (Bálint, p. 235, and see Table 3.13).

In order to reduce the proportion of the poor, official statistics beef up income figures by adding fringe benefits and other transfer payments. Fringe benefits are also awarded in the form of low-cost or free public services. In

Table 3.13 Size of Pensions 1980–84
(according to total number of pensions)

Forints per month	1981 %	1982 %	1983 %	1984 %
1,499 and less	20.8	12.2	1.8	1.3
1,500–1,999	35.8	31.3	33.6	15.5
2,000–2,499	17.6	25.0	26.0	31.9
2,500–2,999	9.5	11.0	13.3	20.8
3,000–3,999	9.5	11.7	14.0	16.3
4,000–4,999	3.6	4.7	6.0	7.4
5,000–5,999	1.7	2.1	2.6	3.3
6,000–6,999	0.8	1.0	1.3	1.6
7,000–7,999	0.7	1.0	1.4	1.9
Total	100.0	100.0	100.0	100.0

Source: Heti Vilaggazdasag, 23 February 1985.

1980, 32.1 per cent of the average total income consisted of fringe benefits and public services (Bálint, 1983, p. 199). As most of these benefits are distributed according to income, the poor compare more favourably on this basis than on that of pure work income. As far as other supplementary sources of official income are concerned, around 14 per cent of the total income is generated by private agricultural activity (Nyitrai, 1984, p. 237). The significance of this sort of ancillary income is highest with the collective farmers (34.5 per cent of the total income), but at the other end of the spectrum, even white-collar workers in leading positions draw a sizeable proportion of their income from this source (Bálint, 1983, p. 206). The real income supplement from 'ancillary' activity is not adequately reflected in the official statistics. Thus, a CSA survey taken in 1977 found that a group consisting of confectioners, cooks and waiters had achieved the highest income supplement (38.9 per cent of the monthly income) whereas mechanics reported a proportion of only 17.7 per cent. Doctors and chemists gave their additional income at 22.6 per cent of the total (Bálint, 1983, p. 213). These figures are most certainly unreliable, as

Table 3.14 Income Growth, by Social Class

	Workers' & employees' income per capita (ft p.a.) (1)	Peasant income per capita (ft p.a.) (2)	(2) as a percentage of (1)
1949	6,212	5,488	88
1950	6,562	5,583	85
1951	6,109	6,466	106
1952	5,869	3,622	62
1953	6,155	5,893	96
1954	7,462	6,081	81
1955	7,855	6,457	82
1956	8,550	6,273	73
1957	9,853	7,242	74
1965			93
1966			94
1967			98
1968	steadily rising		102
1969			102
1970			104
1972			109
1980			104

Source: Balint, 1983, pp. 233–4.

they are based on the unsubstantial replies of the respondents. Real incomes are often many times higher than the level of official incomes, especially if the skills offered are in high demand (as with doctors and car mechanics).

Thus, the existence of official and unofficial markets for goods and services considerably distorted the effects of egalitarian policies from above. The party's argument that the income differentials have diminished is correct for the portion of the income which is amenable to central redistribution. In the case of the differential between workers and employees on the one hand and peasants on the other, it can be said that Hungary's peasant class has been compensated for the sacrifices it was forced to bear during the 'construction of socialism'. The comparison between the two income categories shows the impact and the priorities of Kádárism (see Table 3.14).

However, these effects cannot be attributed to equalization policies alone as the per capita income of the occupational categories stems from vastly different sources (agricultural and industrial work, private ancillary activities and pensions). The imputation criterion used in such comparisons is whether these contributions flow into a collective farm household or not. Therefore, any change in non-agricultural wage or pension policy produces certain effects in the sphere of agricultural incomes as well. It seems that the improvement of incomes in collective farms is mainly due to the expansion of the opportunities for non-agricultural work. If one forms a separate category of households with a dual income (with one spouse working in industry, and the other in agriculture), then the favoured position of this group becomes obvious. Their income was thirteen percentage points above of the average

Table 3.15 Monthly Income per capita by Social Position of Family Head

Occupation of the head of the household	Monthly income per capita		Percentage increase	1977 wages
	1972	1977	1972–7	(ft/month)
Leading position	2,444	3,449	41	5,274
Foremen	1,916	2,700	41	4,185
Highly skilled specialists	2,210	2,837	28	4,410
Other skilled specialists	1,791	2,468	38	3,577
Executive personnel	1,704	2,235	31	2,936
Skilled workers	1,562	2,304	47	3,536
Semi-skilled workers	1,402	2,146	53	3,089
Unskilled workers	1,348	1,954	45	2,745

Source: Balint, 1983, p. 228.

workers' income (Bálint, 1983, p. 227). As far as the income differentials between the various echelons of the production hierarchy are concerned, the most recent available data show that the relatively large difference between the categories is reduced considerably if the income per capita of the earner's household is considered (Table 3.15). Thus, the span between the top and the bottom average income is reduced from 2,529 to 1,495 ft/month. This effect brought about by the variations in household size and ancillary income, as well as the impact of equalization policy.

As far as the generational gap is concerned, there is a clear dividing line coinciding precisely with the mid-life line, i.e, forty years. Incomes are relatively stable up to this point and a tangible increase in emoluments is evident only during the second half of the average Hungarian's working life (see Table 3.16). The data show that the available income for young families is very low. Seen against the dramatic rise in the costs of child rearing, it has even shrunk during the past few years. The prices of the main items of children's clothing have jumped by 180 per cent since 1978. Simultaneously, the real value of child allowances paid by the state has dropped by 11 per cent, a situation that affected two-thirds of young families (*TSz* 1984: 7, 8, p. 74). The

Table 3.16 Monthly Income per capita by Age of Family Head, 1983

Household heads by age brackets	Average	White-collar	Foremen	Prof. workers	Non-agr. workers	Agr. blue-collar
20–29	2,881	3,293	3,277	3,522	2,815	2,663
30–39	2,956	3,366	3,303	3,530	2,838	2,463
40–49	3,592	4,095	3,987	4,319	3,452	3,328
50–59	4,199	5,089	4,737	5,154	4,033	3,991
Average	3,385	3,952	3,817	4,066	3,218	3,214

Source: *Társadalmi Szemle*, 1984, Vol. 39, nos 7 and 8, p. 75.

handicaps are well distributed among the occupational categories. Young workers raise relatively more children than young white-collar workers, the income of the latter reaches the level of an average blue-collar workers' only at the age of 35.

While raising a family and finding an apartment ties down the financial capacity of young Hungarians for years, the problems of the elderly are different. Sixty-five per cent of women between 70 and 74 years of age are widows. Twenty-two per cent of the citizens over 60 live in Budapest, where the danger of social isolation is much greater than in the villages, where about

50 per cent of Hungary's aged live. The high financial pressures on young households results in a lifelong obligation for older generations to sacrifice their income for the survival and the careers of the young. In view of this fact, the percentage of active earners among retirees is astonishingly low: 6.1 per cent of men over 60 and 8.2 per cent of women over 55 were in this category in 1980 (Bálint, 1983, p. 167). However, these figures do not include the private ancillary activities in agriculture and in the service branches. With average pensions well below the poverty level, ancillary earnings are far from being a luxury; they are an absolute necessity for many pensioners and their families.

In spite of the progress that has been achieved during the past 35 years, socialism has not been able to remove the wage differentials between male and female earners (see Table 3.17). This is mainly a consequence of the male monopoly in the higher income categories. The picture is complete only if one considers the full set of interrelated factors that result in discrimination against the female sex. The opportunities for women to obtain or upgrade technical qualifications are still lower. Thus, most of them start working earlier than men. Also, they retire earlier, i.e. they do not reach the possible wage maximum. Thus, the average male industrial worker spends 15.4 years in production, a female worker only 11.9 years. Male technicians are on average, employed for 19.5 years, female technicians for 13 years (Bálint, 1983, p. 146).

Table 3.17 Male–Female Wage Differentials, 1978 (%)

Monthly wage (ft)	Men	Women
Under 1,000	0.2	1.2
1,001–1,500	0.3	1.8
1,501–2,000	1.2	8.3
2,001–2,500	4.0	20.0
2,501–3,000	8.5	21.8
3,001–4,000	30.7	29.5
4,001–4,500	15.7	7.3
4,501–5,000	12.3	4.2
5,001–5,500	8.5	2.4
5,501–6,000	5.8	1.3
6,001–7,000	6.4	1.3
Over 7,000	6.4	0.9

Source: Balint, 1983, p.146.

However, in contrast to this 'veiled' discrimination against the female sex, there also is open discrimination which consists in paying unequal wages for equal work. An unskilled female worker earns 94 per cent of her male counterpart's pay; this 'index of discrimination' is 89 per cent in the case of semi-skilled and skilled workers. The only areas where there is no open discrimination are the administrative and health fields. Wage differentials between sexes are especially high in the technical and economic professions.

Living Standards, Consumption
The differences in property and lifestyle have created an 'anti-rich' mood in Hungary (*Magyar Hírlap*, 15 September 1984) and legitimation problems for the regime under whose auspices such a development could take place. The Hungarian economic miracle has created an upper class (which compares to the American middle class) who have expensive villas, swimming pools, private tennis courts and cars of Western make. Simultaneously, a selective pattern of industrialization has led to the emergence of rural slums, and

Table 3.18 Annual per capita Consumption of Selected Food Items

	1950	1984
Meat and fish (kg.)	34.9	78
Milk and dairy products (kg.)	99.0	185
Fats (kg.)	18.7	33
Potatoes (kg.)	108.7	58
Vegetables (kg.)	139.4 (1960)	155 (1980)
Eggs	85.4	327
Coffee (litres)	0.1	3
Wine (litres)	1.0	30
Beer (litres)	33.0	87
Hard liquor (litres)	1.5	9.9

Source: StZsK, 1984.

decaying villages which are inhabited by the low-class citizens: the poor and the gipsies. However, it should not be forgotten that this is the price Kádárism has to pay for its largely successful policy of reconciliation, and that the glaring inequalities of the past have been eradicated. Consumption levels are high in contemporary Hungary, especially if compared to those of most socialist states. The Hungarian 'economic miracle' has led to a dramatic increase in the purchase of durable consumer goods. Between 1950 and 1980 sales soared by 1,600 per cent. Today, 90 per cent of households headed by active earners are equipped with TV sets, washing machines and refrigerators. The main status symbol, the car, has long conquered the streets, causing traffic jams and parking problems in the cities. Hungary's consumption record is especially good in the foodstuff sector. At the beginning of the eighties the daily intake of food was computed at 13,500 kilojoules per head. The annual per capita meat and fish consumption was 76 kilograms whereas fifteen years ago, it was still 58 kilograms. Consumption of other food items show similar increases (see Table 3.18).

In 1982, Hungary's citizens realized a monetary income of 425 billion ft. Together with credits and non-monetary income sources, 449.2 billion ft were available for consumption. Eighty-eight per cent of this sum was expended for the purchase of food items and durable consumer goods, 6.5 per cent for dwelling space and 4 per cent was saved (See Table 3.27). There is a clear gradient in consumption structure and levels from the high earnings groups downwards. The upper classes can spend 50 per cent of their income after the vitally necessary purchases have been made, the lowest group in the income hierarchy only 15 per cent (Bálint, 1983, p. 246). Luxury items are therefore the prerogative of the high income groups. Thus, although there are already thirty-four cars for one hundred households in the cities and twenty-four in the villages, car ownership is still mainly enjoyed by the upper and middle classes.

Per capita expenditure is highest within the white-collar group, followed by the blue-collar workers, the collective peasantry, the mixed households (worker/peasant) and the pensioners. The real consumption levels of the underprivileged groups certainly are higher than the ones given by the official figures because these do not comprise all sources of income. It is safe to assume, however that the white-collar class stands out with a consumption

Table 3.19 Per Capita Household Expenditure, 1982 (%)

	Workers	White-collar	Pensioners
Foodstuffs	33	27	42
Drugs	9.4	7	10
Textiles	10.6	10	8
Apartment maintenance, land purchase	16	17	n.a.
Transport & communication	10	13	4.6
Recreation & entertainment, education	7.1	11	6.1

Source: Nyitrai, 1984, p. 243.

level that is 31.6 percentage points higher than that of the nearest category, the blue-collar workers. Consumption patterns by social groups show significant differences (see Table 3.19).

The housing situation is one of the most significant indicators of the standard of living in Hungary. At the beginning of the eighties 59 per cent of the workers, 88 per cent of the collective peasantry, 37 per cent of the white-collar group and 70 per cent of the pensioners lived in one-family houses (see Table 3.20). Most of the remaining families now have apartments of their own. In contrast to the post-war years, apartments rented by several families have become a rare occurrence (0.7 per cent of the workers, 0.5 per cent of pensioners). However, subletting is rising rapidly, especially in Budapest. A

Table 3.20 Available Living Space, by Social Class (%)

	1 room	2 rooms	3 rooms	4 rooms and more
Working class	28.4	49.8	19.3	2.5
Collective peasantry	31.5	49.3	17.1	2.1
White-collar	16.5	48.3	28.7	6.5
Small commodity producers	26.6	46.3	22.9	4.2
Average	26.3	49.3	21.1	3.3

Source: Balint, 1983, p. 264.

comparison of the living space at the disposition of the various social groups indicates that the intra-category differences are greater than the inter-category gradient if one takes internal income differentiation, especially between young and older families, into account. Living space is still scarce. On a country-wide average, 3.07 persons have to share one apartment. For blue-collar households, the figure is 3.19; for the white-collar class 2.93 and for the collective peasantry 2.89. The comparison of housing standards shows a considerable inter-class differentiation.

Household appliances and amenities are distributed unequally throughout the population. Seventy-three per cent of the workers, 60 per cent of the collective peasantry, 93 per cent of white-collar workers and 48 per cent of the pensioners live in apartments with a bathroom. Apartments with central-heating or heated from a remote source are owned by 17 per cent of the workers and 8 per cent of the pensioners, as opposed to 27 per cent of the white-collar families (Nyitrai, 1984, p. 245). Data taken in a 1979 survey shows that the higher the level of education and the intellectual complexity of work, the better the household equipment. The greatest difference between the social groups is the possession of a telephone. In Hungary only 6 per cent of the unskilled and semi-skilled workers have a telephone, as opposed to 40 per cent of the professionals (Beskid & Kolosi, 1983, p. 125).

Table 3.21 Housing Standards, by Social Class

	High standard	Average	Low standard
Working class	48.9	13.8	38.3
Agricultural workers	20.7	15.0	64.3
Non-agricultural	48.7	12.9	38.4
Foremen	76.3	10.7	13.3
Collective peasantry	20.9	13.9	65.2
Manual workers	14.4	12.2	73.4
Non-agricultural manual workers	36.6	17.5	45.9
Foremen	47.7	25.4	26.9
White-collar	82.2	7.1	10.7
Technicians	86.3	6.9	6.8
Administrators, economists	82.0	6.8	11.2
Healthcare, cultural workers	75.5	8.4	16.1
Accountants	79.0	10.5	10.5
Small producers	46.9	13.0	40.1
Agricultural	17.0	12.8	70.2
Non-agricultural	56.6	13.1	30.3
Average	51.1	11.8	37.3

Source: Balint, 1983, p. 266.

While the quality of housing in terms of household equipment and facilities is higher in urban areas, the availability of living space is generally much higher in rural regions. A serious apartment problem exists in Budapest, where construction activity is surpassed by the dramatically increasing demand. In Budapest and other urban centres there is a clear trend towards an unequal distribution of housing categories among the social groups: the high prestige value of renting a cheap communal apartment has decreased, the intelligentsia and white-collar groups have become increasingly interested in co-operative housing. Thus, the percentage of white-collar tenants is very high in the 'old' satellite towns on the outskirts of Budapest (e.g. Lágymányos, József Attila), whereas blue-collar domination is characteristic of the newly constructed suburban settlements like Kőbánya-Újhegy

(Tocsis, 1980, p. 35). Family houses are still the predominant form of housing in rural areas and in provincial towns.

Several years ago, the number of people without an apartment of their own was still high in provincial towns, as Table 3.23 shows. Thus, an overall characterization of the inequalities in housing would have to state a clear city-village cleavage in terms of housing standards and the privileged position of

Table 3.22 Housing Forms, by Qualification of Household Head and Region (%)

	One-family house	Multiple dwelling unit	Co-operative apartment house	State apartment
Budapest				
Skilled workers	28.9	7.4	7.6	56.1
Semi-skilled workers	26.2	4.0	6.0	63.8
Unskilled workers	30.7	1.6	3.1	64.6
Provincial towns				
Skilled workers	48.0	16.5	10.2	25.3
Semi-skilled workers	48.6	9.9	8.3	33.2
Unskilled workers	52.5	4.2	4.0	38.3
Villages				
Skilled workers	88.9	1.8	0.6	8.7
Semi-skilled workers	88.1	0.8	0.5	10.6
unskilled workers	90.3	0.3	—	9.4

Source: Társadalmi Szemle, 1984, vol. 39, nos 7 and 8, p. 77.

white-collar workers as far as prestigious housing is concerned. However, better housing becomes progressively more expensive and one must tackle virtually insurmountable barriers (especially in the case of young heads of family) in order to obtain it. As far as the overall financial situation of Hungarian citizens is concerned, there are pronounced intracategory differences. The material living conditions of almost one-third of each group are similar to groups above or below them in the division of labour. Among the active earners, the cluster of workers in heavy manual jobs who must work several shifts and, who consequently, may have unfavourable work schedules and an overlapping group of workers living in villages can be singled out as the main losers in the social equality game (Kolosi, 1983, p. 183).

Table 3.23 Persons without Own Apartment (%)

	Salgótarján (1977)	Pécs, Szeged (1968)
Unskilled and semi-skilled	21.7	12.1 (semi-skilled: 2.6)
Skilled	18.5	11.7
Employees in service sector	17.3	1.7
Administrators	14.1	9.5
White-collar	9.1	8.2
Pensioners		
White-collar	8.6	7.2
Blue-collar	17.8	7.2

Source: Tocsis, 1980, p. 38.

Education

In most countries, education is the main channel towards higher positions in the social pecking order. While social competition undoubtedly promotes higher educational and qualification levels, the overall rise is mainly due to the exigencies of an industrial society. Marxist regimes have been especially efficient in rapidly pushing up the educational standards of the societies under their rule. In 1941, the proportion of general school graduates (completing eight grades) in the population under 15 was 15.1 per cent in 1980 it was 66.2 per cent. During the same period, the proportion of middle school graduates in the population under 18 rose from 5.1 per cent to 23.3 per cent. The percentage of graduates from institutions of higher learning in the population over 25 increased from 1.8 to 6.6 (see Table 3.24).

The Hungarian class structure still roughly coincides with the distribution of educational opportunities. If one takes the percentage of high school

Table 3.24 Highest Qualification Level of Working Class Active Earners (%)

	1949	1960	1970	1973	1980
0–7 grades	80.1	65.9	40.5	35.3	20.7
8 grades, professional school	19.7	30.3	51.9	6.3	67.3
High school diploma	1.9	3.5	7.1	8.0	11.6
University diploma	0.1	0.3	0.5	0.4	0.4

Source: Balint, 1983, p. 41.

graduates and university graduates as an indicator of social placement, then the workers' class, in spite of the educational revolution, emerges as the least privileged and the white-collar group gets the lion's share of the educational offerings. Among the foremen, qualification levels are significantly higher (62 per cent high school, 6.8 per cent university graduates). The city-village cleavage is also reflected in educational levels. Sixty-four per cent of the agricultural workers had not attended school through the eighth grade in 1980 (Bálint, 1983, p. 41). Twenty-three per cent were holders of a medium level high-school or technical school diploma. The comparable figure for the workers was 35.3 per cent (Bálint, 1983, p. 60). As far as the most educated group is concerned, their qualification level has risen most slowly. While a little more than 50 per cent of the white-collar class held high school diplomas in 1949, this proportion rose to 75 by 1973. During the same period the proportion of university graduates within this group went up from 18 per cent to 23 per cent. In 1980, university graduates made up 30 per cent, while on the other end of the white-collar spectrum, the qualification level of 17.6 per cent was not higher than eight grades (Bálint, 1983, p. 74).

Table 3.25 Female High School Graduates, by Type of School (%)

General high school	65.4
Specialized high schools	
Industry	24.9
Agriculture	24.3
Economy	92.1
Commerce	80.8
Catering	48.0
Transport	33.1
Health	97.7
Kindergarten teachers	100.0
Arts	66.7

Source: StZsK, 1984.

In recent years, the access of women to education has by and large matched or even surpassed that of males. The proportion of females in high schools is already 57.6 per cent ($N = 218,000$ in 1982). They form the majority in most technical high schools as well (see Table 3.25). There were 63,200 full-time students at Hungarian universities in 1984. Of these, 51.4 per cent were women. The distribution of female students among the various facilities follows a pattern which is also typical for Western countries. In 1982, the proportion of female university graduates had risen to 40 per cent of all graduates (*NSz*, 25 September 1982). Women, however, are still prevented from making full use of their qualifications. While 35 per cent of the male white-collar workers with a university education hold a leading position, only 13 per cent of their female colleagues do so (Bálint, 1983, p. 74).

Table 3.26 Female University Students,
by Department (%)

Technology	19.5
Agriculture	33.1
Veterinary sciences	17.0
Medical	55.6
Health	95.0
Economics	63.4
Law & administration	56.1
Philosophy	64.4
Science	45.1
Education	73.6
Sports	42.0
Teachers' training	87.2
Kindergarten teachers' training	99.5
Arts	54.4
Average	55.8

Source: StZsK, 1984.

Mortality

In all societies life circumstances determine death circumstances. Also in Hungary, mortality rates are stratum-specific and specific mortality causes correlate with the affiliation to specific social groups. The data show that while overall life expectancy has risen, the differences between groups have remained constant, and partly have even increased. Infant mortality rates show a clear class–pattern (see Table 3.27).

With regard to general mortality, the record of agricultural labourers and of white-collar workers has improved in comparison with that of the blue-collar workers (see Table 3.28). Despite the rapidly progressing urbanization and industrialization of the Hungarian countryside, in 1977 the village dwellers still had a much higher life expectancy than the inhabitants of cities (9–11 years). However, part of the disparity can be explained by the different age structure in the various groups at the time these results were obtained.

Table 3.27 Infant Mortality by Social Group (0–1 year)

	Deaths per 1,000 live births in each group			Percentage of the average		
	Manual workers		White-collar workers	Manual workers		White-collar workers
	agric.	non-agric.	workers	agric.	non-agric.	workers
1948	108	88	46	115	94	49
1950	97	83	49	113	97	57
1953	83	74	50	117	104	70
1955	60	63	48	100	105	80
1957	63	66	45	100	105	71
1960	49	49	36	102	102	75
1963	45	44	33	105	102	77
1965	39	41	31	100	105	79
1966	37	39	29	100	105	78
1970	35	39	28	97	108	78
1973	40	34	29	118	100	85
1977	28	28	21	108	108	81

Source: Klinger, 1980, p. 86.

Juvenile mortality was much higher in the non-agricultural blue-collar group than among agricultural manual workers, which points to a higher incidence of accidents in the former group.

The main mortality causes are typical for industrialized countries: circulatory diseases 78,233; cancer 28,685; cirrhosis 3,451 (1982); accidents 12,559 (*StZsK*, 1984). Distributed over social groups, cancer and heart diseases are typical white-collar diseases, sclerosis is most frequent with the peasant group and diseases of the digestive organs among blue-collar workers. The industrial working class also dominates the accident category. As the author of the study quoted above concludes, 'mortality rates still reflect significant social differences' (Klinger, 1980, p. 89).

The Road to Equality: Mobility

Hungarian society before the Second World War was relatively closed, but there was upward mobility mainly caused by population growth. Rural over-population led to the expansion of the industrial work force, and parts of the blue-collar group rose to white-collar status. Downward mobility was mainly caused by the competition between small producers and large

Table 3.28 Mortality by Social Stratum

	Gross proportion			Standardized proportion[1]		
	Manual workers		White-collar workers	Manual workers		White-collar workers
	agric.	non-agric.	workers	agric.	non-agric.	workers
Per 1000 born in each group						
1900	27.0	25.1	15.1			
1910	26.6	20.9	13.8			
1930–31	18.5	13.9	10.8	17.4	14.4	11.3
1941	14.3	12.3	12.2			
1948–49	12.8	10.7	8.2	12.2	11.5	7.9
1959–60	11.4	10.1	8.6	9.7	10.7	10.1
1969–70	16.5	10.6	7.5	11.2	12.3	9.8
1972–73	21.7	10.2	7.3	11.8	12.1	9.9
1977	24.4	10.7	8.4	12.0	13.0	11.3
Percentage of the average						
1900	104	97	58			
1910	110	87	57			
1930–31	115	86	67	108	91	70
1941	108	92				
1948–49	111	93	71	106	100	69
1959–60	111	98	83	94	104	98
1969–70	143	92	62	97	107	85
1972–73	187	88	63	102	104	85
1977	197	86	68	97	105	91

[1] On the basis of the age distribution of the entire population.
Source: Klinger, 1980, p. 84.

industrial firms which led to the economic downfall of large parts of the former group. Yet, it was extremely hard to rise into the more prestigious social positions. In 1983, 97 per cent of the intelligentsia's children were at the same social level as their parents and 59 per cent of the white-collar group, excluding the intelligentsia, had preserved their parents' status. On the other end of the social hierarchy, the peasantry formed an equally closed stratum: 69.3 per cent of the peasant offspring remained in the same social class. The middle classes were the most open groups. While the self-recruitment quota was 56.8 per cent among the skilled workers, it was as low as 24 per cent within the semi-skilled group. This pattern was broken by the war which opened new opportunities for the underprivileged both inside and outside

Table 3.29 Average Age of Deceased, by Social Stratum and Sex

	Manual workers		White-collar workers	Total
	agric.	non-agric.		
Men				
1948	49.1	42.7	52.1	47.0
1960	63.4	57.1	60.3	60.0
1970	67.3	60.0	61.2	63.0
1973	70.4	59.9	60.6	63.5
1977	71.7	60.7	62.8	64.2
Women				
1948	51.9	48.1	56.0	50.8
1960	66.4	62.6	65.2	64.5
1973	72.5	66.7	65.5	69.0
1977	74.0	67.5	68.7	69.8

Source: Klinger, 1980, p. 88.

the military. The land reform after the war turned hundreds of thousands of agricultural workers into small farmers: around 45 per cent of the rural proletariat's children were engulfed in a large-scale social transformation process (Bálint, 1983). Simultaneously, many industrial workers who had lost their jobs due to wartime destruction migrated back to their native villages to increase the smallholder stratum. The communist takeover brought a sudden reversal of the class barriers that had existed hitherto. A plethora of new positions was created for the sons and daughters of the new 'leading classes' and the old elites were—more or less effectively—prevented from passing on

Table 3.30 Intergenerational Mobility, 1938–49

Father's social stratum	1938 (%)	1949 (%)
Leading position, intellectual	26	19
Other white-collar	26	23
Independent small artisan, shop owner	19	16
Worker	11	21
Farmer	16	20
Other	2	1

Source: Balint, 1983, p. 107.

to their offspring the career chances connected with their social status. Already by 1949 this effect had become visible in the composition of the white-collar class (see Table 3.30).

In contrast to the white-collar group, the skilled workers preserved, by and large, their original composition. Recruitment from the same class decreased from 56.8 per cent in 1938 to 48.6 per cent in 1949. The peasants began to stream into the ranks of the working class. In 1938, 69 per cent of the children of peasants became peasants; in 1949, this figure was 65 per cent. Nevertheless, the direct career paths into the white-collar class were still largely

Table 3.31 Intergenerational Mobility, 1949–64

Father's social stratum	1938 (%)	1962–4 (%)
Intellectual	19	16
Other white-collar	23	16
Independent small artisan, shopkeeper	16	15
Worker	21	27
Farmer	20	24
Other	1	2

Source: Balint, 1983, p. 108

blocked: only 4 per cent of the peasants' offspring made their way into the top stratum in 1949, which represents only a slight increase over the 3 per cent figure for 1939.

Between 1949 and 1964, the tendencies promoting the upward mobility of the formerly underprivileged classes were reinforced. The composition of the top group (see Table 3.31) showed the further opening of career chances for the lower strata quite clearly. The decrease in the number of intellectuals with a white-collar background does not necessarily mean a large-scale or random dismissal of experts having bourgeois origins. Although the party wanted to prevent a status transfer to the next generation by barring access to higher education for the children of 'class enemies' (these prohibitions were only lifted in 1962), it needed the 'bourgeois specialists'. On the contrary, the decrease in those recruited from the same class is due to the rapid growth of the white-collar group. Concurrently with this trend, the new socialist elite showed the first signs of stabilization: fifty-seven per cent of the children in this group stepped into their parents' positions in 1962–4 as compared to 48 per cent (1949). The period from 1949 to 1964 was a time of radical economic and social transformation. The effects of crash industrialization can be observed in the composition of the working class during the period: from 1962 to 1964, 42 per cent of the skilled, 61 per cent of the semi-skilled and 68

Table 3.32 Education of the Population by Sex and Age of Leaving

	No formal education (10 years +)	At least 8 grades (15 years +)	High school (18 years +)	University (25 years +)
Men				
1930	7.4	14.1	7.6	3.3
1941	5.2	16.1	7.0	2.8
1949	4.1	21.9	8.1	3.1
1960	2.6	34.5	11.6	4.5
1970	1.5	55.1	17.8	6.4
1973	1.3	59.9	19.6	6.9
1980	1.0	71.2	24.2	8.6
Women				
1930	11.1	11.8	2.1	0.3
1941	7.5	14.1	1.6	0.4
1949	5.5	19.5	3.3	0.5
1960	3.7	31.3	6.3	1.1
1970	2.3	48.0	13.5	2.3
1973	2.2	51.7	15.9	2.9
1980	1.7	61.7	22.4	4.8

Source: Balint, 1983, p. 38.

per cent of the unskilled workers were of peasant origin. Only a minority of the unskilled and semi-skilled workers remained on the same social level (16.5 and 19.2 per cent); most of them entered the 'higher' groups.

The period from 1964 to 1973 was characterized by the dramatic expansion of career opportunities for women. While the class composition of high school and university student bodies did not change essentially, the percentage of female students grew constantly. Thus, the number of girls with a working-class background attending middle schools and universities grew by 200 per cent and that of peasant girls by more than 200 per cent. Table 3.32 shows this turning point in the 'battle of the sexes'.

Hungarian sociology has registered the results of the equalization policies and of the general social development in post-war Hungary with satisfaction, but does not fail to underline the still existing inequality in career opportunities. According to calculations by R. Andorka, if one lets the chances of a

Table 3.33 Relative Chances of becoming an Intellectual or Leader

Father's occupation	1938	1949	1962–4
Farmers	1.0	1.0	1.0
Unskilled workers	0.6	1.9	2.3
Skilled workers	2.9	3.3	4.0
White-collar	24.6	19.6	10.6
Leading position, intellectual	0.3	34.3	20.9

Source: Andorka, 1975.

farmer's child to join the top (intellectual or leader) group be 1, then the chances of the other groups would be as shown in Table 3.33. Thus, the gap between the unskilled worker and the intellectual has been reduced considerably, but it certainly is still high enough (Andorka, 1975; Bálint, 1983, p. 112).

In addition to the strong increase in female mobility, the period between 1962 and 1973 is also characterized by a growing exchange of the labour force between the industrial and the agricultural sectors. On the one hand, peasant class children left agriculture in increasing numbers (only 29.9 per cent of boys and 46.4 per cent of girls remained in the villages) and on the other hand, the number of agricultural blue-collar workers with an industrial worker background began to grow. This phenomenon was due to the industrialization of agricultural work.

Recent data show that among the working class, the category of semi-skilled and unskilled workers is the most stable in Hungary. Eighty per cent of

Table 3.34 Intergenerational Mobility, 1979

Father's occupation	Present occupation			
	Unskilled or semi-skilled workers (%)	Skilled workers (%)	White-collar workers (%)	Professionals (%)
Individual farmers	13	9	5	2
Unskilled or semi-skilled workers	52	42	33	17
Skilled workers	24	37	39	32
White-collar	2	3	8	13
Professionals	3	4	10	32
Merchants, craftsmen	6	5	5	4

Source: Akszentievics, 1983, p. 58.

this group started as unskilled workers. Yet, there is considerable upward mobility into the white-collar stratum: fifty-six per cent of the white-collar stratum comes from the manual worker group. Intergenerational mobility shows a similar picture, as is shown in Table 3.34.

One of the ways in which the overall mobility of a society can be assessed is to use family occupational homogeneity as an indicator. The proportion of families where parents and children are in the same occupational category is very low in Hungary. It is about 10–12 per cent among manual workers, 9 per cent among professionals and 2 per cent among white-collar workers. The data show that the general tendency is upward mobility (Akszentievics, 1983, p. 66). Upward mobility among skilled workers takes the highest value (42 per cent), followed by the white-collar group (32 per cent), and professionals (29 per cent). Unskilled and semi-skilled workers are at the bottom of the list (26 per cent). The data on marriage patterns show relatively high homogeneity, especially with the skilled and the semi-skilled workers' group (38 per cent). Marriage is a channel of mobility, especially for women: e.g. 37 per cent of the white-collar workers have a skilled worker wife. These findings are consistent with the trends in female mobility through educational

Table 3.35 Marriage and Mobility

Present occupation of spouse compared with that of respondent	Occupation of respondent			
	Professionals (%)	White-collar workers (%)	Skilled workers (%)	Unskilled, semi-skilled workers (%)
Upward-tending:				
men	—	10	4	34
women	—	23	7	71
Homogeneous:				
men	30	52	43	66
women	75	19	73	29
Identical level, but not homogeneous:				
men	—	20	20	—
women	52	52	7	—
Downward-tending:				
men	70	18	33	—
women	25	6	13	

Source: Akszentievics, 1983, p. 69.

channels (see Table 3.35). Friendship is a mobility channel for both sexes. The proportion of 'downward-directed friendships' is very small (Akszentievics, p. 71). Probably the most puzzling findings of the relevant surveys is the high proportion of unskilled or semi-skilled workers who reported having no friends. One explanation lies in the definition of 'friend', a concept that developed in an individualizing culture. Having no friends certainly does not imply having no regular contact with other people. One may well be integrated into a community and have 'no friends'.

Social Problems

Alcohol Abuse, Deviance, Suicide

The social transformations that have swept Hungarian society removed some stress factors such as material insecurity for most people, but created new ones for the whole society as well. As mobility increases, family and village solidarity is weakened, new options, promises and a rapidly changing environment put a heavy strain on people's adaptation capacities. The negative social consequences of modernization are by no means limited to urban centres. They have not spared the formerly 'intact world' of the Hungarian village. In spite of the social progress or as a consequence of it, neurosis and alcoholism are on a steep rise in rural Hungary as well. While the number of neurotics among the population over sixteen grew from 30.1 per cent (1961) to 42.2 per cent (1971), 25.8 per cent of the village dwellers (42.2 per cent of the adult population!) were categorized as neurotics during the second half of the seventies. The figures were highest for two Budapest workers' districts (54.1 per cent and 57.4 per cent). The incidence of mental disorders is significantly higher in Hungary than in other capitalist or socialist societies (Juhász, 1980).

Alcoholism has been a socially accepted form of escapism for centuries. In spite of the obvious damage caused to labour productivity by this phenomenon, no regime has been able to prevent the growth of alcoholism in Hungary. An annual 45 billion ft is spent on alcohol consumption and 12 litres of pure alcohol are drunk per head. The increase in the consumption of alcoholic beverages reflects not only the overall increase in consumption levels, but also an increase of stress factors (see Table 3.36).

In 1975, the overall percentage of alcoholics was 3.5 per cent of the total population and 8.8 per cent of the male population over sixteen. This proportion was even higher in the villages, where 12.4 per cent of the adult population were classified as alcoholics (Juhász, 1980, p. 70). But alcoholism is

Table 3.36 Alcohol Consumption, 1961–84 (litres per capita)

	1961	1964	1968	1975	1984
Wine	13.2	9.5	15.2	21.4	30.0
Beer	17.2	38.5	43.3	130.4	87.0
Brandy	3.7	5.9	6.4	10.7	9.0
(Expenditure as % of per capita income)	(12.0)	(10.4)	(8.0)	(7.7)	(11.0)

Source: Juhász, 1980, p.70; *StZsK*, 1984; Andorka, 1985.

not limited to the lower classes. As it has in the West, social drinking has also permeated the white-collar stratum. The groups that seem to be specifically predisposed to developing regular drinking habits are skilled workers and young urban professionals with a rural background, i.e. people of humble social origin with pronounced career ambitions (Andorka, 1985).

Apart from the increasing mortality figures in the relevant disease categories, alcoholism also has a strong impact on the delinquency statistics. Forty-two per cent of the persons convicted by the Hungarian criminal courts committed illegal acts under the influence of alcohol (*NSz*, 1 September 1984). Delinquency, the main indicator of social deviance, is on the rise. In 1983, 150,000 criminal acts were recorded in all Hungary, which

Table 3.37 Suicide Rates in Selected Countries,
per 100,000 persons

Hungary	45.6
Denmark	30.0
Austria	27.6
FRG	27.6
France	19.6
Japan	17.1
Poland	12.7
USA	11.5
Australia	11.0
England	8.9
Italy	6.4
Israel	6.0
Ireland	5.7
Spain	4.1
Greece	3.3

. *Source*: *US News and World Report*, 2 April 1984.

meant an increase of 8.4 percentage points since the preceding year. The increase is mainly due to the rise in criminal acts against property (59 per cent of all crimes), which are characteristic of juvenile delinquency (two-thirds of all convicted minors were accused of crimes against property). Judging from data given by Minister of Justice Imre Markója, the fluctuation between the criminals and the 'normal' population seems to be very high indeed: in 1983, 49.4 per cent of the persons tried by Hungarian courts had a previous conviction. The percentage of people that had resumed a normal life after a conviction or a prison term is not known, but is said to be 'significant' (*NSz*, 1 September 1984). From 1983–4, the number of convictions decreased by 3.5 percentage points (*StZsK*, 1984).

One of the most conspicuous social phenomena in Hungary is the high suicide incidence. In 1984, 4,767 cases were officially recorded. The real number is believed to be much higher. Yet even so, Hungary has the highest suicide rate in the world (Hungarian SR, RFER, 3 July 1984, p. 8). High suicide rates are no achievement of modernity, although the excess stress of contemporary society has undoubtedly pushed up the figures (see Tables 3.37 and 3.38). There is much speculation, but no convincing explanations for the high incidence of suicide that cuts across all strata, towns and villages. Religious affiliation explains why the divorce rate is twice as high in Hungarian cities as in the villages but fails to account for the high suicide rate in most villages.

Hungarian Nationalism and Anti-Minority Attitudes

The most cherished stereotype about the Hungarians is that they are passionate, spread-eagle nationalists. Indeed, the history of the last few centuries seems to prove the truth of this assumption. The Magyars have the appearance of unruly revolutionaries who suppress the peoples within their own domain while rejecting alien rule most vehemently. A widely accepted theory about the 1956 uprising has it that the 'enforced Sovietization or Russification . . . was the greatest contributor to the revolt of 1956' (Voelgyes, 1982, p. 88). However, what is defined as Hungarian nationalism by observers must be understood as a reaction which developed in a situation of external military pressure and internal competition between different ethnic groups, among which the Magyars felt threatened by the prospect of becoming a minority in their own country. Moreover, the 'nationalist' stereotype is stratum-specific, in that it is a generalization of the nineteenth-century gentry's outlook to the whole population. In the autostereotype of the workers and peasants, features like 'diligence' 'hard work' and 'slyness' dominate (Heller, 1974, p. 154). Recent surveys show a strong connection between occupation, education and the strength of national identification.

Table 3.38 Suicides in Hungary, 1921 to 1984

Year	Number of Suicides (yearly average)	Suicides per 100,000 people
1921–5	2,289	28.0
1931–5	2,910	32.9
1945	3,006	33.3
1946	2,144	23.8
1948	2,178	23.8
1950	2,074	22.2
1952	2,407	25.3
1953	1,999	20.8
1954	1,772	17.7
1955	2,015	20.5
1956	1,923	19.4
1958	2,312	23.4
1960	2,592	26.0
1962	2,532	25.2
1963	2,720	27.0
1964	2,903	28.7
1965	3,020	29.8
1967	3,150	30.8
1968	3,457	33.7
1970	3,582	34.6
1971	3,697	35.7
1972	3,851	37.0
1973	3,854	36.8
1974	4,307	41.1
1975	4,020	38.1
1976	4,304	40.6
1977	4,390	41.2
1978	4,525	42.3
1979	4,770	44.9
1980	4,809*	45.2
1981	4,880*	45.6*
1982	4,659*	43.5*
1984	4,764*	44.7

* *Statistical Yearbook*, 1981, 1982; *StZsK*, 1984.
Source: Gergely, 1981, pp. 14, 58, 122.

For most contemporary Hungarians, Magyardom is not considered to be a problem in most situations with the exception of travel abroad. Of course, most Hungarians also evaluate Hungarian nationality positively and prefer it to other nationalities. A relatively high percentage (40 per cent on an average, 51 per cent in Budapest) of respondents to a 1979 survey said it had worn a Magyar cockade on the 15 March (the date of the 1949 uprising against the Habsburgs). Most of these people were in intelligentsia positions (Csepeli & Lányi, 1981, p. 23).

Hungary is still a relatively closed society. Forty-five per cent of the respondents of the survey quoted above had never been abroad. Thirty per cent had been to socialist countries and only 7 per cent to Western countries. Only 1 per cent are familiar with both Eastern and Western systems. However, the tourist regions in the country (especially Budapest and the Lake Balaton area) are exposed to foreign cultural influence to an unusually high degree. In 1983, 10,463,000 tourists crossed Hungary's borders, among them 1,605,000 Austrians. This fact and the fact that Hungarian is virtually not spoken outside of Hungary (with some notable exceptions in neighbouring countries) have forced Hungarians to emphasize the study of foreign languages. Thus, only 16 per cent of Hungarians have never studied a foreign language. Fifty-two per cent had studied Russian exclusively, 23 per cent German and 11 per cent English (Csepeli & Lányi, 1981, p. 23).

Modern sociology treats 'nationalism' as a vehicle for the expression of specific socio-economic interests and demands emerging in connection with the social development in the European territorial states. Thus, Magyar nationalism was mainly the ideology of aristocratic-bourgeois elites who wanted to embark on the path of modernization while remaining free from foreign (i.e. Austrian) interference. The Magyars do not seem to be more nationalist than other peoples in similarly conflicting situations. The fierce anti-semitism that characterized the interwar years actually prevented the German extermination campaign from becoming effective until 1944. Today, national or racial prejudices have become weaker: about 30 per cent of Hungarians would resent mixed marriages (with members of national minorities, Jews, gypsies and blacks). Of the minorities that had lived in Hungary before the war, only the gypsies stand out as a sizeable group. There are about 80,000 Jews (0.75 per cent of the population); the proportion of national minorities is equally low: Germans 1.6 per cent, Slovaks 1.1 per cent, Romanians 0.2 per cent, Serbs, Croats and others 0.5 per cent (Kende, 1984, p. 83; Bugár, 1984, p. 175). The national minorities have their own associations, radio and TV studios and press organs. There are regular radio and TV programmes in the Serbo-Croatian, German and Romanian languages (*NSz*, 1 November 1984; 4 May 1984). Signs in German have been placed along the streets and on public buildings in nearly one hundred communes.

The gypsies, who have been a problem for all settled societies because of their nomadic lifestyle, seem to be in a gradual acculturation process. The inevitable conflicts between a peasant and a 'savage' society are still reflected in contemporary Hungarian, which is rich in idioms referring to gypsies. In most cases, the undertone is clearly negative. Thus, to swallow something the wrong way is expressed by 'it has gone the gypsy alley' (*cigányútra ment*), to give somebody a licking by 'dress somebody in gypsy trousers' (*felhúzni a cigánynadrágot*) and 'that's not the way to do it' is translated by 'this is not how they beat gypsies' (*nem úgy verik a cigányt*). There are 240,000–500,000 gypsies in Hungary (Jokisch, 1981, p. 5) who fall into different groups with different ethnic and linguistic identities as well as different lifestyles and motivation to adapt to the prevailing social patterns. The Hungarian government has tried to promote the full integration of the gypsy population into the social, educational, political and economic systems. A 1961 CC decision proclaimed the 'dissolution of settlements that do not meet the social standards'. Seventy per cent of these settlements were inhabited by

Table 3.39 Anti-gypsy Attitudes, 1978 (%)

	yes	No	Undecided
Budapest	38	58	4
City	56	43	1
Village	73	25	2
Village with substantial gypsy population	81	7	12

	All Hungary	Village with subst. gypsy population
The state should support those who live in worse conditions than others	33	30
The state should support those who deserve the support through their work and behaviour	50	59
The state should not specially support anybody; everybody should care for his own happiness according to his abilities and diligence	17	11

gypsies (Pártos, 1980, p. 6). All of these efforts, however, still face great difficulties and are resisted by those groups which are not willing to forsake their traditional way of life.

Among the gypsy population over 14 years of age, 39 per cent are illiterate, and only 21 per cent of the 15–19 age bracket finished the eighth grade. Two per cent are skilled workers. Most of the gypsies are employed in low-grade, strenuous and unhealthy jobs. The overall unemployment rate among male gypsies in the working age bracket is 25 per cent (Pártos, 1980, p. 11).

Public opinion shows, by and large, understanding for their problems. However, there is a sharp city–village gradient and a pronounced anti-gypsy attitude in villages with substantial gypsy population. Thus, a 1978 survey obtained the answers shown in Table 3.39 to questions testing anti-gypsy attitudes (Pártos, 1980, p. 16). The new socialist minority policy has been able to rid itself of the heritage of the past which, however, is still alive in society at large. Minority rights are not impaired by official policy in contemporary Hungary, but by everyday social discrimination.

4 The Economy and Economic Reforms

Natural Resources

The most significant characteristic of the Hungarian economy is its dependence on world markets and foreign trade. This fact has dominated the economic policies of all governments and administrations which have ruled Hungary since 1918. For Hungary, the breakup of the Habsburg Monarchy meant the loss of important raw material resources, a fact that necessitated the development of a competitive export industry. Faced with a dramatic fall of the prices of agricultural products, Hungary could no longer rely on its traditional role as an agricultural exporter.

Hungary is poor in raw materials. Its greatest natural riches are coal, bauxite and uranium. Hard coal (with a caloric value of 4,500–5,000 kcal/kg) is mined under relatively difficult conditions in the southern range of hills (Pécs, Komló), soft coal and lignite are extracted in the central and north-western hill regions (e.g. Tatabánya). As coal has been replaced continuously by oil in the spectrum of the country's energy sources (in 1982, its proportion was as low as 29 per cent), Hungary meets, by and large, the demand for coal from its own mines, whose yields are expected to last for about one century. However, the replacement of coal as an industrial fuel by oil has had far-reaching consequences. Hungary produces only very small amounts of oil and natural gas, and the known resources are expected to last no longer than about ten years (Dietz, 1984, p. 162). Although the country possesses about 10–12 per cent of the world's known bauxite reserves, it can only convert about one-third of it to aluminium because of the lack of hydroelectric power. This is due to the insufficient fall of the country's rivers. The rest of the bauxite mined in the Bakony mountains must be transported to the Soviet Union for conversion. The Bakony Forest also contains rich deposits of manganese. The uranium won in Southern Hungary feeds Hungary's nuclear power plant in Paks which went into operation in 1982. Apart from the lack of fossil energy the most strongly felt lack of raw material concerns iron ore: only one-fifth of Hungary's demand can be covered from domestic deposits. The big steel mills at Dunaújváros, Ózd, Miskolc and Budapest are largely dependent on imported iron. As far as agriculture is concerned, Hungary can feed its population with most food products that are produced from its fertile soil. In spite of the extensive reforestation programme after the Second World War, large amounts of pulp and timber must still be imported to meet the growing demands of an incipient welfare and consumer society.

The uneven distribution of raw materials influences the geographical distribution of the industrial centres. Hungarian planners have divided the country into six economic regions, of which Budapest and the Northern Transdanubian are the most important. The former comprises one-third of the population, yields 30 per cent of the industrial production and possesses the most important industrial enterprises in addition to the central commercial, scientific and cultural centres, whereas the latter is a huge industrial agglomeration, linking mining with important export industries: the region produces 95 per cent of the radio sets, 62 per cent of the TV sets, 47 per cent of the buses and 80 per cent of the semifinished aluminium products.

Characteristics of the Economic System

With a per capita GNP of US$2,100 (this figure does not reflect the large-scale unofficial transactions), Hungary is about to cross the threshold of a developed industrial state. From the second half of the nineteenth century, several industrialization drives created an infrastructural network that today comprises about 5,000 miles of railroad tracks (15 per cent of which are electrified) and 15,000 miles of roads (of which 84 per cent are hard surface), set up giant industrial centres and pushed Hungary into the technotronic age in a few advanced branches without, however, changing much of the traditional rural life style and the 'peasant' habits of a majority of the population. Many essential features of Hungary's socialist economy can be explained by the survival of the 'peasant calculus'. Like their forefathers, who were mostly subsistence farmers, the managers of Hungarian industries try to ensure the survival of their firms by creating excessive reserves or by channelling excessive subsidies into the bottomless pits of production sites with hopelessly outdated technology. They are not used to defining the firm's success in terms of meeting market demands, competitiveness and entrepreneurship. And not unlike the millions of farmhands who had tried to survive under harsh conditions of exploitation, the industrial workers of today try to beat the system by adopting go-slow tactics or a hardly disguised refusal to work for a low wage. However, these traditional attitudes that were, at the same time partly combatted and partly reinforced by a modernizing socialist elite trying to combine both security and higher efficiency, are bound to change sooner or later because Hungary cannot isolate itself from the world market for too long. The openness of Hungary's economy is its main long-term characteristic. As early as the end of the 1920s, 20 per cent of the national income was exported. The Rákosi leadership tried to turn Hungary into an industrially self-sufficient country, giving political-strategical considerations an absolute precedence over economic rationality. Hungary's economy is still struggling with the heritage of political utopianism and industrial megalomania. Rákosi's heirs could not afford to turn a deaf ear to consumer demands and the foreign trade constraints. The policy to make Hungarian industry more competitive were designed to meet both goals. With the gradual opening of the Hungarian economy (between 1950 and 1981 exports grew by a factor of twenty and imports showed a twenty-one fold increase) domestic economic policies are increasingly contingent upon developments in world markets. Since the beginning of the NEM in 1968, a fairly consistent policy has been pursued to link domestic to world markets. Hungary needs the non-socialist markets to import Western technology and to supply the economy with additional energy (70 per cent of the total energy imports come from socialist countries; c.f. Dietz 1984, p. 179). Hungary joined GATT in 1973 and became a member of the World Bank and the International Monetary Fund in 1982. Today, Hungary derives 51 per cent of its domestic Net Material Product from foreign trade (in GNP terms 45 per cent are imported, 40 per cent exported). Due to differences in the calculation method (a part of the service sector is not included in 'material production'), the Hungarian net material product is about 7–8 per cent smaller than the GNP (cf. Hilker, 1983, p. 257).

The 1968 reform had reckoned with a stable international economic environment; the NEM had been a complex package of active reform policies. However, with the rapidly deteriorating terms of trade, Hungary's economic leaders have come under heavy pressure and must resort to reactive policies. Between 1973 and 1980, Hungary lost 80 per cent of a year's national income because of the unfavourable development of the terms of trade. The rise of oil prices, the recession in the West, the sharp fall of the prices for export goods (aluminium by 40 per cent between 1980 and 1982, bauxite 10 per cent and grain 19 per cent) together with the revaluation of the dollar have narrowed the planners' options considerably. Today, undisputed priority is assigned to the objective of strengthening the country's export capacity no matter what the social and political implications may be. One can speak of a deliberate policy to expose the domestic market to the chilly winds of international competition. Whether this policy can be successfully implemented is another matter.

Since 1947 (the nationalization drive and the beginning of the first three-year plan), Hungary has had a planned economy on a broad basis of state and collective ownership of the means of production. Today, the socialist and collective sectors produce 95 per cent of the national income and employ 95.8 per cent of the active earners. Judging from the official data, the state is the decisive economic factor in Hungary: 73.7 per cent of the national income is produced by state enterprises, 20.9 per cent in collectives operating in the industrial, agricultural and the service sectors, 3 per cent is produced by ancillary private plot farming and the rest (2.4 per cent) is the domain of the full-time private activity. However, as will be shown, the real impact of private production and entrepreneurship is inadequately reflected in these figures.

The composition of the national income shows the extent of the change that Hungary has undergone under socialism. Before the First World War, 58 per cent of the national income was produced in the agricultural sector. Today, this percentage has gone down to a mere 19.1 per cent. Industry is the most important economic branch, both as far as its contribution to the national income and the proportion of the employed workforce is concerned (46.6 per cent to 38.7 per cent). In contrast to Western industrialized states, the weight of industry is higher and that of the service sector is lower (34.2 per cent of the national income, 38 per cent of the work force). However, the work force percentages should be corrected in favour of both the service and the industrial sectors because many agricultural enterprises have ancillary service and industrial units attached to them, which distorts the statistical picture in favour of agriculture with regard to the character of work.

Hungary had a central planning system until 1 January 1968. According to this Soviet-type model, a—rarely consistent—system of central regulations that were binding on individual enterprises was to provide the political leadership with the possibility of direct intervention from above. These direct control and monitoring devices included detailed production, supply and investment plans, material balances that were to safeguard the availability of inputs for the production of the most important commodities and price and wage indicators. However, the main goals of socialist planning—control, security and technical progress—could be met only partially. All participants in the system tried to minimize their risks. The enterprise managers bargained for 'soft' plans and the ministries turned into agents of 'their' enterprises in the fierce all-out competition for centrally distributed funds. The workers were paid excessively low wages, but enjoyed employment security and hence did not care much about production efficiency. The real risk-taker was the state budget that incurred high and officially acknowledged deficits. The aim of the 1968 reform was to shift responsibilities from the centre to the enterprises themselves, but a sudden change would have been disastrous for

Hungary's rather inflexible production structure. Therefore, the abolition of direct central controls was counterbalanced by 'temporary' measures. Although the plan specifies only global growth figures (national income, domestic consumption, industrial and agricultural production, construction and real incomes) and is no longer binding on individual enterprises, the pertinent legal regulations and above all the largely unbroken traditions of central planning still provide enterprises with ample opportunities of avoiding a too high degree of independence and entrepreneurship. The 1977 Enterprise Act provides for only a few means of direct administrative interference, such as the permission to start or to discontinue business operations. Enterprise guidance is to be carried out by the main economic decision-making centres (the Council of Ministers assisted by the Planning Authority, the economic ministries and the local councils) through a set of indirect measures, such as fiscal and budget policy, price and wage limits, credit and tariff policy and preferential direct investments. However, in spite of the 1980 merger of the industrial branch ministries into a single institution the old communication lines are still largely intact. The main difference from the pre-1968 situation seems to be that bargaining over plans has been replaced by bargaining over credits and subsidies. The principle of central risk absorption is still in force. A Hungarian economist describes the survival of the command economy in new forms as follows:

In the old system of directives enterprises had to draw up reports on the progress of plans, the size of stocks, supply data on wages and staff etc. at regular intervals. The same indicators are today asked for by most of the ministries, though not with the old regularity, but by letter, telephone or telex, according to the 'urgency' of the information. Sectoral ministries implementing instructions and meeting expectations themselves take an active part in preparing the enterprise plan: they state their expectations as regards exports, stocks and profit etc. They allocate 'quotas', they permit and prohibit; they issue instructions as well as 'guiding principles' (e.g. for the development of enterprise organizational work, information on the future need for various machines, proportion of manual staff) and, as supreme authorities in the owner's right, they reserve for themselves the right of a decision in a number of questions (e.g. in investment activities). The ministries intervene in the distribution of most of the resources to be allotted to enterprises, and their opinion is decisive— unless the enterprise has good connections at levels superior to the ministry . . . (Laky, 1980, p. 106.]

According to J. Fodor, a top manager in the Hungarian Aluminium Trust, the planning process was simplified by the creation of the Ministry of Industry. Still, the file containing the planning figures requested by the Ministry weighed about fifty kilos (*NSz*, 13 September 1984). The 1984 regulations have not abolished the power of the ministries to issue instructions to 'their' enterprises, but have tried to reduce the latter to an emergency tool to be employed only in the case of economic failure. For the first time, the liability of ministries to refund enterprises for damages caused to them by incorrect instructions has been made public (*NSz*, 13 October 1984). There are increasing signs that change is under way. The first step toward a functioning bankruptcy institution was taken as early as 1978 with a decree–law (37/1978) authorizing the Ministry of Finances to initiate bankruptcy proceedings against indebted enterprises. The Twelfth Congress of the HSWP (March 1980) reiterated and reinforced this decision. In February 1984, the Pest County Building Industry Enterprise in Vác was liquidated without a legal successor, followed by the dissolution of the IGV (Office Equipment and Fine Mechanics Enterprise) in Budapest and Városnámény, altogether employing 1,200 workers (*Hetivilággazdaság*, 24 March 1984 and *NSz* 14 August 1984). The decision to close these enterprises for good was taken after a prolonged debate involving the Planning Authority, the Ministry of Finance, the National Material and Price Office and the Industry and Foreign Trade Ministries on the basis of a detailed scheme dealing with the utilization of the firms' material assets as well as the transfer of their employees to new jobs. The fact that middle-sized enterprises were also liquidated can be interpreted as a warning sign for the industrial giants that they are considered sacrosanct no longer.

Hungary's industrialization process had always been guided and monitored 'from above'. Political and social interests, mobilizing and instrumentalizing state authority have traditionally outweighed (macro and micro) economic rationality. One of the hereditary maladies of the Hungarian economy is its tendency to form industrial giants that monopolize whole industrial branches. This propensity towards cartellization and centralization is still strong in spite of the efforts to curb the growth of big business. In 1968 the state enterprises numbered 812 and by 1977 this figure had decreased to 713. This trend continued until 1980 when the number of industrial enterprises was 699. Due to decentralization measures, the figure was 724 at the beginning of 1983. However, it is unclear how much of a real de-cartellization has taken place. Most of the 'new' enterprises are affiliate firms of some mother corporation that have gained legal, but not economic dependence. The big enterprises represent a formidable economic and political power. Over 70 per cent of the industrial work-force is employed in large firms. As a result of the loosening of wage and price controls and the resuscitation of markets in the wake of the 1968 reform, Hungary's industrial giants experienced great difficulties in organizing production for a rapidly changing demand and in paying higher wages than smaller industrial establishments (above all, the mushrooming private enterprises). As a result, the movement of qualified workers away from big industry into the equally comfortable but better paid jobs in small and middle-sized enterprises started to irritate the managers of industrial giants. In 1971 and 1972, they decided on what has been called by Hungarian observers the 'counterattack of the big enterprises' (Szalai, 1982, p. 27). In a carefully orchestrated manoeuvre, the grievances of big enterprises were submitted to the Party Central Committee that had to act as an arbiter in the conflict. The autumn 1972 CC Plenum decided to 'seed' 180 large enterprises (fifty corporations) that were to be put under the special control of the Council of Ministers and were to receive preferential treatment. After much infighting, the list of 'seeded' (*kiemelt*) enterprises was drawn up. As a rule, those enterprises were included that had a protector in the CC (Szalai, 1982, p. 27). Together, this group turns out 50 per cent of the industrial production and 60 per cent of the export commodities. As a reaction to the growing centralization, trust-control measures have been introduced since 1980 that have led to the creation of an additional 150 legally independent firms. In 1981, the establishment of small private production units was legalized. Prior to this date, private enterprise was legal only in the service and commercial sectors as well as in agriculture.

Small and Private Enterprise

Hungary's neglected but rapidly developing service sector is practically run by small business. The insight that big business is incapable of developing market competition, is very inefficient and fails to meet rapidly changing consumer demands has been spreading also in the party headquarters and has prompted a decision of the HSWP's Twelfth Congress to use the reserves of private labour and initiative more effectively 'in harmony with the common interest' (A MSzMP XII . . ., 177). Following this decision, new regulations were passed in the autumn of 1981 that significantly increased the legal elbow room of small business. The limitations concerning the quantity and quality of the commodities produced and the capital invested as well as employment ceilings have been dropped altogether or significantly loosened. According to the new regulations, small business can be operated by state firms, small co-operatives, so-called 'professional co-operative groups' and 'economic work communities'. In addition to these corporate forms of small business, private individuals can operate small firms in all fields of economic activity. Small co-operatives have 15–100 members who must be factually employed (the political leadership has no intention of creating a large-size private capital market) whereas the PCGs are specialized groups within a co-operative with an independent financial status. The EWCs, Hungary's most recent answer to the structural deficits of the service sector can be founded by 2–30 private entrepreneurs for a common purpose, above all for activities in the fields of repair, construction, cleaning, painting and other everyday servicing. In addition, EWCs can also be founded by workers, employees or pensioners of a state firm. Normally, they are run by the more active and highly qualified workers, who have found deficiencies in the performance of their firms. In practical terms, the EWCs are private businesses using state facilities. The report of a control committee that had reviewed the operation of EWCs in Budapest states dryly: 'The problem of separating work for the factory and for the EWC is still waiting for a solution, especially as far as desk work is concerned. The manual workers frequently start their better paid EWC job during working hours' (*NSz*, 9 May 1984). However, the formation of EWCs seems to be in the enterprises' interests as well because most of them are formed on their initiative. Given the lack of qualified workers, they are interested in a better utilization of existing capacities. The growth figures are indeed impressive: at the end of 1983 about 5,800 EWCs employing about 60,000 people were operating throughout the country, with about 60 per cent of them in Budapest (Inotai, 1984, p. 19 and own computations). Fifty per cent of the EWCs are active in production, above all in the fields of cutting, casting and tool making. The repair and maintenance of machines is the main service activity. However, impact on production and employment has hitherto remained minimal (far below 1 per cent). Although individual private entrepreneurs must still apply for permission (*iparengedély*), their freedom has grown considerably as a consequence of a new policy that actively encourages private business. Since 1981, unprofitable state enterprises, such as restaurants and food stores, can be leased by private artisans with tools and raw materials. A significant income tax progression starts only at an annual income level of 200,000 ft (about four times the average worker's income). Private entrepreneurs may hire three employees, employ up to six family members and train no more than two apprentices. As of 1981, they may also conclude supply contracts with state enterprises. They are thus moving from a peripheral position in the economy closer to the centre. Although most individual contractors lack sufficient capital for wholesale trade, there seem to be greater possibilities for the various co-operative models.

At present, there are about 170,000 people working in private individual firms. Fifty-five per cent of the value produced by private enterprise is realized in the service sector, 30–35 per cent in construction (only about one-third of the new dwellings is built by state contractors) and 10–15 per cent in commodity production. Sixty per cent of the individual entrepreneurs run their firms on a full-time basis, 29 per cent beside other work and the rest are pensioners. Because of their low income, 27,000 (23 per cent) of the small entrepreneurs are not taxed. Their role is especially important in Hungary's many small villages where profit opportunities are limited (*NSz*, 13 November 1982). On the other hand, burgeoning private business has definitely increased the opportunity of quick enrichment for a selected group among private businessmen. According to the official statistical data the median income (the income of the lower 50 per cent) of private entrepreneurs was about 4,500 in 1982, which was a little over the average income of the gainfully employed population. Twenty-eight per cent drew an annual income of 60,000–1,000,000 ft, 13 per cent earned between 100,000 and 200,000. Only eleven small businessmen had realized an annual income of 900 thousand ft and above (before taxes) which amounts to a monthly income of 20,882 ft (*NSz*, 13 November 1982). Thus, the popular generalization that private business is a gold mine and is undertaken by prospective or actual millionaries is a myth supported by a few outstanding examples. Because of the public criticism that is levelled at the small entrepreneurs—mainly because of the high prices they charge for goods and services that are also available in the state sector, the National Union of Small Artisans (OKISZ) tries to enforce a rigid discipline among its members, withdrawing annually 300–400 permits. Tax evasion seems to be a common occurrence. According to J. Molnár, the OKISZ chairman, only 38 per cent of the tax declarations had been judged acceptable in 1981 (*NSz*, 13 November 1982).

From Black to Grey: the Unofficial Economies

Although Western observers agree that Hungary has the most accurate and candid statistical reporting system in the communist world, economic indicators can be taken at face value only to a certain degree. The obviously high level of consumption and the mass scale construction of private homes cannot be reconciled with the relatively low official average income levels and the data on the supply of the population with consumer goods. Therefore, a significant part of production, distribution and consumption is not included in the official figures. It contains a broad spectrum of illegal, semi-legal, tolerated and officially encouraged non-official activities.

The hard core of 'black income' earners consist of people who have, besides their official full-time job, one or more additional occupations which they exercise after or during work hours. This type of supplementary income is drawn by highly paid specialists, like architects or dentists, who often earn much more in their secondary jobs, but also by unqualified workers who engage in chore and moonlighting activities, repairing cars or painting rooms without applying for a permit and without reporting to the tax authorities. Official statistics estimate 250,000 such individuals (*NSz*, 13 November 1982). However, the aforementioned gap between the low official wages and the real consumption levels and the social pressure for higher consumption suggests a much higher degree of a 'black' economy. Statistically, there is not much room for non-official economic activities. According to official data, of the about 6.5 million people of working age, about five million are employed, of the remaining 1.5 million, 300,000 have no income. In addition to the poor work discipline (cf. Volgyes, 1982, p. 58) one has to take into account the many loopholes from which unofficial entrepreneurship can profit. Although owners of private capital are not officially allowed to use it as a source of 'income without work', social practice has rendered this principle obsolete. Owners of capital goods use them to draw subsidiary incomes whose quantity varies according to the relative scarcity of the item in question. Renting out rooms to subtenants has become widespread in the big cities, where becoming a 'night lodger' (*bejáró*) is often the only possibility to finding accommodation. The authorities close their eyes to such illegal practices, especially since private room renting is important for tourism. Surveys taken in Borsod county in 1977 showed that 54 per cent of the overnight stays were offered by private citizens (Borsod-Abaúj-Zemplén megye Statisztikai Évkönyve 1977). The income accruing from illegal renting practices can be estimated to be an annual 1–1.5 billion ft (Zsille, 1983, p. 19).

Probably the most widespread feature of the 'black' economy is the habit of demanding and offering *bakshish* (a Turkish word for 'tip') for services rendered. The multitude of more or less euphemistic expressions that describe this social phenomenon (like *hálapénz* —gratuity, or *csúszópénz* — sliding money that is quickly passed over the counter or over the desk) is indicative of its social significance. Those who profit most from this institution are people whose special abilities are high in demand: doctors demand and get enormous sums for operations, lawyers are paid over and above the legally fixed fees (Volgyes, 1982, p. 59). The struggle against the 'bribe economy' that the Council of Ministers had proclaimed in 1979 has hitherto been largely unsuccessful. The main reasons for this state of affairs are the inflexibility and the bad quality of the services offered by state enterprises and institutions. The official system of rendering services to customers according to the registration of the order and of equal quality to all is in practice crosscut by a shadow market system which rewards the economically more powerful. A survey taken in Veszprém County showed during the three years that had passed since the C.o.M.'s proclamation, the situation had worsened in several commercial branches. 'Some articles in short supply, especially building materials are impossible to come by without "sliding money", frequently not even *csúszópénz* can help . . . it can be assumed that the free prices in private commerce are rising so high because they must allow for *csúszópénz* as a cost factor'. The proportion of patients who stated openly that they had paid their doctors in spite of the principle of free treatment rose from 38 per cent to 60 per cent between 1980 and 1983 (*NSz* 4 October 1983).

Every economy in the world must rely on the 'self-supply' activities of its members. No market or other official supply system can replace the gratuitous services of housewives, the do-it-yourself activities rendered in and for one's own home. In Hungary, such activities are of an unusual magnitude. The self-sufficiency strategies of large enterprises have their corollary with the endeavours of the private citizens to have their private repair outfit at home and to be armed for all possible emergencies. Most citizens have a private source of food supply as well. The most important activity in the do-it-yourself sector seems to be the construction of family homes. According to the official figures, the proportion of homes constructed by the official industry was a little over 50 per cent, the rest must be attributed to private means. As far as investments into the construction of dwellings are concerned, private capital financed around 65 per cent. Summarizing and evaluating the data, a Hungarian sociologist belonging to the Budapest School concludes that 80–90 per cent of the national income is generated by the 'black economy' (Zsille, 1983, p. 25). This may be an exaggeration, but the leadership is certainly aware of the problem. Speaking from the rostrum of the Thirteenth Congress Kádár formuled the official standpoint of the party in this highly sensitive matter:

It is a social necessity and a justified claim that the economic tasks in all production spheres be met primarily during the official work hours and only then. I should like to add that there is a work and a social aspect of this problem: the working people must be able to create the necessary material basis for life during official working hours.

This is the standpoint of the CC and the government. If this objective cannot be reached at once, we must head in this direction . . . [A MSzMP XIII Kongresszusa, p. 181.]

The policy of the HSWP, then, is to paint the 'black' economy white, to turn unofficial and illegal activities into official and legal occupations. However, for some time to come, the underground economy will be a simpler and more profitable playground than the new forms of private entrepreneurship offered by the government. Up to now, 300,000 individuals (5 per cent of the work force) have accepted the offer (*NSz* 22 June 1984). There seems to be no detergent strong enough to wash out the 'black spots' from the economic fabric. It seems fairly realistic to expect the further expansion of the 'grey economy' relying on the tacit connivance of the state.

Industrial Relations

According to the Constitution of the HPR, the trade unions 'defend and strengthen the power of the people, defend and represent the interests of the working people' (§ 4 sect 3). A similar tone is struck in the resolutions of the Thirteenth Congress which circumscribes the trade union's tasks more closely:

The trade unions must enhance their activity to protect and to represent the workers' interests and must demand higher discipline in the fulfillment of work duties ... They must contribute to the active participation of the workers in enterprise management and policy implementation by renewing socialist competition, and the socialist brigade movement, by developing the creative potential of the workers and by deepening democracy at the working place ... [A MSzMP XIII. Kongresszusa, p. 98.]

Under the impacts of events in Poland, the Hungarian trade unions invigorated attempts to portray the organization as a strong and representative political force. Speaking at the party Political Academy in Budapest, the Chairman of the National Trade Unions Council, Sándor Gáspár warned: 'The Polish crisis, and earlier the 1956 events in Hungary and other examples show clearly what a heavy price must be paid for a formal operation of interest representation' (*NSz*, 15 December 1983). Gáspár demanded a vitalization of the workers' representation in the enterprises tacitly implying that the much-hailed 'enterprise democracy' was not working satisfactorily. Beyond any doubt, the role of Hungarian trade unions on the national decision-making level is much more impressive than that of other East European trade unions. Dissenting opinion, criticism of government policies by TU functionaries are no rare occurrence in Hungarian industrial politics (Gáspár, 1983). In the early 1970s, the trade unions tried to prevent or to emasculate NEM policies that seemed to be unacceptable to them, e.g. greater income differentiation and strict limitations on wage increases (Robinson, 1973, p. 231). There is actual co-decision-making in the areas of working-place safety regulations and social benefits. Here the Ministries and the branch trade-union organizations negotiate with each other on an equal footing. The frequency of Ministry-trade union contacts is on the rise: in 1981, the

Minister of Industry had 150 meetings with trade union functionaries (Tóth, 1982, p. 2). A series of central decisions was taken upon the initiative of the trade unions and partly against the initial standpoint of the government. Thus, when the National Trade Union Council decided, in 1972, on the expansion of the sanatorium network for industrial workers, the government had already decreed an investment stop. During the initial phases of the negotiations, the Ministry of Health refused to go beyond declarations of intent. Finally, it had to agree to co-finance the construction of three major health resorts (*NSz*, 1 May 1982). The 1972 wage increase for the blue-collar workers in the face of a growing economic crisis and the appearance of the first negative consequences of the NEM is a classical example of trade union influence (Heinrich-Huber, 1979, p. 162). In 1974, the trade unions posed as the champions of de-bureaucratization in establishing a trade union legal counselling service. The Labour Code was changed in response to a decision of the Twenty-Third Trade Union Congress, giving the trade union representatives in the enterprise a veto right in labour, wage and social matters (*NSz*, 1 May 1982). The real power test for the trade unions is still to come, namely when large-scale firing of redundant workers becomes necessary. Export of redundant labour is a likely remedy, although it has not removed unemployment in the Yugoslav case. Hitherto, cases of 'work force regrouping' as the Hungarian political parlance has christened dismissals, can still be handled easily. At the beginning of 1983, there were 70,000 workers in Hungary who were unemployed for longer than six months. It is assumed that most of them live by doing odd jobs (*NSz*, 22 January 1983). Government and trade unions have agreed on a common strategy that obliges both partners 'to encourage justified labor force regroupings, but to implement them with great circumspection, and to take the workers' material and social interest into due account' (*NSz*, 1 May 1982).

In contrast to the national level, enterprise itself offers little opportunity for successful trade union policy. Although the law provides for the election of shop stewards ('trustees') by the workers and in spite of the impressive array of veto and co-determination powers accorded to them, enterprise trade union representatives regularly go along with management decisions. The law makes clear that management decisions which violate the rights of the workers or the 'Principles of Socialist morality' may be vetoed by the trade union enterprise organization. Thereupon the decision is suspended and reviewed by a joint arbitration committee. Hungarian trade union leaders claim that the veto institution is a substitute for the right to strike which is still an anathema to the official doctrine. The proportion of actual strikes is very low (Pravda, 1984, p. 62). The number of vetoes has increased in recent years; in 1979 it was 281 against an annual fifty during the early seventies. Most arbitration cases are decided in favour of the workers (Pravda, 1984, p. 63). Since 1976, changes in the wage structure must be approved by the trade unions. Also, enterprise trade union representatives must be consulted before the director or other managers are appointed. As of 1 January 1985, enterprise directors are elected in most firms by the Enterprise Council, a body in which the workers have at least a 50 per cent representation. This body will also be empowered to take important decisions. It remains to be seen how these changes will influence the traditional attitudes of non-participation and indifference toward the trade union among the workers. Hungarian studies stress the dominant influence of economic constraints that as a rule override sectoral workers' interests (Balogh, 1977, p. 69). The sense of efficiency is low both among the workers and trade union functionaries: a survey among trade union enterprise functionaries found that only 20 per cent could enumerate the competencies of trade union enterprise bodies correctly (Vass, 1978, p. 78). When the managers of the Budapest Chemical Works had the workers decide on the distribution of the annual wage and premium increases, the workers wanted to avoid conflicts and spoke out for the maintenance of the old system (Héty, 1980, p. 165).

Hungary's planners are interested in putting brakes on inflation and reducing the quantity of money circulating in the economy. Therefore, enterprises that pay wages or bonuses over the centrally set ceilings are subject to a progressive and prohibitive taxation. However, the lack of labour (and especially skilled labour) forces managers to offer prospective employees certain privileges as a compensation for the low wages. These privileges include a general connivance with laxity in work discipline, unofficial permission to work in outside jobs during work hours, utilization of a factory resources and the like. The real bargaining power of the working class is the planning system itself which is orientated towards employment security and produces no incentives for the management to economize on labour reserves. Moreover, about 35 per cent of the industrial work force are commuters from nearby villages, who can always rely on private plot farming as a means of subsistence (Fuchs–Demko, 1977, p. 465). Thus, workers are less dependent on industrial work, a fact that increases their bargaining power. The high fluctuation rates, absenteeism, a low work morale and alcohol abuse during work hours illustrate this phenomenon. The top managers of Hungarian enterprises are probably more vulnerable than their Western colleagues who can display force more openly in the face of strike threats and other attempts at blackmailing. He has to persuade workers to produce the quantities envisaged by the plan. His position is especially precarious if shipments to

COMECON partners or strategically important deliveries are delayed. In such cases, not only his premium but also his political career—most plant directors are communists—are jeopardized. As the size of the wage fund is regulated, extra payments and bonuses that are used to 'buy' one recalcitrant group decrease the wage frame of the others. Thus, removing one source of conflict can create a series of other intra-enterprise conflicts. Management dilemmas are likely to persist under the new wage regulations as well. Hungarian sociologists stress the better opportunities to achieve higher incomes for better trained workers, for those who own an apartment large enough to store equipment and those who have resided long enough in urban centres to have a sufficiently large network of acquaintances to offer customers for moonlighting jobs. Apart from that, the position taken in the production processes themselves plays a key role. One study found that electrical engineers occupy a strategically most important position. In case of technical breakdowns the functioning of the entire plant is jeopardized without their co-operation (Héthy, 1980, p. 194).

The workers themselves do not follow a conscious and consistent anti-management policy. Their attitudes resemble the century-old survival strategies developed by their peasant and farmhand ancestors. They do not regard violations of work discipline as illegal acts, but as a just compensation for low official wages. Settling private matters, like shopping or the necessary everyday contacts with administrative authorities during work hours, has become a semi-legal institution. Hungarian observers agree that work discipline has deteriorated dramatically in the past twenty years. An empirical survey taken at the end of the seventies showed that 51 per cent of the respondents claimed the habit absenteeism. A total of 25.12 days per year and must be subtracted from the annual sum of work days (Pogány, 1980, p. 346).

The Planners' View: Enterprise Guidance in Hungary

Throughout the history of NEM, Hungarian planners have stated their intention to create a qualitatively new setup (Inotai, 1984, p. 13). Yet, even leading executives in the Planning Authority evaluate the results of the leadership's efforts with a weeping and a laughing eye:

As far as the economic mechanism, the affluence of our capital and consumer goods supply and the qualification of our labour force is concerned Hungary has closed up to the most developed countries in the past thirty-five years. But these quantitative changes did not or did not always keep pace with the necessary qualitative pre-requisites, the results of technological progress and the demands of the markets. [Hoós, *NSz*, 19 August 1984.]

Indeed, the planners' long-range intentions have regularly been thwarted by unexpected developments in world markets and by the inertia of the planning system itself. Instead of opening the Pandora's box of radical change and wholesale revamping of the entire system, the planners had to rely on a muddling-through strategy which resulted in the appearance of a two-step-forward-one-step-backward policy. Therefore, the overall picture of the reform is somewhat contradictory and inconsistent.

The economic reform that had been partly dismantled between 1972 and 1978 and that, after 1978, could not unfold because of the difficult external conditions, has gained momentum in recent years. The leaders' intention is clearly to shift power from the state to the enterprises and from the sectoral to the functional institutions. Market supervision is to be carried out by the Material and Prices Office, the regulation of enterprise income by the Ministry of Finance and the regulation of money flows by the banking system capped by the National Bank. In 1981, the nomination rights concerning some 900 leading positions were transferred to the enterprises. The relationship between the state agencies and the enterprise is to be put on a new basis: instructions are to be replaced by contractual agreements and bargaining processes. The position of both partners is to be delineated more precisely in the relevant legal norms. The same principle is to be applied to the enterprise party organization that has operated in a legal vacuum up to now. The legal institutionalization of the Party in the enterprise will most certainly entail a reduction of its hitherto practically unlimited powers. But deconcentration policies also aim at cutting down to an operable size the unwieldy production apparatus itself. Since 1980, some 150 enterprises have gained independence from the giant trusts, a step that has also reduced personnel redundancy: the job of 150 administrators working in the trust bureaucracy is now performed by five civil servants in the Industrial Ministry. There is still a relatively large province in the Hungarian economy that is directly administered by the state. Direct state guidance concerns defence industries, the production of energy and building materials, meat and grain industry, the communal public utilities, some important CMEA suppliers and a few trade enterprises. Twenty per cent of all enterprises producing 8-10 per cent of the total production value are still under direct state control (Wass von Czege, 1985, p. 44).

The system of indirect guidance is also undergoing further changes. The objective of changes in taxation and financial policy is to enforce a reduction of investments in fixed assets achieving an increase in venture capital for investments in other, more productive firms instead. Thus, the 'peasant tradition' of creating unnecessary reserves is to be broken. Yet, changes are gradual and leave the general framework of planning via incentives intact.

The planners' goals are specified in several main documents: the five-year plan, the annual plan and the state budget. While the plans contain only rough developmental estimates for the main indices of growth and are not legally binding on individual enterprises, the budget contains more detailed instructions for state organs to realize the planners' ideas through expenditure and taxation. A series of financial incentives is used to guide the enterprises into the direction envisaged by the political leadership.

(1) Price policy: It is the explicit aim of the planners to introduce world market prices into domestic markets in order to stimulate efficiency. However, most Hungarian enterprises could not withstand the direct impact of international competition. Therefore, large-scale subsidies (around one third of the budget expenditure) have to be provided for the survival of these enterprises, and for price control. The high liquidity of most enterprises, which in turn is a consequence of excess subsidies, led to soaring investments in the past. Technology was imported from Western countries, often in unnecessary quantities and incompatible with the domestic infrastructural conditions. As these imports had to be financed through foreign credits, the balances of trade and payments showed a dramatic deterioration. In this situation, the political leaders had to decree a strict austerity policy which was ushered in by price increases roughly counterbalanced by social measures for the poorer strata of the population. Hungary's complex price system includes fixed, limited, maximum and free prices. Since April 1984, 'competitive prices' have ruled for about 60 per cent of the industrial products. This means that for most items, import (world market) prices are the level of reference, and for most export commodities sold in Hungary, the export prices. Although a price policy has contributed to a drastic improvement of the trade balance and a remarkable decrease of the foreign debt, the absolute size of the subsidies increased from 1979 to 1983 by 74 per cent (RFER, 16 May 1984, p. 8). Hungary's planners will have to continue oscillating between the Scylla of high prices and the Charybdis of high subsidies. For price formation fair competition clauses are in force. Beginning in 1985, differentiated turnover tax rates have been levied on basic food items (11 per cent), textiles (20 per cent) and automobiles and spare parts (30 per cent) (*NSz*, 6 November 1984).

(2) Tax policy: In the past few years, tax policy has mainly served to skim off excessive enterprise liquidity and to stimulate technical progress. The valid regulations, put in force in 1980, provide for a 24 per cent social security

contribution paid out of the wage fund. But as the 5 per cent production fund tax (a tax on fixed assets) was abolished simultaneously, capital is relatively cheaper than labour. In the past, such a policy has usually led to a mere quantitative increase of capital as compared to labour without increasing capital effectivity. Of the enterprises's gross profits, 63.9 per cent are taxed away, the rest flows into development and participation funds from which investments and wages are financed.

(3) Wage policy: In order to dampen inflation, wages are strictly controlled. Prior to 1985, wage increases were subject to a progressive taxation up to 800 per cent (amounting to a fine) if the increase exceeded 14 per cent. The main weakness of the old system was that average wages were taxed. Thus, managers who decided to give extra remunerations to high-performance workers or brigades had to hire an appropriate number of workers in the low-pay category to maintain the previous wage average. Beginning in 1985, wages have been taxed individually and only wage increases are taxed by the average. This will increase the managers' flexibility in hiring top specialists, but is unlikely to remove a potential source of intra-enterprise conflict. For enterprises in the low-profit zone, the system of central wage regulation will be maintained (*NSz*, 6 November 1984).

(4) Credit policy: Eighty per cent of the state budget investments are centrally planned and implemented. Usually, they go to large-size or infrastructural projects. The remainder is allotted to investments planned by individual enterprises in the forms of loans and grants that usually have strings attached. Enterprises may also request credit from the banks. Between 1976 and 1980 the credit program was strictly export-orientated. Since then, the arrangement has been changed to a priority branch system, i.e. the National Bank establishes credit ceilings for each sector of the economy. Within the available contingent there is competition between the enterprises.

(5) Investment guidance: Fifty-five per cent of all public investments are decided on the enterprise level. The policy in recent years has been to crack down on overinvestment which was mainly a consequence of oversubsidizing. However, the present low investment rates will have to be increased in the near future, otherwise technological innovation will not be posible.

In summary, the system of financial enterprise guidance is cost and production-orientated. Market elements have certainly changed the face of Hungary's planned economy. Customers have most certainly profited from the changes. Yet hitherto, the structural problems were only pushed ahead or aside and not solved. On the other hand, Hungarian and Western critics must realize that the social and political risks of incisive reforms have been an insurmountable dilemma for the leadership. At present, the precarious balance between the economically necessary and the politically feasible can still be maintained. However, the scales show a tendency of tipping over to the economic side.

Agriculture

Development
Through most of its history, Hungarian agriculture has suffered from the contradiction between highly favourable climatic and soil conditions and a social system of agricultural production which prevented the effective exploitation of these prerequisites. Until the middle of this century, medieval and nineteenth century structures of agricultural production were preserved. Although the system of large estates had been able to generate the domestic investment capital that had primed the pump for the industrialization drive after 1867, the reliance on grain exports turned out to be the Achilles' heel of the Hungarian economy in the 1930s when a drastic slump in grain prices caused a catastrophic situation, both economically and socially. The big landowners could not or did not want to modernize production because of the low prices, and for the bulk of the rural population survival was the main problem. Fifty per cent of the agricultural land belonged to 1 per cent of the population. On the other end of the ownership spectrum, 25 per cent of the population were dwarf holders (below 3 hectares) owning 10 per cent of the land. One-third of Hungary's population were seasonal workers, farm hands and village poor. The land reform of 1945 brought a radical change in owner-ship structures. All holdings over fifty-seven hectares were confiscated and redistributed among the poorest levels of the agricultural population. The formation of collective farms and state farms began in 1949 and had to rely on large-scale intimidation and coercion; in communist parlance, on the 'distortion of Leninist co-operative norms'. The collectivized peasantry used the two brief liberalization periods of 1953 and 1956 for mass desertion from the collective farms. Thus, in 1956 two-thirds of their members turned their backs on collectivized agriculture which they had always resented and which had never met the high-strung expectations of the political leadership either. The reconciliation with the peasant was the primary goal of Kádár's new agricultural policy. New guidelines were drawn up as early as in July 1957. In realization of this new policy, the mandatory deliveries were abolished and

substituted by contracting at reasonable prices. Simultaneously, the state invested large sums into the remaining collective farms. Between 1958 and 1961, a new socialization drive collectivized the farms again, this time without the violence and the coercion that had characterized the pre-1956 period. Today, Hungary's agricultural system is both effective and stable, it has shown itself capable of feeding the population and producing surpluses for export. It has led to prosperity in the villages. The consistent broadening of the opportunities for private production and sale has greatly contributed to the legitimacy of the system among the rural population. In its agricultural policy the regime has demonstrated its ability to learn from past mistakes, trading ideological purity for pragmatist attitudes.

Hungarian Agriculture Today
In 1984, 70.6 per cent of Hungary's territory was under cultivation, of which 50.4 per cent was arable land, 17.6 per cent forests and 5 per cent was used for fruit production. As far as the structure of agricultural production is concerned, the proportion of crop production and horticulture is one-third; cattle breeding and animal products accounts for another third, whereas 25 per cent is produced in the agricultural industrial and service sectors. This means that Hungary's agricultural enterprises are involved in large-scale non-agricultural activities, although most ancillary industrial establishments (such as brick factories, canneries, repair shops and the like) serve their mother agricultural enterprises and do not produce for the market. Therefore, the high proportion of Hungary's agricultural work force (over 20 per cent) in total employment does not mean that all of them perform agricultural activities. However, this type of rural industry provides the farm population with year-round employment and helps to reduce the number of commuters to industrial urban centres.

Hungary's agriculture is the most successful among the socialist countries. Hungary is a net exporter of agricultural products and it can supply its own population with most food items. In contrast to other socialist agricultures, the increased emphasis on meat production has not led to setbacks in the Hungarian crop and vegetable sectors. Due to a relatively high level of mechanization and the use of artificial fertilizers (around 235 kg/ha) hectare yields are approaching Western standards, e.g. in the 1980 bumper wheat harvest 4,760 kg/ha (West: around 5,000 kg/ha). Apart from grain, the most important crops are maize, sugar beet and oil seeds.

While field crops are mainly produced by state or collective farms, most other agriculural goods are turned out by all three sectors of Hungary's agricultural system: state, co-operative and private sectors are combined in what can be called a 'system of crosscutting relationships' (Volgyes, 1982, p. 53).

In 1984, the public sector consisted of 128 state farms, organized and directed after the model of state industrial enterprises, 1,408 co-operatives of which 1,279 were agricultural producer co-operatives (*mezőgazdasági termeloszövetkezet*), sixty-four specialized co-operatives, fifty-one co-operative unions and sixteen fishery co-operatives. The state farms have the same legal status as other state enterprises and their workers enjoy the same social benefits as industrial workers. Because of their large size (they hold 10.5 per cent of the arable land, 7,700 hectares on an average) and because of their financial power they also form the backbone of agricultural experimental research. Some state farms have a long tradition, e.g. the Mezőhegyes and the Bábolna farms, that were founded as state enterprises in the eighteenth century and today are marketing their high-quality produce (among other things, fowl and horses) all over the world. The producers' co-operatives are founded by voluntary contributions (mostly land) by their members for the purpose of common production. They are smaller (4,000 hectares on an average) and their members have a special legal status, which however is continuously advancing to that of the state farm workers. In 1982, around 16.1 per cent of the agricultural work-force was employed on state farms and 74 per cent (around 700,000 people) on the collective farms (*NSz*, 17 January 1984). The rest are private producers. Around 95 per cent of the cultivated land is owned by the public sector institutions, namely, by the state. Private agricultural production can be pursued in three ways: by individual full-time professional farms (around 50,000 individuals, 6 per cent of the agricultural work-force), by state farm and collective farm members, cultivating their private plots that are put at their disposal by the farm and as auxiliary household plots for everybody. Indeed, private farming is no privilege of the rural strata in Hungary. Twenty-six per cent of the private producers are farmers, 28 per cent are workers, 23 per cent are both or white-collar and 23 per cent are old age pensioners. The private plots are cultivated by one and a half million families. In addition, 700,000 families cultivate small pieces of land not exceeding 1,500 sqauare metres or raise one or two animals, producing for their own needs and not for the market. Altogether, half of the population is involved in private agricultural production. (*NSz*, 14 August 1984).

According to official data, around one third of the total agricultural production stems from the private sector and above all from the household plots (*háztáji gazdaság*). About 50 per cent of Hungary's pigs (total 11,000,000) are bred by private citizens and 90 per cent of the raspberries were raised on private plots in 1983. Private production has contributed considerably to the strength of Hungarian agriculture. Hungary produces an annual 144 kilo-grammes of meat per inhabitant, which ranks her fourth on the world list after Denmark, Australia and New Zealand. Each year, Hungary realizes an income of US$100 million resulting from the world market sales of agricultural produce from her private plots (Fehér, 1980, p. 10). During recent years, the proportion of private production in the total agricultural output has decreased in spite of an absolute increase of 1.3 per cent. While the con-tribution of the private sector was at 35.9 per cent ten years ago, it was down to 33.68 per cent in 1984. This decrease reflects the investment emphasis in the public sector, but also the relative economic inefficiency of private plot production which is based on self-exploitation. Forty-four per cent of the collective farm members are pensioners, which means that the bulk of private plot cultivation activities is undertaken by them. The age structure of private plot farmers reveals a similar picture: five per cent are under thirty years of age, 29 per cent between thirty and fifty, 21 per cent between fifty and sixty, and 45 per cent older than sixty. During the last years, the proportion of old age pensioners has been increasing (*NSz*, 14 August 1984).

As the state profits from this voluntary self-exploitation, official policy aims at the integration of the public and the private sectors. Private plot farming is assisted by the state and collective farms by permitting private producers to use the firms' technical equipment and facilities. The sale of private produce is likewise organized and financed by the public sector. The fact should not be overlooked that co-operative farms are organized on a democratic basis, which under the present conditions, allows the articulation and the consideration of private farming interests. No co-operative could permit itself to rule against the vital economic interests of its members. It is interesting to note in this connection that the democratization experiments currently undertaken in state industrial firms extend to agricultural enter-prises as well. As in the industrial sector, the reforms are aiming at a more meaningful participation of state farm personnel through direct elections of the management and other mechanisms. Only the most important state enterprises are to remain under close administrative supervision and tutelage.

5 The Regime's Policies

The policies of the HSWP are a product of political action under heavy economic, social and foreign policy constraints. The relative independence which has been accorded to market forces renders active, ideologically-orientated policy-making almost impossible. Under the impact of the world economic crisis Hungary's leaders had to resort to a muddling-through model of decision-making, postponing to a distant future the realization of goals that are at variance with keeping the economy afloat. The distribution of budget resources over the various policy areas shows the predominantly reactive pattern of Hungarian politics. The biggest slices of the cake must be allotted to social security and enterprise as well as price subsidies—both areas that are hardly amenable to political guidance:

Revenues (607.8 billion ft)	(%)	Expenditures (610.3 billion ft)	(%)	as % of national income
Payments by enterprises and co-operatives	66.2	Social insurance	21.6	
Turnover tax	14.9	Enterprise subsidies	16.1	
Social security contribu-tions	21.6	Price subsidies	7.0	
		Education and culture	10.5	9.1
Income of budgetary organs	9.0	Law and public order	10.1	8.8
Direct taxes and fees	3.2	Health and social services	6.4	5.8
		Defence	6.1	5.3
		Accumulation	9.4	
		Other	12.6	

Figure 5.1 The 1985 budget of the HPR (*Source*: *NSZ*, 20 December 1984.)

Given the pressing economic constraints, the regime's budget showpieces deserve attention. The expenditure for education and culture rose by 10.9 per cent and those for health and social services by fourteen percentage points since the preceding year. However, the exigencies and demands constantly surpass the available means, causing a long-term relative deterioration in the main policy areas.

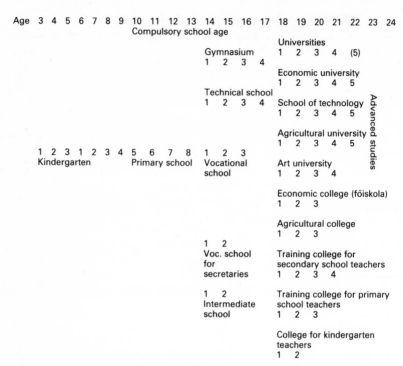

Figure 5.2 The Educational System of the HPR

Domestic Policies

Education and Culture

Hungary's educational system has a long Central European tradition. Under the enlightened absolutism of the Habsburgs the basis for a modern educational system was laid. A 1777 decree Ratio Educationis paved the way for universal basic education and the elimination of illiteracy. Higher education had already existed since the Middle Ages. Hungary's first university was founded in Pécs in 1367, but instruction in Hungarian was not offered there as the school system was a vehicle for the propagation of German and Latin culture. Magyar schools were established all over the country only after the Compromise of 1867. Nationalism had started out as an educational movement: consequently the schools were now used as agencies of Magyarization. The 1919 Soviet republic proclaimed a state monopoly on school instruction, trying to break the century-old dominance of clerical schools. During the Horthy period, education improved slowly but consistently. Ninety-two per cent of the school-age children attended, on the average, four to six grades. Ten per cent of the children in the eligible age groups attended secondary schools. Illiteracy was pushed down to 3 per cent of the economically active population (Császtvay, 1984, p. 271). With the separation of church and state after the Second World War, the church lost its educational predominance. Today, only a small number of secondary schools (kollégium) is run by the Hungarian Catholic Church and they strictly abide by the state curricula. The educational policies of the CPH had a dual aim: on the one hand, industrialization demanded a rapid upgrading of the workers' qualifications and on the other hand, traditional educational privileges were to be abolished. Therefore the main thrust of the party was directed at the broadening of technical training on all levels and a reversal of the social access conditions to higher education in favour of the working class and to the detriment of the bourgeoisie. The 1961 reform basically followed the Soviet (Khrushchevian) pattern of linking education and production. The compulsory school age was extended to 16 years. One year later, the legal discrimination clauses against 'class enemies' were dropped. The main result of these efforts was a rapid quantitative increase in the educational level of the population. However, this development was not matched by a similar rise in qualitative standards. The schools were inadequately equipped, classrooms and teaching faculty were relatively scarce, and the curricula oversized. This relative overstrain on facilities and pupils alike is still characteristic of today's educational system. The contemporary arrangement is based on a CC decision passed in June 1972, emphasizing the continuous modernization of the curriculum and instruction methods. Post-graduate university education extends over a period of three years. Titles confered are 'candidate' and 'doctor'. Doctoral diplomas are issued to physicians, dentists and lawyers after five years of regular university studies.

Close to 90 per cent of the children in the 3-6 age group attend kindergarten, where pre-school education is offered during the last year. Fifty-nine per cent of the approximately 170,000 children who finish primary school continue their education in vocational schools, secondary technical schools and gymnasiums. Close to one half of them (47 per cent) attend secondary schools leading to a high school diploma (maturity exam). Sixty-five per cent of the high school students have a worker or peasant background, while only 20 per cent of the vocational school students come from other than the working classes (Bencédy, 1982, p. 19). The high schools, however are relatively selective institutions: the dropout rate is 30 per cent. The most selective educational body in Hungary is the university: admission is granted on the basis of a high school diploma and successful completion of an entrance exam which is passed annually by around 42 per cent of the 35,000 applicants for university and college studies. In contrast to Western free-access universities, there are few dropouts during the studies. The proportion of university students, in the eligible groups was 9.9 per cent in 1984 (*StZsK*, 1984). Naturally, the educated classes enjoy a more advantageous position in the competition for higher educational standards. The HSWP's answer to this educational privilege was the institution of a large network of evening and correspondence courses on all levels, specially tailored to compensate for the working classes' weaker starting conditions. Thus, roughly one-third of the students registered at Hungarian universities and colleges (i.e. around 37,000 people) are non-regulars. One can assume that most of them come from a working-class background. The obvious disadvantage of this arrangement is the high disparity in terms of standards, skills and qualifications that exist between the two systems.

In the curricula, one can observe a strong emphasis on mathematics and sciences. In the primary school curriculum there are two areas of concentration: Hungarian language and literature (24.9 per cent of a total of 7,293 hours) and mathematics (17.5 per cent) are the two points of gravity.

	Hours per week				
(year)	I	II	III	IV	Total
Hungarian language	2	2	1	1	6
Hungarian literature	2	3	3	3	11
History	2	2	3	4	11
Fundamentals of the socialist world-outlook	—	—	—	2	2
Russian	4	3	3	2	12
Second foreign language	3	3	—	—	6
Mathematics	5	4	3	3	15
Physics	2	2	3	3	10
Chemistry	2	4	—	—	6
Biology	—	—	4	2	6
Geography	3	2	—	—	5
Music	1	1	1	—	3
Drawing	1	1	1	—	3
Physical education	3	3	3	3	12
Technical education	2	2	—	—	4
Class head's period	1	1	1	1	4
Vocational advising	—	1	—	—	
Non-obligatory subjects	—	—	7	9	16

Figure 5.3 The High School Commission

Students choose their course of studies on the basis of career and interest considerations. Graduation figures by departments, however, reflect the specific priorities in educational planning.

Like every communist movement, the Hungarian Communist Party has tried to popularize culture. Whereas the efforts of Stalinist Hungary to propagate Russian culture were strongly resented by the population at large, the increased emphasis placed by the post-1956 leadership on Hungarian traditions and the gradual opening *vis-à-vis* Western cultural influences has certainly increased the regime's legitimacy. Culture has a specific place in socialist societies as a vehicle for expressing demands, anxieties and thoughts

Table 5.1 Graduations by Department

Departments	% of graduating students
Technology	26.1
Agriculture	5.6
Economics	10.7
Law	5.5
Medicine	4.4
Teachers' training	12.6
Arts etc.	1.9

that are less apt to be communicated through other channels. The unusually rich cultural offering and the widespread network of cultural institutions is therefore widely used. There are 10,500 public libraries that make an annual 53,000,000 volumes available to its readers; 2,605 cultural centres and 464 museums. 120,000,000 books are published each year (Császtvay, 1984, p. 291). Approximately 21 million literary works are in circulation, roughly 50 per cent of which are by Magyar authors, 10 per cent of which are translations from American literature and only around 6 per cent which are from Soviet authors. There is a rough equilibrium between the two ideological camps. In the film industry, of the 193 films that were shown in 1984, 115 were produced in socialist and 78 in non-socialist countries (*StZsK*, 1984).

The Kádár regime had a hard time in winning over literati and artists, who were browbeaten, embittered and who had withdrawn into sullen silent opposition after 1956. Many of them had left the country, and some, like the writer Gyula Háy, served long prison terms. With the overall decompression, tension loosened in the Hungarian cultural scene as well and a political line that sought to combine little freedoms and party guidance began to emerge. Hungary's cultural policies were moulded by György Aczél, who managed to reintegrate the larger part of the alienated opposition into the government camp, using his network of acquaintances (he is a former actor and a friend of Kádár) and his political talents. Aczél's main guideline is the categorization of artistic creation into three provinces: the supported, the tolerated and the prohibited (Aczél, 1971, p. 11). While the 'supported' category includes all that is considered to advance the party's cause ideologically, 'tolerated' refers to everything that promises high sales and 'prohibited', according to Minister of Culture Béla Köpeczi, refers to 'products that directly attack the Socialist order, incite war or racial hatred or belong to the category of pornography (Köpeczi, 1983, p. 16). Köpeczi describes the basic purpose of Hungarian cultural policy as follows:

We take note of the fact that we live in an open world, that a free flow of information exists and that cultural exchange has become a vital necessity. But we select in regard to value. It is true that we also publish criminal novels and best sellers, but the essential feature of our cultural policy is the propagation of values. [Köpeczi, 1983, p. 16.]

It is natural that the above-mentioned categories cannot be separated from each other neatly. Thus, many 'supported' books, articles and films are more critical than for example works of dissident writers that fall under an indictment just because the author's name has been branded before. Moreover, the categories are also flexible over time. Much that is officially published now could have been published only in samizdat form ten years ago. Increased distance to past periods of the regime's history leads to greater leeway by critics. Thus, the Rákosi era is now criticized freely in such films as *The Witness* or in books like Erzsébet Galgóczy's *The Otter Trap* and István Gáll's *The Manager of the Stud Farm*. The latter does not conceal its sympathy for its anti-heroes, a group of Horthy officers who are employed on a state stud farm because of their skills and experience and who are forced into open revolt by narrow-minded and overly apprehensive communist bureaucrats.

Music is probably the art sector which is least controllable and amendable to party tutelage. Broadcasting is not jammed in Hungary and Western (Austrian) television can be received by half of the population. The party has realized it cannot win the battle for youth by cracking down on new waves and trendy styles. Thus, music groups have mushroomed all over Hungary that, just as in the West, provide an adequate form of artistic expression for the problems of the younger generation and absorb protest potential.

Religious Policy

The traditional social and political influence of religion and the Catholic Church in Hungary conflicted sharply with the interests and the ideology of the communist movement. Thus, the first phase of Church-state relations after the communist takeover was characterized by a series of repressive measures against the churches (two-thirds of the religious believers belonged to the Catholic Church, one-third to other religious denominations in 1949). Church property was confiscated, and almost all religious orders disbanded. The churches were menaced with the prospect of becoming relics and had to choose between complete subjugation or stubborn resistance. Hungary's Roman Catholic Primate József Cardinal Mindszenty opted for the second alternative. Sentenced to life imprisonment in 1950 and freed during the 1956 revolution, he spent fifteen years in the United States' embassy in Budapest and became a symbol of religious resistance. However, the Kádár leadership discarded the policy of direct confrontation and tried to establish a modus vivendi based on bargaining with the Church leadership. In 1964, Hungary concluded an agreement with the Vatican, in which the Church pledged its allegiance to the Hungarian constitutional and legal order, in as far as there were no contradictions to the principles of Christian faith. The Hungarian state was granted the right to influence the nomination of incumbents to certain Church positions. But only when, in 1974, Pope Paul VI declared the Primate's diocese in Esztergom vacant was the major obstacle for the further improvement of Church-state relations removed and the era of open confrontation ended. Today, the basis of co-operation between the Church leadership and the state has broadened considerably and both sides display moderation and compromising attitudes. The Hungarian Constitution guarantees the freedom of religion and worship and proclaims the principle of the separation of Church and state (Art. 63). However, although the legal status of the churches under civil law is that of a corporation, they never managed to escape from massive state interference, and find themselves in the peculiar position of being asked to perform state functions like providing education and peace propaganda. At the present, the state recognizes twenty churches and religious associations: the Catholic, Reformed and Lutheran Churches, the Israelite Religious Association, ten religious communities united in the Hungarian Council of Free Churches, the Greek Orthodox and the Hungarian Unitarian Churches plus the Hungarian Buddhist Mission. Church policy is handled by the State Office for Church Affairs, whose head, State Secretary Imre Miklós, a professor of philosophy, displays remarkable circumspection and political skill.

The dependence of the Church on the Hungarian state is reflected in its precarious financial position. Since the Church tax was abolished in 1949 and other sources of income have been confiscated, the churches have to be financed via voluntary donations and state subsidies. The Catholic Church receives nearly 80 million ft per year in the form of state aid to priests and to religious schools. Thirty per cent of the state budgetary expenditure for the maintenance of historical buildings goes to the Church. In addition to that, an annual two million dollars of voluntary financial aid are transferred from abroad. Since 1945, around 630 churches have been built in Hungary (of which 144 between 1970 and 1980). There are ten church schools: eight Catholic, one Reformed and one Jewish. A total of 497 students were pursuing theological studies in the 1983-4 school year. In 1984, there were seventeen religious papers, whose Hungarian sales amounted to 200,000 copies. During the past years, about 200,000 copies of the Bible were printed by state publishing houses. Religious services are broadcast (one hour per week) but the churches have no access to television. As far as religious instruction is concerned, a period of two hours per week is provided in state schools for those children whose parents request it. In addition to school tuition, there is voluntary religious instruction in churches or parish halls (*Magyar Nemzet*, 6 May 1984). The churches are also represented in public institutions: there are five Church delegates in the Diet, two in the Presidential Council, sixty-five in the local councils and six in the PPF National Council. For the Church leadership, these achievements are indeed impressive. The Catholic Primate László Lékai, an advocate of a gradualist policy, expressed the feelings of the Church hierarchy by pointing out that: 'Our Churches live in an atmosphere of tranquility, affection and mutual respect. . . . We take care to preserve this social and national unity, for it is our greatest treasure' (*L'Humanité*, 27 October 1984). Nevertheless, in spite of the visible *détente* between Church and state there are problems which are irritating to both partners. The most explosive issue is the question of conscientious objection, which is openly propagated by the so-called basic communities. These are informal groups organized and led by local priests. At the time being, around 150 conscientious objectors are serving prison terms for their refusal to participate in armed military service (RFER Hungarian SR/11, 11 October 1984). Generally, the state uses the repression mechanisms of the Church itself to crack down on recalcitrant priests. Thus, Father György Bulányi, who had supported conscientious objection was suspended from his priestly duties by the church authorities.

As far as the religious attitudes of the population at large are concerned, no precise statements can be made. Some general conclusions can be drawn from the results of a Budapest survey that was conducted in 1978. Of the 531 respondents, 44 per cent declared they were religious believers, 44.8 per cent were atheists, and 10.9 per cent undecided. Those who identified with a specific church mostly came from the lower strata: 42 per cent had no basic education, 56 per cent were first-generation workers, 38 per cent had moved to Budapest from the villages, 79 per cent of them were older than fifty years. The 'independent believers' had a better education and were somewhat younger, whereas atheists were predominantly of young urban professional origin (Tomka, 1981, p. 16). Certain clues are also yielded by the data on participation in religious ceremonies. In 1948 the national average of abstention from the Sunday mass was 12 per cent (42 per cent in Budapest). In 1972, 12.3 per cent of the entire population declared it went to church at least once a week. Most of these were over sixty years of age (Tomka, 1982, p. 303). In the above-mentioned 1978 Budapest survey even 8.7 per cent of the nonbelievers declared they went to church (albeit 'seldomly') and 61.7 per cent said they had not been to church 'for a considerably long time' (Tomka, 1981, p. 14). As far as church ceremonies are concerned, data are available only on confirmation frequency: in the eighteen to twenty-nine age bracket of the Budapest respondents, 48 per cent had received confirmation, and 72 per cent of the thirty to thirty-nine year olds (Tomka, 1981, p. 15). One can conclude that the proportion of baptized citizens is much higher. Most young couples follow the church wedding tradition and only very few funerals are held without religious ceremonies.

A general conclusion one can draw from the scant data is that religious attitudes are subject to attrition because of social processes and not because of the effects of anti-religious propaganda. The commitment to peace, however, is a deeply-ingrained feeling with the population. According to the empirical surveys, a majority of Hungarians (62 per cent) feel that a nuclear war would leave Hungary in shambles; only 5 per cent believe that it would leave their country unscathed. Ninety-seven per cent recommend the improvement of trade, exchange and co-operation as an antidote to war between the superpowers, 74 per cent are for the immediate dissolution of the military blocs. Those who implicitly subscribe to the prevailing Hungarian model by advocating its application throughout the world are relatively numerous (80 per cent), an equally large proportion is for the world-wide expansion of the socialist system as a peace-saving device. Only a minority (18 per cent) come out for world-wide capitalism as the solution of the peace problem (Dobossy, 1984, p. 646). Thus, a credible peace policy and peace propaganda by the state and the churches could undoubtedly elicit more than lip-service support from within the population.

Military Affairs

Due to its geographical-strategic position in the centre of Europe, Hungary has a long military tradition. However, the trends favouring the further militarization of society and the high esteem for the military were reversed after the disastrous defeat of the Second Hungarian Army as it participated in Hitler's campaign against the Soviet Union. Since then, the Hungarian military has ceased to play a decisive role in strategic confrontations. The troops fighting with the 1956 insurgents were too weak to resist the Soviet onslaught longer than for a few days. Yet, the Danube basin has not lost its potential strategic importance. For the Soviets, it can serve as a turnpike for possible military action in all directions, and it is the key area for dominance in the Balkan peninsula. Although it does not enjoy actual priority as a theatre of military operations in the Soviet military scenario (Hungary borders on neutral Austria and non-aligned Yugoslavia), its importance could be enhanced by specific conflict constellations.

In Hungary, there are approximately 80,000 Soviet troops belonging to the 'Southern Group' which are distributed among more than forty garrisons. There are two tank and motor rifle divisions; the Air Force comprises 350 airplanes and helicopters (Pilster, 1979, p. 485). The post-1956 Hungarian Army is fully integrated into the Warsaw Pact Organization. It had to be completely rebuilt and reorganized after the revolt and is now considered a loyal and reliable ally of the Red Army (V. Kulikov in *NSz*, 8 December 1984). Most of the leading officers are graduates of Soviet military schools. Hungarian units participated in the 1968 invasion of Czechoslovakia and take part regularly in the Warsaw Pact joint manœuvres. The regular forces comprise 105,000 troops, of which 58,000 are conscripts who serve a tour of duty of eighteen months (for the Air Force twenty-four months). The paramilitary forces include 15,000 border guards (of which 11,000 are conscripts), a part-time Workers' Militia of 60,000 members, the Hungarian National Defence Union and the Civil Protection Organization with an unknown number of full-time members. The Army consists of one tank division with about 1,200 tanks (mostly Soviet T-54 and T-55), five motor rifle divisions, one artillery brigade, one rocket brigade equipped with Scud surface-to-surface missiles, anti-tank and anti-aircraft units as well as the Danube flotilla. The Air Force can muster 145 combat aircraft and some twenty-four armed helicopters (*Air Force Magazine*, December 1984, p. 98). Western military specialists evaluate the fighting capacity as high (Pilster, 1979, p. 487). However, the absence of a real threat and the spreading of consumerist attitudes throughout society underscore the general impression that military defence is not—in contrast to the Soviet Union—accorded top priority by citizens and political leaders. The Hungarian Army is mainly used as a troubleshooter in the national economy: it participates in the realization of top-priority investments, producing an annual value of 5.3 billion ft and contributing 510 thousand working days to the fall harvests (*NSz*, 23 March 1985).

The Workers' Militia was founded in 1957 as the military branch of the new regime which was maintained by Soviet bayonets. The Kádár regime wanted to demonstrate that they were not afraid of issuing weapons to the workers. Once the regular troops had consolidated, the Workers' Militia was reduced to the function of guarding important industries and other strategically important objects. In practice, the Militia is used as a task force in emergency cases, such as natural disasters. It is subordinated to the Ministry of the Interior, but guided and controlled by the Military Committee of the party CC. About 70 per cent of the Militia members are workers, 10 per cent are collective farmers and the rest are recruited from the state and party bureaucracies (Gosztony, 1977, p. 311); 4.7 per cent are women (*NSz*, 23 March 1985). The Hungarian National Defense Union corresponds to the Soviet DOSAAF organization. Its tasks are the promotion of leisure activities which are of military interest, like military and motor sports. The protection and preparation of citizens for cases of emergency is the task of the Civil Protection Organization (Polgári Védelem), which is in practice used for similar purposes as the Workers' Militia. Military education in Hungarian schools is galvanized into the regular curriculum. Chemistry teachers, for instance, must cover topics like chemical warfare, and class heads in the course of instruction are expected to deal with topics like 'the military oath' and 'the war efforts of imperialism and European security' (Gosztony, 1977, p. 329).

Environmental Policy

The plain fact that an industrialized lifestyle is hazardous for the environment is relevant to the social organization of production and distribution. Only to the extent that the way in which ecological problems are handled is primarily determined by the prevailing political, economic and social patterns. Hungary parted with the principle of unlimited techno-optimisim in the mid-seventies, when the negative consequences of economic growth became clearly visible. The Environmental Protection Act was passed in 1976 in order to curb the increasing damage to the environment which was reflected in the rising costs of external diseconomies that had to be covered by the state budgets.

Hungary's geographical features make water pollution the most pressing environmental problem. Due to a shortage of sewage purification plants, surface waters are heavily polluted (*NSz*, 31 August 1983). Nearly 900 communes have been registered as suffering from 'unhealthy water supply'. The main pollutant is nitrate stemming from artificial fertilizers (*NSz*, March 1981). Obviously, water pollution is the price for Hungary's high agricultural productivity. Hungary is in the top group of European air polluters. With an annual 750,000 tons Hungary ranks sixth as far as sulphur emissions per square mile are concerned, exporting twice as much as it imports from other European countries (*NSz*, 24 May 1984). Rising sulphur dioxide emissions are mainly caused by a policy that aims at the substitution of oil by coal in the face of soaring oil prices. But domestic fuel and a rapidly expanding stock of automotive vehicles (automobiles alone numbered 1.3 million in 1983) also contributed to the sulphurization of the soil and to acid rain. An equally serious problem is rubbish disposal. Forty million tons of waste material is produced annually, mainly in industry and agriculture. The quantity of hazardous waste is five million tons per year (*NSz*, 31 August 1983). A relatively low level of technology, together with the profit motives of industry has thus far stood in the way of a more rational utilization of fuels and raw materials. Consistent programmes for the recycling of wastes would yield gigantic savings (*NSz*, 22 March 1981). However, in the estimation of industrial managers, it makes more economic sense to pollute the environment, because the fines against polluters are much lower than the purification costs. Thus, only 10 per cent of the calculable environmental damage is recovered through fines or penalties (*NSz*, 22 March 1981). That the needs of the economy receive priority before those of the environment was made clear by Gy. Gonda, the head of the Hungarian delegation to a multilateral conference on pollution (Munich, June 1984) who stressed that 'In our present situation we are not in a position to undertake a commitment regarding the percentage reduction of total sulphur dioxide emissions in Hungary. We may reconsider our position within four to five years when our economic situation improves' (RFRE, Hung. SR 19, 20 July 1984, p. 3).

In contrast to Western countries, popular ecological movements have appeared only sporadically in Hungary. A notable exception is the movement against the project to build the Gabčikovo–Nagymaros hydraulic power dam on the Danube between Bratislava and Budapest. The plan to build several power plants in this region, which is important for both agriculture and tourism emerged shortly after World War II. Hungary's precarious fossil fuel situation prompted the idea to use the river network for hydropower. But because of the insufficient fall of Hungary's rivers, even a maximal exploitation of its capacity would not meet the rising energy demand. Therefore, a coalition of energy experts, hydrologists, construction engineers and politicians tried to promote the project, grossly exaggerating its planned performance and understating the potential hazards. 'By this method', concludes a Hungarian critic, 'Hungary was downgraded to an uninhabited and uncultivable desert, where the hydraulic engineers could transform nature as they pleased' (Vargha, 1981, p. 63). The plans drawn up during the 1950s did not materialize due to the high production costs, and this despite the open interest the Soviets displayed in the project (Vargha, 1981, p. 6; *Novoe Vremya*, **13**, 1981, 23 March, p. 18). Finally, Czechoslovakia and Hungary agreed in an interstate treaty concluded in 1977 to jointly build the dam and the plants. Criticism to the effect that the project would fail to reach its aims (the improvement of navigation on the Danube, flood protection and power production), and would on the contrary cause great harm to the water supply of the area and to its agriculture, destroy an important tourist attraction and have other negative economic and ecological effects became intensive after the signing of the Czechoslovak–Hungarian agreement. The weight of the counterarguments raised against the project was so great that the Hungarian government seriously considered dropping the scheme in 1983 (RFER, Hungarian SR **7**, 1 June 1984, p. 15). Eventually, in May 1984 a full-fledged ecological movement formed around a letter written as a protest against the projects and signed by fifty prominent writers, historians, economists, actors, architects and film producers. Ten thousand people are reported to have signed the petition endorsing the letter's demand to 'stop the construction of the dam system, even at the price of revoking the interstate agreement by December 1984 (AFP, Vienna, 7 May 1984; *Die Welt*, 23 November 1984). Nevertheless, the Hungarian government has reaffirmed its willingness to resume construction in 1985. The international dimension of this project seems to be the most serious problem befuddling the Hungarian authorities. Hungary concluded the first East–West environmental agreement with Austria in June 1984, and the visible achievements successes of the Austrian ecological movement may now provide fresh ammunition for Hungarian ecologists.

Foreign Policy

The most conspicuous aspect of Hungarian foreign policy is Hungary's inclusion in the Soviet defence system. Although Hungarians were unwilling to accept Soviet domination during the decade following the end of the Second World War, they have since learned a lesson from the Soviet punitive action in 1956 and accept Soviet presence as a fact they are unable to change. Hungary's faithfulness towards the Warsaw Pact system is never seriously questioned, although the population at large regards the close relations to the Eastern superpower as a mixed blessing, at best. The political leaders have always stressed their determination never to undertake any moves which might jeopardize vital Soviet interests. From the Soviet perspective, the Kádár group is accepted as a faithful ally, since they demonstrated their unconditional dedication to the Soviet cause in 1956. The Soviets have thus few objections against the relative autonomy that Hungary practically enjoys in the field of economic policy, and also—to a more limited degree—in foreign policy. As Kádár is aware of the connection between the Cold War and Hungarian Stalinism, he has worked successfully to promote détente even at times when the spectre of a new Cold War appears. Thus, Kádár keeps expressing the hope that 'the tensions that came into being between the two superpowers are of a temporary nature'. He even speaks of a demilitarized Europe, which would exist after the 'simultaneous dissolution of NATO and the Warsaw Pact Organization' (*NSz*, 3 July, 1977). For Hungary, *détente* has been a security factor that will have to replace military security in the long run (*Magyar Hírlap*, 17 October 1973). In the words of Gyula Horn, the head of the CC's Foreign Relations Department, 'one must join the antiwar side, whatever one's ideological and political commitment' (*MTI Weekly Bulletin*, 15 August 1984).

The specific features of Hungarian foreign policy, in the final analysis, spring from one overriding interest, namely not to jeopardize the Alliance Policy. Since the basic rationale of this strategy consists in exchanging political support for higher consumption levels and minor freedoms Hungary must be open towards the West economically and partly also politically. The Kádár group therefore started to put out feelers towards the West at a time when they were still outlawed by the media and by public opinion in Western countries. The Hungarians spotted Finland as a neutral country and a loyal Soviet neighbour to demonstrate their determination to promote East-West *détente*. Following unsuccessful attempts at winning Austrian sympathies, the dialogue with the capitalist neighbour was started anew in 1964 after being interrupted by the 1956 events. Meanwhile, Austro–Hungarian relations are regarded as a model for relations between Western and socialist countries. Co-operation has extended to practically all fields of political, social and economic life. Of course, this unusual intimacy is not only explained by a joint interest in reducing political tensions in Europe, but also by the existence of problems that call for a co-operative solution, like the common waters, questions of environmental protection, tourist traffic and the like. In recent years, Hungary has intensified its contacts with NATO countries as well, particularly with Western Germany which is Hungary's most important Western trade partner.

Kádár's *westpolitik* is not received with enthusiasm everywhere in the Soviet bloc. While the Soviets generally hold his cautious and well-orchestrated foreign policy performances in high esteem and have explicitly endorsed Hungary's economic policy on numerous occasions, the regimes that have opted for different strategies are implicitly threatened by Kádár's successes. This concerns, above all, the Czechoslovak leadership, which views Hungarian economic reform with a jaundiced eye and has not refrained from openly criticizing Hungary, as it did on the occasion of the visit of the British Premier M. Thatcher to Budapest in February 1984 (RFER Hungarian SR/5 13 April 1984, p. 9). The most serious conflict, however has emerged with Hungary's southern neighbour around the issue of Romania's treatment of the Transylvanian Hungarian minority, numbering approximately two million people. Using the vehicle of nationalism, Romania's leader N. Ceaucescu has tried to forge national unity around the Romanian Communist party. This has led to a considerable deterioration in the position of the minorities. The traditional polemics over Transylvania have thus resurfaced, this time between two socialist governments.

Hungary's integration into COMECON

The transition from self-sufficiency under Rákosi to gradual opening in the post-1956 stage also implied a much higher degree of interdependence between Hungary and its socialist allies, particularly with the Soviet Union. Because of its deficient raw material base, Hungary is forced to import most of the primary products needed to meet the requirements of its industries and to ensure a stable supply for the economy and the population. Thus, in terms of percentage of total imports, Hungary imports from the Soviet Union 95 per cent of the natural gas, 90 per cent of its oil, 90 per cent of its iron ore and 75 per cent of its fertilizers (*NSz* 9 November 1984). All in all, 30 per cent of Hungary's foreign trade is with the Soviet Union, which in return imports

Table 5.2 Ranking of Hungary's Foreign Trade Partners

	1970 (rank)	1984 (rank)	1970 (%)	1984 (%)
Hungarian exports to				
USSR	1	1	35.2	30.1
West Germany	4	2	6.9	7.4
East Germany	2	3	9.5	5.9
Czechoslovakia	3	4	8.1	5.2
Austria	8	5	3.1	5.3
Poland	5	6	5.9	4.2
Yugoslavia	7	7	2.3	3.4
Hungarian imports from				
USSR	1	1	33.2	29.1
West Germany	5	2	5.1	10.7
East Germany	2	3	10.5	6.4
Austria	6	4	3.9	5.1
Czechoslovakia	3	5	7.9	5.0
Poland	4	6	5.8	4.4
Yugoslavia	13	7	1.8	3.9

Source: *StZsk*, 1984.

food products, computer technology and buses from Hungary. For political and economic reasons, the Soviet Union has been Hungary's biggest trade partner, but the Western countries are gaining ground, as is clearly reflected in the data in Table 5.2. As far as the import and export of the various product groups are concerned, Hungary's dependencies on foreign trade with three of the main economic regions of the world are illustrated in Table 5.3.

In comparison with these figures, the quota of foreign trade with socialist countries was higher by about 10 percentage points during the 1960s and the early seventies. The long-term tendency since the inception of the New Economic Mechanism has therefore been a decrease of this ratio. Moreover, about 5 per cent of Hungary's intra-COMECON exports and imports are compensated for in dollars. Hungary's inter-dependence with world markets and therefore with Western countries shows a pronounced upward trend. Hungary has been a member of GATT since 1973 and it joined the World Bank and International Monetary Fund in 1982. Moreover, it is working on a comprehensive trade agreement with the EEC. Official net indebtedness in convertible currency stands at $4,100 million (*NSz*, 16 March, 1985).

Table 5.3 Foreign Trade Structure, 1983 (%)

	Socialist	Developed Western Countries	Third World
Import			
Total imports (324,818 mill ft)	53	36.4	10.2
Energy carriers, electricity	32.2	0.4	48.2
Raw materials, semi-finished products, spare parts	34.1	68.3	14.9
Machines, means of transport, other investment goods	21.5	18.6	0.3
Industrial consumer goods	10.2	6.8	7.4
Food products	2.0	5.7	29.0
Export			
Total exports (324,486 mill ft)	57.2	29.9	12.9
Energy	0.7	17.7	0.04
Raw materials etc.	23.6	33.6	32.7
Machines etc.	45.1	6.2	43.9
Consumer goods	16.7	17.7	9.8
Food products	13.9	24.5	13.3

Source: StZsk, 1984; own calculations.

Dependency on Western markets was most certainly agreed with the Soviets. Soviet endorsement of Hungarian Western trade policies shows that the Soviet Union has by and large accepted Hungary's special position: as long as domestic tranquility and stability are safeguarded, the Soviets are ready to give Hungary a large degree of domestic and, increasingly, foreign policy autonomy, even at the expense of a liaison with a capitalist mistress. The Hungarian leadership and the Hungarian people view both the Soviet Union and the West from the perspective of Hungarian national interest and with a matter-of-fact instrumentalist attitude. They have learned the lesson of 1956: that any challenge to loyalties arising out of Warsaw Treaty Organization membership or to Soviet defence interests is anathema. Certain aspects of Western life certainly hold a great attraction and command the attention of many Hungarians (especially Western fashion and economic efficiency) but Hungarians very rarely endorse or reject the Western model in a wholesale manner. This 'new pragmatism' is probably the most significant result of the country's development since 1956. The average Hungarian no longer identifies with the proud nobleman who inflames the nation's passions and dies a heroic death on the battlefield of revolution. As a belated triumph of the traditional peasant mentality, this figure is being replaced by the new success image of people who have made a fortune or upgraded their social status by virtue of hard work, cunning or flexibility. The Hungarians have realized that in order to survive and to progress they must be realistic about the situation. As a Hungarian saying has it: '*ez van, ezt kell szeretni*'—this is what you have, so like it.

Bibliography

Aczél, György 1971. *Eszmeink erejével (With the Power of Our Ideals)*, Budapest, Kossuth.

Ádám, Antal 1984. 'Allamszervezet' ('The State Organization'), in *Mit kell tudni Magyarországról (Essential Facts About Hungary)*, Budapest, pp. 121–56.

Akszentievics, György 1983. 'Mobility and Social Relations', in Kolosi, Tamás and Wnuk-Lipiński, Edmund (eds), *Equality and Inequality Under Socialism: Poland and Hungary Compared*, Sage Studies in International Sociology, Vol. 29, London, Sage, pp. 50–78.

Andorka, Rudolf 1985. 'Alkoholizmus és társadalom' ('Alcoholism and Society'), *Népszabadság*, 14 May, p. 4.

Andorka, Rudolf 1975. 'A társadalmi mobilitás történeti tendanciái' ('The Historical Tendencies of Social Mobility'), *Központi Statiszitkai Hivatal Statisztikai Idoszaki Közlemények*, Vol. 343.

Angelusz, Róbert & Tardos, Róbert 1983. 'Felfogások a szociálpolitika néhány általános kérdéséről' ('Attitudes on Some General Questions of Social Policy'), *Szociológia*, Vol. 1, no. 2, pp. 117–34.

Bálint, B. András 1974. 'Népmozgalmi statisztika' ('Demographic Statistics') *Heti Vilaggazdaság*, 31 March.

Bálint, József 1983. *Társadalmi rétegzodés és jövedelmek* (Social Stratification and Incomes), Budapest, Kossuth Könyvkiadó.

Balogh, József 1977. 'A vállalatgadasági és politikai funkciónak kapcsolata' ('The Relation of Economic and Political Functions of the Enterprise') *Társadalmi Szemle*, Vol. 32, no. 12, pp. 67–70.

Benczédi, József 1982. *Das ungarische Bildungswesen*, Budapest.

Berend, Iván T. & Ránki, György (eds) 1979. *Underdevelopment and Economic Growth: Studies in Hungarian Economic and Social History*, Budapest, Akadémiai Kiadó.

Beskid, Lidia & Kolosi, Tamás 1983. 'Differences in Welfare' in Kolosi, Tamás and Wnuk-Lipiński, Edmund (eds), *Equality and Inequality Under Socialism*, London, Sage, pp. 106–45.

Bugár, Péter 1984. 'Egyházak és hitfelekezetek' ('Churches and Religious Communities') *Mit kell tudni Magyarországról* (Essential Facts About Hungary). Budapest, Kossuth Könyvkiadò, pp. 157–88.

Császtvay, István 1984. 'Oktatás' ('Education') in *Mit kell tudni Magyarországról* (Essential Facts About Hungary). Budapest, Kossuth Könyvkiadò, pp. 264–81.

Csepeli, György & Lányi, Gusztáv 1984. 'Onmeghatározás és magyarság' ('Self-Definition and Magyardom'), *Világosság*, Vol. 22, no. 1, pp. 18–24.

Demszky, Gábor 1984. 'Wahlrechtsreform ohne Alternative', *Gegenstimmen*, vol. 5, no. 17, pp. 26–9.

Dietz, Raimund 1984. *Die Energie wirtschaft Osteuropas und der UdSSR, Studien über Wirtschafts-und Systemvergleiche*, Vienna, New York, Springer.

Dobossy, Imre & Lázár, Guy 1984. 'Mit hoz a jövo. Közvéleménykutatás a háború és béke kérdéséről' ('What Will the Future Bring: Opinion Polls on the Question of War and Peace') *Világosság*, Vol. 25, no. 10, pp. 642–7.

Domanovski, Sándor 1979. *Gazdaság és Társadalom a középkorban* ('Economy and Society in the Middle Ages') Budapest, Gondolat.

Enyedi, György 1975. 'Development Regions on the Hungarian Great Plain' in Burghardt, A. F. (ed.), *Development Regions in the Soviet Union, Eastern Europe and Canada*, New York, Praeger, pp. 65–74.

Erényi, Tibor 1975. 'The Activities of the Social Democratic Party of Hungary during the First Decade of the Century', in Vass Henrik (ed.), *Studies on the History of the Hungarian Working Class Movement, 1867–1966*. Budapest, Akadémiai Kiadó, pp. 55–88.

Fehér, Károly 1977. *Information über die ungarische Landwirtschaft und Nahrungsmittelindustrie*, Budapest, Ministry of Food and Agriculture.

Fuchs, Roland J. & Demko, George 1977. 'Commuting in the USSR and Eastern Europe: Causes, Characteristics and Consequences', *East European Quarterly*, Vol. 11, no. 4, pp. 463–75.

Gáspár, Sándor 1983. 'A szakszervezetek a szocialista épitomunkában' ('The TUs in Socialist Construction') *NSz*, 15 December.

Gati, Charles 1971. 'Modernization and Communist Power in Hungary', *East European Quarterly*, Vol. 5, no. 3, pp. 325–59.

Gergély, András & Száz, Zoltán 1978. *Kiegyezés után (After the Compromise)*, Budapest, Gondolat.

Gergély, Mihály 1981. Röpirat az ongyilkosságról (Leaflet on Suicide). Budapest, Medicina Kiadó.

Gosztony, Péter 1977. 'Die paramilitärischen Organisationen in Ungarn' in Gosztony (ed.), *Paramilitärische Organisationen im Sowjetblock*, Bonn, Hohwacht, pp. 295–332.

Hajdu, T. 1979. *The Hungarian Soviet Republic*, Budapest, Akademiai Kiadó.

Halay, Tibor 1980. 'Egészégügyi fejlodés és társadalmi fejlodes Magyarorágon' ('The Development of Health Care and Social Development in Hungary'), *Sozociológia*, No. 1, pp. 47–52.

Hankiss, Elemér 1984. 'Második Társadalom? Kisérlet egy fogalom meghatározása és egy valóságtartómány leírása' ('The Other Society? Attempt to Define a Concept and to Describe a Province of Reality') *Valóság*, Vol. 5, pp. 25–44.

Hare, P. H. Radice & N. Swain (eds) 1981. *Hungary: A Decade of Economic Reform*, Winchester, Mass., Allen & Unwin.

Hegedűs, András & Márkus Mária *et al.* 1974. *Die Neue Linke in Ungarn*, Berlin, Merve.

Heinrich, Hans-Georg 1980. *Verfassungwirklichkeit in Osteuropa, Forschungen aus Staat und Recht*, Vol. 52, Wien & Springer.

Heinrich, Hans-Georg & Húber, Mária 1981. 'Hungary—Quiet Progress?' in Homes, Leslie (ed.), *The Withering Away of the State? Party and State Under Communism*, London, Beverly Hills, Sage, pp. 151–74.

Heller, Agnes 1974. 'Wie ist der Ungar jetzt?' in Bállint, Balla (ed.) *Historische Entwicklung und sozialer Wandel, Soziologie und Gesellschaft in Ungarn*, Vol. I. Stuttgart, Klett, pp. 138–55.

Héty, Lajos 1980. *Az üzemi demokrácia és a munkások (Enterprise Democracy and the Workers)*. Budapest, Kossuth Könyvkiadó.

Hilker, Töns Heinrich 1983. *Ungarns Wirtschaftsmechanismus in Wandel zwischen Plan und Markt*, Frankfurt, Peter Land.

Hoós, János 1984. 'Gazdaságfejlesztés, gazdaságirányitás' (Development and Guidance of the Economy'), *NSz*, 19 August.

Huszar, Istvan 1984. 'Pártirányitás és gazdaságpolitika' ('Party Guidance and Economic Policy'), *Társadalmi Szemle*, Vol. 39, no. 6, pp. 3–13.

Illés, Iván 1981. 'Nemzedékek nyomában' ('Tracing the Generations') *Valóság*, no. 11, pp. 49–55.

Inotai, András 1983. 'Wirtschaft und Wirtschaftspolitik in Ungarn, Entwicklung und Aussichten', *Aus Politik und Zeitgeschichte*, 50, 17 December, pp. 13–28.

János, Andrew C. 1982. *The Politics of Backwardness in Hungary 1825-1945*, Princeton, Princeton University Press.

Jokisch, Karl 1981. 'Zigeuner-Fremdgebliebene unter uns', *Aus Politik und Zeitgeschichte*, no. 12, 21 March, pp. 3-17.

Juhász, Pal 1980. 'A neurózis és az alkoholizmus néhány szociológai vonatkozása' ('Some Sociological Aspects of Alcoholism and Neurosis'), *Szociológia*, no. 1, pp. 69-80.

Kende, Péter 1984. 'Van-e ma zsidókérdés?' ('Is There a Jewish Question Today?'), *Valóság*, no. 3, pp. 19-38.

Kenez, Peter 1971. 'Coalition Politics in the Hungarian Soviet Republic', in Janos, Andrew C. & Slottman, William B., *Revolution in Perspective: Essays on the Hungarian Soviet Republic of 1919*. Berkeley, California University Press, pp. 61-84.

Kirschner, Béla 1966. 'Society and Nation in the Hungarian Republic of Councils', in Vass, Henrik (ed.), *Studies on the History of the Hungarian Working Class Movement, 1867-1966*, Budapest, Akadémiai Kiadó, pp. 125-54.

Klinger, András 1980. 'A halandóság társadalmi összefüggései' ('The Social Factors of Morality'), *Szociológia*, Vol. 1, pp. 81-90.

Kolosi, Tamás 1983. Concluding Remarks in: Kolosi, T. & Wnuk-Lipiński, E. (eds). *Equality and Inequality Under Socialism*, London, Sage, pp. 181-96.

Kovrig, Bennet 1979. *Communism in Hungary. From Kun to Kádár*, Hoover Institution Press, Stanford University.

Kulcsár, Kálmán 1984. 'A társadalmi struktura' ('The Social Structure') in *Mit kell tudni Magyarországról* (Essential Facts About Hungary), Budapest, pp. 157-88.

Lackó, Mihály 1981. 'Értelmiség és demokrácia a két háború között' ('The Intelligentsia Between the Two Wars'), *Világosság*, vol. 22, nos. 8 and 9, pp. 521-6.

Laky, Tibor 1980. 'The Hidden Mechanisms of Recentralization in Hungary', *Acta Oeconomica*, vol. 24, nos. 1 and 2, pp. 95-109.

Lukács, József 1982. 'A parbeszéd elveirol' ('On the Principles of the Dialogue'), *Világosság*, vol. 23, no. 5, pp. 265-71.

A MSzMP határozatai és dokumentumai (*Decisions and Documents of the HSWP*) 1978, Budapest.

A MSzMP IX kongresszusának jegzőkönyre/Protocols of the HSWP 9th Congress/ 1967, Budapest.

A Magyar Szocialista Munkáspárt XII Kongresszusa (*The 12th Congress of the HSWP*) 1980, Budapest.

A Magyar Sozcialista Munkáspárt XIII Kongreszusa (*The 13th Congress of the HSWP*) 1985, Budapest.

A Magyar Szocialista Munkáspárt Központi Bizottságának elozetes jelentése a XIII Kongresszus küldötteinek (*Preliminary Report of the CC of the HSWP to the Delegates of the XIII Congress*) 1985, Budapest.

Milei, György 1975. 'The Historical Path of the Emergence of the Hungarian Party of Communists', in Vass, Henrik (ed.), *Studies on the History of the Hungarian Working Class Movement, 1867-1966*, Budapest, Akadémiai Kiadó, pp. 89-124.

Nemes, Dészo 1960. *Magyarország felszabadulása* (*The Liberation of Hungary*), Budapest, Kossuth Könyvkiadò.

Nyitrai, Ferencné 1984. 'Gazdasági élet' ('Economic Life'), in *Mit kell tudni Magyarországról* (*Essential Facts About Hungary*), Budapest, pp. 189-247.

Orbán, Sándor 1972. *Két agrárforradalom Magyarországon (Demokratikus és szocialista átalakulás 1945-1961)* (*Two Agrarian Revolutions in Hungary (Democratic and Socialist Transformation)*), Budapest, Akadémiai Kiadó.

Orolin, Zsuzsa 1980. 'Szegénység-alacsonyjövedelműség-hátrányos helyzet' ('Poverty-Low Income Under-privileged Position'), *Szociológia*, no. 1, pp. 131-45.

Pártos, Ferenc 1980. 'A cigány és nem cigány lakosság véleménye a fobb társadalompolitikai célkitűzésekről' ('The Opinion of the Gypsy and Non-Gypsy Population on the Main Goals of Social Policy'), *Szociológia*, vol. 1, 1–18.

Pilster, Hans-Christian 1979. 'Der Warschauer Pakt und Südosteuropa, Österr'. *Militarische Zeitschrift*, no. 5, pp. 395–492.

Pintér, István 1975. 'The Major Features of the Alliance Policy of the Hungarian Party of Communists between 1936 and 1945', in Vass, Henrik (ed.), *Studies on the History of the Hungarian Working Class Movement, 1867–1966*, Budapest, Akadémiai Kiadó, pp. 219–52.

Pogány, György 1980. 'Teremelési kultúra, munkaerkölcs, munkafegyelem' ('Production Culture, Work Ethics and Discipline'), *Szociológia*, nos. 3–4, pp. 339–60.

Pravda, Alex 1984. 'Gewerkschaften in kommunistischen Staaten. Die Sonderfälle Polen und Ungarn', *Journal für Sozialforschung*, vol. 24, no. 1, pp. 47–75.

Robinson, William 1973. *The Process of Reform in Hungary*, New York, Praeger.

Ságvári, Ágnes 1966. 'Issues Concerning the Alliance Policy in the Era of the People's Democratic Transformation' in Vass, Henrik (ed.), *Studies on the History of the Hungarian Working Class Movement, 1867–1966*, Budapest, Akadémiai Kiadó, pp. 289–323.

Sajó, András 1981. 'Jogi nézetek a társadalomban' ('Legal Views in Society') *Világosság*, vol. 20, no. 1, pp. 25–32.

Shawcross, William 1974. *Crime and Compromise: János Kádár and the Politics of Hungary Since Revolution*, New York, Dutton.

Szabó, Márton 1984. 'A hierarchikus tudatról' ('On Hierarchical Consciousness'), *Valóság*, no. 2, pp. 28–37.

Szajkowski, B. 1982. *The Establishment of Marxist Regimes*, London, Butterworths.

Szalai, Erzsébet 1982. 'A reformfolyamat új szakasza és a nagy-vállalatok' ('The New Period of the Reform Process and the Big Enterprises'), *Valóság*, no. 5, pp. 23–35.

Szalai, Júlia 1981. 'Hiány és társadalmi szelekcio' ('Deficiency and Social Selection'), *Valóság*, no. 8, pp. 60–70.

Tocsis, Iván 1980. 'Lakásigénylések és lakáselosztás Budapesten' ('Housing Demand and Allocation in Budapest'), *Szociológia*, no. 1, pp. 19–42.

Tomka, Miklós 1981. 'A vallásosság-nem vallásosság tipusai' ('The Types of Belief and Non-Belief'), *Világosság*, vol. 22, no. 1, pp. 10–17.

Tomka, Miklós 1982. 'Vasárnpok, ünnepek, vallásgyakorlat' ('Sundays, Red Letter Days, Religious Practice'), *Világosság*, vol. 23, no. 5, pp. 300–6.

Tóth, Ágnes 1983. 'Törekedjünk harmoniára. Megjegyzések a népesedés politikához' ('Let Us Strive Towards Harmony. Remarks About Population Policy'), *Valóság*, no. 8, pp. 69–77.

Tóth, Lajos 1982. 'Together With the Trade Union', *Hungarian Trade Union News*, no. 4, pp. 1–3.

Váli, Ferenc 1961. *Rift and Revolt in Hungary*, Cambridge, Mass., Harvard University Press.

Vargha, János 1981. 'Egyre távolabb a jótól' ('Deterioration Progresses'), *Valóság*, no. 11, pp. 56–69.

Vass, Henrik 1975. 'The Main Features of the Development of Social Relations in Hungary (1956–1966)', in Vass, Henrik (ed.), *Studies on the History of the Hungarian Working Class Movement, 1867–1966*, Budapest, Akadémiai Kiadó, pp. 377–406.

Vass, Miklós 1978. 'Ismerik-e a dolgozók a demokratikus jogokat?' ('Do the Workers Know the Democratic Rights?'), *Társadalmi Szemle*, vol. 33, no. 2, pp. 77–9.

Vincze, Edit. S. 1971. 'The Struggle for the First Independent Proletarian Party: The First Congress of the Social Democratic Party of Hungary (1868–1890)', in Vass, Henrik (ed.), *Studies on the History of the Hungarian Working Class Movement, 1867–1966*, Budapest, Akadémiai Kiadó, pp. 19–54.

Voelgyes, Iván 1982. *Hungary: A Nation of Contradictions*. Westview Profiles, Nations of Contemporary Eastern Europe, Boulder, Westview Press.

Wandruszka, Adam & Urbanitsch, Peter 1980. *Die Habsburgermonarchie 1848–1918, Vol. III. Die Völker des Reiches*, Vienna, Osterreichische Akademie der Wissenschaften.

Wass von Czege, Andreas 1985. 'Verschiebungen von Macht und Einfluß im ungarischen Wirtschaftssytem der 80-er Jahre', *Berichte des Bundesinstituts für Ostwissenschaftliche und Internationale Studien*, 10.

Zabov, Zoltán 1980. 'Das Verhältnis Staat-Staatsbetrieb in Ungarn' *OEW*, vol. 25, no. 1, pp. 54–63.

Zsilák, András 1966. 'The Changes in the Social Structure of Hungary and the Main Question Concerning the Alliance Policy', in Vass, Henrik (ed.), *Studies on the History of the Hungarian Working Class Movement, 1867–1966*, Budapest, Akadémiai Kiadó, pp. 233–350.

Zsille, Zoltán 1982. *Die Bedeutung der parallelen Wirtschaft in Ungarn. Die schwarze Ökonomie in der Gesellschaft der toten Arbeit*, unpublished, Vienna.

Index